THE DIARY OF A YORKSHIRE GENTLEMAN

THE DIARY OF A YORKSHIRE GENTLEMAN

JOHN COURTNEY OF BEVERLEY, 1759–1768

Edited by
Susan and David Neave

Susan Neave

David Neave

First published in 2001 by
Smith Settle Ltd
Ilkley Road
Otley
West Yorkshire
LS21 3JP

ISBN Paperback 1 85825 171 0
Hardback 1 85825 150 8

Typeset in Monotype Bembo

Designed, printed and bound by
SMITH SETTLE
Ilkley Road, Otley, West Yorkshire LS21 3JP

Contents

For Barbara and Jim Needham

Preface and Acknowledgements

The diary of John Courtney of Beverley, in the East Riding of Yorkshire, offers a remarkable insight into the daily affairs of an eighteenth-century gentleman. The first two volumes, which are published here, were written between 1759 and 1768, when John was a young man living with his widowed mother. There are two further volumes covering a later period in his life (1788-1805), the publication of which is also planned. The diary forms part of the archive collections of the University of Hull (DPX/60/1-4). Related material in the same deposit includes a late eighteenth-century letter book, a book of rentals, and a household account book.

We are grateful to the university for allowing publication of the diary, and in particular to the archivist, Brian Dyson. Additional material on the Courtney family was provided by Denys Clement, to whom we are indebted. Thanks are also due to the staff of the East Riding of Yorkshire Council Archives and Records Service, and of Beverley Local Studies Library, and to others who have provided information over a long period of time.

Shortly after beginning to transcribe the diary, some ten years ago, we moved to our present house in Wood Lane, Beverley. Although we were aware that the splendid late seventeenth-century house visible from our upstairs windows was the one in which John Courtney spent most of his married life, it was only later we realised that our own house had been built on his kitchen garden. This knowledge has made the task of editing the diary (and occasionally taming the garden) especially enjoyable.

Susan and David Neave
University of Hull
2001

Introduction

John Courtney, the author of the diary, was born in 1734. His father John (1679-1756), the son of a London stonemason, had made a successful career in the East India Company, culminating in his appointment as Governor of Surat. It was perhaps through his friendship with John Robinson of Buckton, near Bridlington, a merchant in Surat, that he came to Yorkshire and met a young widow, Elizabeth Bourdenand, daughter of Thomas Featherstone of Beverley. They married in 1732 and on 22 February 1734 she gave birth to John, their only child.

John spent his childhood in Beverley, where he was educated at the local Grammar School under one of its most influential masters, Revd John Clarke. When Clarke moved to Wakefield School in 1751 John followed him there for his final year of schooling, before going up to Trinity College, Cambridge. His father died in 1756 and by 1759, when the diary begins, John was back in Beverley, living with his widowed mother in a house in Walkergate. Much time was spent in the company of her close family — an unmarried sister ('aunt Peggy'), her brother Ralph Featherstone, who acted as John's mentor, and Ralph's wife, Ann.

In the first volume of his diary John records a visit to Cambridge to receive his law degree. He chose not to enter the legal or any other profession, although his uncle was anxious to obtain for him a preferment in the Church of England, a prospect that John greeted with little enthusiasm. A wealthy young man, there was no need for him to pursue a career. Instead he dabbled in financial matters, investing money through his broker in London, keeping an eye on the family property and, after the death of his uncle, managing the affairs of his mother and her relatives. In his later years he was very active in public service, sitting on committees concerned with matters such as the local militia, drainage schemes and charities, a role which was just beginning to develop in the years before his marriage.

No likeness of John survives, and the diary offers few clues as to his physical appearance. As a young man he had smallpox, which often left facial scarring. He dressed in the fashionable style of the time — he was frequently in mourning for family or royalty and describes the clothes he ordered on these occasions — and wore a wig. Throughout his twenties and early thirties he was much preoccupied with the need to find a suitable wife, falling instantly in love with almost every eligible young woman to whom he was introduced. His offers of marriage were rejected on several occasions.★

Much of his social life centred on Beverley, a thriving provincial town patronised by the local gentry. Here he attended race meetings held on the common on the edge of the town, the theatre, balls, assemblies and concerts. He was one of the subscribers to the new assembly rooms in the town, which opened in Norwood in 1763, and dined regularly with prominent townspeople, including the local doctors and clergy. He was especially keen on music, and had an organ built and installed in his house, where he occasionally held concerts. He also made regular visits to York, Scarborough, Harrogate, Bath and, of course, London. In York, where he attended the Assizes, he saw the author Laurence Sterne in a bookshop, and at Harrogate and Bath he met Tobias Smollett. It is tempting to think that John Courtney appears somewhere in Smollett's satirical novel, *The Expedition of Humphry Clinker*. In London John visited the pleasure gardens at Ranelagh and Vauxhall, saw members of the royal family at St James's chapel, and went to the Theatre Royal, Drury Lane, where he watched Garrick perform. Of particular interest are the visits to his cousin, Miss Julian Bere, who lived with the artist William Hogarth and his wife Jane in Leicester Square. On one occasion Hogarth showed John his famous election pictures.

The diary offers a fascinating glimpse of the social life of an eighteenth-century gentleman. But there is much more. There are good descriptions of local elections. Items of national interest are noted from time to time, such as the death of George II and the declaration of war against Spain. An eclipse of the sun is recorded. There are graphic accounts of illnesses (often fatal) which befell friends and relatives. Long-distance journeys are described, and there are the inevitable comments on the weather.

The second volume of the diary ends on 23 June 1768, John's wedding day. After the marriage ceremony John took his bride, Mary Smelt, to his mother's house in Walkergate, Beverley, where they lived with Mrs Courtney until her death in 1770. The following year John purchased Newbegin House, a late seventeenth-century property set in substantial grounds on the west side of the town. It was in this house that he and Mary brought up their large family. John began to keep his diary again in 1788, after a break of almost twenty years, and continued to do so until the year before his death. He died on 3 March 1806 at the age of 72.

* For a summary of John Courtney's search for a wife see K J Allison 'John Courtney went a-courting', *East Yorkshire Local History Society Bulletin* no 42, Summer 1990, pp 15-18.

Editorial note

The following editorial conventions have been adopted in this edition. Archaic spellings have been retained, to preserve the flavour of the period, but the use of capital letters has been modernised. Most abbreviations have been extended, and punctuation has been modified to make the text more readable. A standard format has been used for the dates of the diary entries.

The diary entries have been published in full, with the exception of those which deal with repetitive matters, usually of a financial nature. Bills were sometimes copied into the diary; these have been omitted, as have most notes referring the reader to other documents which no longer exist.

In the first month of his diary John Courtney focuses on legal and financial matters. Thereafter the diary became much more varied in content.

Diary of Occurrences Etc.

MDCCLIX [1759]

Monday Jan 1   Went to Hull this day at noon.

Tuesday Jan 2   This morning when I was at Hull there came to me John Spring[1] of Brig[g], one Mr George Smith, steward or agent to the Right Honourable Edward Weston Esqr together with one Mr William Lucas of London Mr Westons attorney. Mr Lucas informed me that Mr Weston had filed an amicable Bill in Chancery against me; as I, as eldest son and heir at law succeeded my father as trustee to Mr and Mrs Springs children; and that Mr Weston having bought an estate of J Spring, he afterwards found he could not have a clear title to it, without filing a Bill in Chancery against me; that Mr Weston would be at all the expence, and I must put in an amicable answer; I told Mr Lucas I knew very little of the affair, but that I would consult with my uncle Mr Featherston[2] about it. He said they were just going to Beverley; they left me; and soon afterwards I returned to Beverley. After dinner my uncle Featherston and I went to the Kings Head, where we talked the matter over with Messrs Spring, Lucas, and Smith. My uncle went to St Marys[3] and took out a copy of the register of my fathers death. After which we told them we would meet them at Hull on the morrow; and that I should take lawyer Cayleys[4] opinion in this matter. Received an answer from Thomas Stonestreet of London Esq by the post and also a letter from John Robinson of Buckton.[5]

Wednesday Jan 3   My uncle Featherston and I went to Hull in the morning and with Mr Lucas, Mr Smith and Mr Spring waited on Mr Cayley. Mr Lucas opened the case; and I then showed Mr Cayley the counterpart of the marriage articles on J Springs marriage with Susannah Midford, and asked him whether I succeeded my father in the trust, notwithstanding my mother was sole executrix. He answered me, that I did succeed him as his heir at law. I then asked him whether by the answer which they brought for me to put in, I became engaged as guardian to Mrs Springs children. He said I was. Mr Cayley desired to see the copy of the Bill. Mr Lucas said that it was ingrossing when he came out of town and alledged several other reasons why he did not bring and why it was not neccessary that he should bring a copy of the Bill. Mr Cayley observed it was a very unusual way of proceeding. He then perused the draught of the answer which Mr Lucas had brought for me to sign, and gave it his oppinion that they had made me say too much. I then declared that I should chuse to be released from acting as a trustee, and Mr Cayley said that if that was my resolution I must not sign that answer. After many words upon my uncle Featherston assuring me he would indemnify me against all expence, that the children might put me to by calling me to an account hereafter in relation to this affair, I declared I would accept of the trust, and desired Mr Cayley would make what alterations and amendments in the answer he thought expedient. My uncle and I then, (after promising to meet them at Hull again on the morrow) returned to Beverley. We had Mr Goulton, Parson Johnston, Mr Lister and my uncle to supper tonight.[6]

Thursday Jan 4   My uncle and I went to Hull in the morning, where I waited on Mr Cayley and asked him whether my putting in my answer without seeing a copy of the Bill did anyway affect me in regard to my oath. He said it did not, for I swore only to the facts in the answer. I then begged his oppinion whether or no if Spring and his wife should abscond, I as guardian to the children should be obliged to be at any expence on their account. He replied that he thought I should not; but that the parish would be in that case obliged to maintain them and as to the £200 settled on them I could [sic] any part of that towards their mantainance. By this time, my uncle and Mr Lucas came in to us. My uncle told Mr Cayley he had forgot to bring my fathers register along with him and I by Mr Cayleys advice sent my servant Thomas Routledge to Beverley with a letter to Revd Mr Johnston desiring he would let my servant the bearer see a copy of the register taken out; to which he was to swear at Hull. Mr Cayley then read over the answer as by him altered and amended to which I carefully attended. There was an expression often occurring therein to which I objected, which was such a thing was so and so as in the Bill is mentioned; I told them I could not swear that such things were mentioned in the Bill, having not seen a copy of it; Mr Lucas observed I might be certain they were mentioned in the Bill, or else the answer would be to no purpose; I reply'd that there was the highest probability that they were mentioned in the Bill, but that I neither could nor would swear positively that they were mentioned therein. Mr Cayley then said he would put in a few lines as a salvo for this expression, and accordingly inserted these words, 'But nevertheless this deforciant for greater certainty as to the contents and purport of all the deeds abovementioned craves leave to refer to the same respectively when produced'. Still this did not satisfy me, so putting the answer in my pocket, we came from Mr Cayleys, Mr Lucas etc going to their dinner at Cross Keys, and uncle F and I to the Black Swan, Mr Jobs. I there read over the answer very carefully, and after much thought told my uncle I could not think of swearing to the answer as it then was worded. I gave him my reasons and he was convinced of their weight. Accordingly we went after dinner to the Cross Keys, and I told Mr Lucas I could not swear to the answer, except he would alter the expression, as in the Bill is mentioned, to as in the Bill may be mentioned; he said the court would object to it. Well then said I Mr Lucas, I beg you would resolve me one question; why will the court object to the words may be mentioned — he seemed a little confounded and endeavoured to evade my question, by beginning a tedious harangue about something else, I repeated my request that he would resolve me this one question, upon which he took the answer in his hand, and began to read it to himself, upon which finding I was not likely to obtain a satisfactory answer I told him that if the court did make any objection to it, this would be the reason why they would do so; vizd that it appeared from the words that the deforciant had not seen a copy of the Bill, and therefore 'tis plain I ought to see a copy of the Bill. He then said it would be a great trouble and expence to Mr Weston and the ruin of Spring and his family in case I did not put in this answer, to which I reply'd that I could not help it and that I absolutely would not swear to the answer except this alteration was made. My uncle just then seeing Mr Barry an attorney of Hull[7] called him in, the matter being explained to him, Mr Barry said he did not see but that they might make the alteration I desired; for as it was an amicable Bill, it would scarce be objected to. To this Mr Lucas at last consented, and altered it. I then looked over the deeds mentioned in my answer (which Mr Cayley had before overlooked and told me they were right); After which I signed my name and then took the oath. After which Mr Lucas desired we would all quit the room but my uncle F and his (Mr Lucas's) servant who was a commissioner as well as his master, in order to their taking my uncles deposition etc as he was a witness to the marriage articles or some of the deeds. When they had done with my uncle which was not 'till near 5 o'clock evening we set out from Hull, and got home before 7 o'clock. Tom my servant returned from Hull about 10 o'clock, and acquainted me had swore to the register; and delivered me the drafts of the answer inclosed in a cover from Mr Lucas, who desired me to get it copy'd and send <u>him</u> it to London by next Tuesday's post. Vide his letter. Vide the copy of my answer to the Bill, in which is a plain account of the matters of fact in regard to the settlement, mistake of Spring's attorney, etc.

Friday Jan 5   I gave the draft of my answer to Mr Edward Clapham to copy it out. Received a letter from Revd Mr Whisson, my tutor at Cambridge.[8] Supped at Mr Goultons.

Saturday Jan 6   Mr Clapham brought me the draft and a copy of it, to which he set his name, and I paid him half a crown for his trouble.

Sunday Jan 7   By this days post I sent Mr Lucas the draft inclosed in two franks directed to him in the Inner Temple London desiring he would let me know when he received them.

Tuesday Jan 9   Supped at Parson Johnstons.

Saturday Jan 13   In the afternoon my uncle Featherston brought me a letter he had just received from Andrew Perrott of Hull, Esqr,[9] who says Mr Cayley told him my uncle had 3 or 4000 pounds to put out this Spring, (and that he had mentioned it to <u>Mr Cayley</u>) and Mr Perrott says in his said letter, he should be glad to take it and give land security, as he is determined to mortgage his estates, rather than to be in the power of any person to surprise him, as some have done by demanding their bond debts upon an hours notice; and that he will then pay all his bond creditors of[f] unless they agree to give 3 months notice before payment be made. I wrote to Mr Perrott by Mr Ferraby.[10]

Sunday Jan 14   Received a letter from Mr Lucas that he had received the drafts. This afternoon Mr Furnes,[11] who is a partner with Mr Perrott came to treat with me about the money. He mentioned an estate Mr Perrott had at Hes[s]le, which was let in Mr Perrotts fathers time at £68 a year since that at £74 and now for 100, but 10 pound was remitted last year. On this estate Mrs Perrott has her jointure, but has agreed to give it up. So that this is proposed as a security for my £2000. My uncle and I talked over the matter with Mr Furnes, and I told him I believed I should be at Hull tomorrow, and I would then call upon Mr Perrott and talk with him farther about it. Mr Furnes said that Mr Perrott, was he believed worth twenty thousand pounds.

Monday Jan 15   In the morning I went to Hull, and in the afternoon waited on Mr Perrott, whom I found confined to his room by a complaint on his foot. Mrs Perrott and he were in great distress, and told me how cruelly they had been used by peoples reporting such malicious storys in regard to Mr Perrott's circumstances, which was the reason of their present want of money to answer the demands their bond creditors might make. It gave me great concern to see such good natured worthy persons in such distress especially Mr Perrott, who with a true Christian charity prayed God to forgive those who had thus inhumanly injured him. He mentioned the rents of the Heasil [Hessle] estate which let in his fathers time for £68 per annum afterwards for £74, and now for £100, but he returned the tenant £10. I told Mr Perrott I understood but very little of those matters but that I should leave this affair to my uncle Featherston who had more experience, that as my uncle was going to Sledmire[12] tomorrow, it would be some days before we could both come to Hull about this affair; but we would do so as soon as we conveniently could. Mrs Perrott came up to me and said, this is my jointure, but I willingly give it up to make Mr P easy, and I have such a good oppinion of you that I am glad you are to have it. Both she and Mr Perrott had been crying before I came in, as was easy to perceive. It was a melancholy sight!

Tuesday Jan 16   I got from Hull this morning before eleven o'clock; that I might talk with my uncle F before he went to Sledmire. I acquainted him with what Mr Perrott had told me about the rents, and also that he told me he had not lost ten pounds by all the bankruptcies in England. My uncle advised me to write Mr Perrott that he might depend on my two thousand pounds, if the title was good. I accordingly wrote a letter to him; but in the evening before I had sent it away, Mr Furnas came to me and brought a letter from Mr Perrott to my uncle; and at the same time told me Mr Perrott desired I would be so kind as not to engage the £2000 'till Friday the 26th instant for that he (Mr Furnas) would go to London and talk with lawyer Perrott, a relation of Mr P and try if they could get a larger sum upon it. I told Mr Furnas that to oblige Mr Perrott I would not engage the £2000 'till Friday the 26th instant.

Wednesday Jan 17   I considered that it might give Mr Perrott a pleasure if I acquainted him with the certainty of my letting him have the money in case the title was good, I made some addition to the letter I had wrote yesterday before Mr Furnas came and would have sent it to Hull, but Philip Wilkinson, by whom I intended sending it, does not go 'till tomorrow.

Thursday Jan 18   This morning I sent the letter I had wrote to Mr Perrott, by P Wilkinson. This day from some hints dropt in conversation I found there was at this time, a very great hazard in lending a person money, even on land security. For if that person has committed any act of bankruptcy, such as denying himself to any body who came to demand their debts, etc, etc, prior to the mortgage, in that case, the person who has lent him the money, on the said mortgage, only comes in for his share with the rest of the creditors; as the borrower becomes a bankrupt from the very first denial or other act of bankruptcy, and consequently has no power to mortgage. If this is the case, I do not see how I can be secure in letting Mr P have my money, for though I dont know that he has committed any act of bankruptcy yet such a thing may not be easily or suddenly discovered in case he has.

Friday Jan 19   In evening I received a letter from Mr Perrott by P Wilkinson dated yesterday. I wrote to Mr Lucas.

Saturday Jan 20   I went to my uncles and talked over Mr Perrotts affair, my uncle said he did not, when this business was first entered into forsee the hazard in case bankruptcy; but that we might go to Hull on Tuesday next the 23d instant take counsellor Beatniffes[13] opinion, without mentioning any names; and if he said there was no security to be had then I must not lend Mr Perrott the money which I promised him, if the title was good, which will not then be the case. I am afraid poor Mr Perrott will be distrest, when he finds that he cannot get money even upon his land. I am sorry for him, but prudence will not permitt to hazard so large a sum as two thousand pounds. Mr Goulton agrees about the hazard in case of act of bankruptcy. I did not tell him who the person was.

Tuesday Jan 23   Early in the morning my uncle Featherston and I went to Hull. We were both very much embarrassed, and did not know how to act in this affair. However, we judged it better not to go to Mr Beatniffe. So called at Revd Mr Sykes's[14] my uncle talked to him about my lending Mr Perrott the money, though he did not acquaint him with our present embarrassment. We then waited on Mr Perrott, who said he hoped we would dine with him and then might transact the business; my uncle after a long silence, and asking Mr Perrotts pardon for what he was going to say; told him that some persons had told us, that I should not be secure; if he had committed any acts of bankruptcy. Mr Perrott said that everything had gone on just the same, and that he hoped it would never come to that, but if Mr Featherston and I were not satisfied, he must apply somewhere else; but that it was a disapointment to him, and people perhaps might think that things were bad with him, as we had not agreed. My uncle told him the case was as he had informed him and got up, and we came away; I having not spoke twenty words all the time I was there. My uncle dined at Mrs Collings's,[15] but I would not dine there; nor anywhere, but galloped home, more chagrined than ever I was in my life, that I was obliged to deny Mr Perrott; and had I known as much as I now do, I never would have meddled in this affair. I wrote to Mr Stonestreet this day.

Wednesday Jan 24   In morning I went to my uncle F who told me that the Revd Mr Sykes would take the two thousand pounds that Mr Perrott was to have of me, and that Mr Sykes would let Mr Perrott have the said £2000 on the 27th February next, and receive Mr Perrotts mortgage for the same; and that Mr Sykes would give me his bond for the said £2000, which he would keep for three or six months, by which time he expected he should have such a sum paid him in. That if he did not take my £2000 as above mentioned, Mrs Collings, would, and give me her bond paid him for the same. My uncle further told me that Mr Sykes went and acquainted Mr Perrott he would lend him two thousand pounds, which should be paid him on the same day I was to have paid him the same sum; but did not tell him he had borrowed the money of me. I am very glad that Mr Perrott will not be disapointed of the money. This affair has given me very great vexation and uneasiness on many accounts.

Friday Jan 26   Supped at my uncle Featherstons.

Saturday Jan 27   Mr Constable sent his servant with seven guineas for my spinett which he got this day was sevnight. I returned a receipt for the same by the servant.[16]

Monday Jan 29   Supped at Mr Meekes — his daughters christening.

Tuesday Jan 30   Received a letter from Revd Mr Whisson my tutor.

Wednesday Jan 31   This evening I spent at Mr Meekes who gave a ball at his own house to a select party, on account of his daughters christening (on Monday last). After drinking tea, we began to dance and danced 'till supper, after which we began again and danced 'till 12 o'clock.

Thursday Feb 1   This day I went into mourning for the Princess of Orange.[17] I should have done so last Sunday, but my cloaths were not ready. William Meeke, Esqr of Wighill Park with his son, and Mr Francis Meeke with his wife and son dined with us this day.

Sunday Feb 4   This morning by the post I received a letter from Thomas Stonestreet Esqr. Between 10 and 11 o'clock in morning I set out for York, at which place I arrived between 3 and 4 o'clock in the afternoon; not having called any where on the road. I laid tonight at Mrs Gibsons in Lendall.

Monday Feb 5   This evening I went to the York assembly[18] the first time I ever was there. Danced with Miss Kitty Thompson.

Tuesday Feb 6   I was at the play this evening.

Wednesday Feb 7   I dined with Mr and Mrs Burton. Went to the card meeting and from thence to a private ball at Mr Tancreds, where we danced 8 couples, and had an elegant supper.

Thursday Feb 8   At the play in evening.

Friday Feb 9   This evening went to the concert (first time). Afterwards danced. Heard Miss Formantell sing.[19]

Saturday Feb 10   At the play in evening.

Monday Feb 12   I was at the assembly again this evening and danced.

Tuesday Feb 13   This morning at a quarter before 11 o'clock I left York, and got to Beverley a quarter before 4 o'clock in the afternoon, having not called anywhere to bait on the road.

Friday Feb 16   Received a letter from Mr Taylor attorney at law.[20]

Saturday Feb 17   Fast day, this. Wrote to Revd Mr Mark Sykes at Hull.

Assembly Rooms, York. Engraving by W Lindley, 1759. John Courtney visited the assembly rooms that year.

Sunday Feb 18   This afternoon my mother and I made a visit to the Revd Mr Ward and family for the first time. I had not been in that house since the year 1751 when Revd Mr Clarke left it![21]

Monday Feb 19   This morning Mr Taylor agreable to his letter received on Friday last came and paid me my pounds four thousand one hundred and fifty principal and pounds seventy seven sixteen shillings and three pence, being half a years interest due the 27th of this month. After which I set my hand and seal to a deed acknowledging my receipt of the £4150, and my relinquishing all claims on Mr Heblethwaites[22] estate which was mortgaged to my father and Peter Wyche Esqr[23] etc, I also signed and sealed a memorial of the same deed; and also signed a receipt for the half years interest. Mr Heblethwaite has had this £4150 ever since the 16th February 1737. He paid 4 per cent till [blank] since which time he paid only 3¾ per cent. NB My uncle and Mr Edward Clapham counted the money and weighed the peices they thought looked light, which Mr Taylor changed. I also counted it, and put it up in purses as follows (about 5 hours in counting etc): No 1 £1000; No 2 £1000; No 3 £1000; No 4 £1000; No 5 £337 16s 3d [total] £4227 16s 3d. Revd Mr Mark Sykes came to dinner, and Mr Taylor staid dinner. After Mr Taylor was gone, upon Mr Sykes giving me his bond for fifteen hundred pounds, and his note for £five hundred both dated the 27th of this month, interest at 4 per cent. But the five hundred pounds to be repaid in a month with interest. I say on Revd Mr Mark Sykes giving me his bond and note as above, I delivered him 2 purses no 1 and no 3 each containing a thousand pounds. Which he took without counting as my uncle told him 3 of us had counted it. I sent two purses no 2 and no 4 each containing £1000 to my grandmothers by my aunt Peggy,[24] for greater safety, till Mr Dixon of Leeds (to whom Mr Goulton has wrote) shall send some persons to Beverley to receive the said £2000, and give me Mr Dixons bills for the same, in order to send to Mr Stonestreet in London to buy me stock. If he cant send to Beverley I am to meet them at York.

Thursday Feb 22   My birthday. I am now 25 years old. Laus Deo!

Friday Feb 23   Mrs Goulton received an answer today from Mr Dixon, dated the 19th instant which should have come by Tuesdays post wherein he says he would send his agents to York, where they would be this day at noon. So I was obliged to send my servant Tom to York, with a letter directed to Mr Dixons agents at the George in Coney Street, York, desiring they would come on to Beverley and I would pay their nights expences here, which Mr Goulton, Mr Dixons friend thought the best way as the letter had miscarried. My servant set out from hence at 10 o'clock in the morning.

Saturday Feb 24   This morning about 10 o'clock my servant Tom returned from York; and told me Mr Dixons agents were come to town; and about 11 o'clock they came to our house and delivered me the bills; and I delivered them two purses no 2 and no 4 each containing one thousand pounds; which they counted and found no 4 wanted 3 shillings which I gave them accordingly, and they put up the two thousand pounds in their own purses; and about 12 o'clock went away with it. I told them I would pay their charges as I had promised if they thought Mr Dixon would expect it; but they said there was no occasion.

Sunday Feb 25   By this days post I wrote Mr Stonestreet and inclosed to him 4 of the above bills. I wrote to Mr Dodsworth[25] also by this days post.

Tuesday Feb 27   By this days post sent Mr Stonestreet a duplicate of my letter of Sundays post.

Sunday Mar 4   Received an answer from Mr Stonestreet, that he had got my letter and the four bills amounting to nine hundred and ninety pounds. By the post I this day sent him inclosed in a letter 4 bills more amounting to one thousand and ten pounds.

Monday Mar 5   Mrs Collings of Hull, or Preston, or Hedon, sent for me today to Mrs Thirsks; and upon her giving me her bond I let her have seventy pounds, and gave up a note she had given my uncle for thirty pounds; which he let her son have, about 4 months ago; which note my uncle gave up to me. (Vide my book of accounts folio -)

I say Mrs Collings gave me a bond for the said hundred pounds so that now she has two hundred pounds principal in her hands. NB Mrs Collings paid me 1 years interest on my £100 due 18th October 1758. Four pounds. NB As to the interest due on the £30 mentioned above the note being without date I chose to let it alone 'till she looked at her papers at home and till I saw my uncle. Supped at Mr Goultons.

Tuesday Mar 6   Received a letter from Thomas Stonestreet Esqr acquainting me that the 4 bills I sent him the 25th of February; were accepted and inclosing a letter of attorney for me to execute, to empower him to purchase bank stock, and receive the growing dividends; which is to be witnessed by 2 housekeepers,[26] mentioning where they live; also 2 warrants, one to empower Mr Stonestreet to receive my dividends on my £500 in East India stock; and the other to empower him to accept all such Old South Sea annuity stock as he shall buy for me, and to receive my growing dividends thereon — I accordingly went together with my uncle Featherston, to Mr Goultons where I signed, sealed and delivered the letter of attorney, which Mr Goulton, and my uncle witnessed. After having signed the warrants I wrote an answer to Mr Stonestreet, in which I inclosed the letter of attorney and two warrants, and also inserted a copy of the 4 bills I sent him last Sunday the 4th instant. I also desired Mr Stonestreet would (when he received my whole remittance) buy for me fifteen hundred pounds bank stock, and lay out the residue in Old South Sea annuities.

Wednesday Mar 7   This morning I went to Hull and paid Cornelius Cayley Esqr Counsellor at Law £204 at my uncle F desire. Mr Cayley delivered up Mr Horsefields bond for £200; this bond I am to keep 'till Mr Horsefield gives me his bond for the same. Capt Popple being to go to York tomorrow, I gave him a note to Mr Scot the peruke-maker, and two guineas which I desired Mr Popple would give Mr Scot; being what I owed him for an undrest bag wig, and a bob wig — the price of each one guinea.[27]

Saturday Mar 10   This day adjusted accounts with my uncle Featherston. Ballance due to me which he has now in his hands, is two hundred and fifty pounds.

Sunday Mar 11   By this days post received a letter from Thomas Stonestreet Esqr acquainting me that he had received the four bills I sent him the 4th instant inclosed in a letter to the amount of one thousand and ten pounds, which he also informs me were accepted and delivered into the bank to be received when due. So that now all the 8 bills, my whole remittance are accepted. NB I paid 8 pence for Mr Stonestreets letter (though a single one,) for I sent my servant Tom to the post house, he paid for it, and when I oppened it and found it a single letter, I sent him back to tell Mr Berriman he must return me 4d. But Berriman refused, I spoke to the letter woman, but have heard nothing more; I shall speak to Berriman myself. I wrote to Revd Mr Whisson of Trinity College, Cambridge my tutor.

Wednesday Mar 14   I went to Mr Berriman, and on my showing him Mr Stonestreets letter, and giving him the outside cover, he returned me the 4 pence overcharged.

Saturday Mar 17   This day about 1 o'clock as I was running from Mr Ferrabys shop in a great shower of rain; I ran against a corn screen, which a fellow was carrying on his head and received such a blow on my breast on the right side, that I fell backwards, but got up immediately, though found I could not speak wanting breath for about a minute; I walked home, and I hope am not much worse though feel some pain. Capt Popple gave me Mr Scots receipt for £2 2s.

Sunday Mar 18   Received a letter from Thomas Stonestreet Esqr acquainting me has received letter of attorney etc. Bank transfer books will not be opened till 19th of April.

Thursday Mar 22   Master Sykes, son of Revd Mr Mark Sykes, of Hull, came and paid me five hundred pounds, which Mr Sykes had on giving me his note. He also paid me a months interest due on the same, from 27th February 1759 to 27th March, that being the time Mr Sykes was to pay it in.

Friday Mar 23   Mr Robinson of Buckton who came to Beverley on some business, gave me this day five pounds twelve shillings and six pence, which he desired I would pay to Mr John Boss for out rent, who he believed would come to the Tyger[28] in this town about the 5th of April.

Thursday Mar 29   This evening Mr Enter had his concert at assembly room, where was a very splendid show of ladies and gentlemen, and a very agreable ball.[29] There were about 100 people at the concert 'tis imagined.

Tuesday Apr 3   Received letter from Revd Mr Whisson, my tutor.

Friday Apr 6   We had a little concert at our house, Mr Raguenaus etc after which we had a ball, we had the following young ladies vizd: 1 Miss Smelt 2 Miss Waines 3 Miss H Waines 4 Miss Goulton   5 Miss Raguenau 6 Miss Marianne Raguenau 7 Miss Legard 8 Miss Jenny Legard 9 Miss Popple. Mr Popple danced with Miss Waines, Mr Montet with Miss Popple, and I with Miss Goulton Master Raguenau with Miss Marianne R.[30] Rest of ladies with themselves. We did not leave of[f] the dancing till 10 o'clock. NB Treated them with negus,[31] cakes etc. My uncle brought me a bill for £500 payable to him which I am to have, on paying Mr Pease[32] the drawer that sum, which is what I received of Parson Sykes March the 22d for which I wanted a bill that I might send it up to London.

Saturday Apr 7   This morning I went to Hull, and delivered Mr Pease five hundred pounds for the bill received yesterday.

Sunday Apr 8   This afternoon the Revd Mr Ward with his wife, sister and daughter returned the visit which my mother and I made them the 18th February last. This is their first visit.

Sunday Apr 15   Received an answer from Mr Stonestreet; he has received the five hundred pounds bill, which I sent him this day sev'night, and it is accepted and delivered into the bank.

Thursday Apr 19   Revd Mr Territt[33] and Mr Meeke dined with me.

Sunday Apr 22   Went into second mourning for Princess of Orange.

Tuesday Apr 24   Received a letter from Mr Stonestreet he has purchased for me fifteen hundred pounds bank stock for which he gave (with the brokerage) sixteen hundred seventy eight pounds, two shillings and six pence. He was to wait on Mr Dodsworth on the 17th instant but his old maid told him he was too ill to see him.

Thursday Apr 26   This day I gave to Mrs Walker, desiring her to give it Mr Walker, five pounds, twelve shillings and sixpence; which Mr Robinson left with me. I say Mr Walker will pay the said sum to Mr J Boss, as I shall not be in Beverley when he comes.

Saturday Apr 28   My face much swelled, 'tis a complaint vastly stirring; this prevents our journey to Cambridge on Monday.

Sunday Apr 29   I wrote to Mr Stonestreet and desired he would inform me how Mr Dodsworth did; and that he would direct for me a letter to Cambridge and one to Beverley, as told him, my face was so much swelled that did not know when I could get to Cambridge.

Monday Apr 30   Mr Walker gave me Mr J Boss receipt for £5 12s 4d for Mr Robinsons out rent.

Tuesday May 2   Having given my uncle Mr Richard and Joseph Sykes[34] 2 notes 1 for £400 and other £200, Mr Joseph Sykes on my uncle Featherstons delivering up the same gave him 3 notes signed only by himself each for £200. Which notes my uncle delivered me, and which he is to indorse being payable to him.

Sunday May 6   This day after dinner reading the news I was vastly concerned at finding Mr Dodsworth died last Monday. In the Whitehall Evening Post, the following account is given vizt; 'On Monday died in Mansell Street Goodmans Fields, in the 77th year of his age, John Eaton Dodsworth Esqr many years one of the Directors of the Bank of England. He has left the bulk of his fortune to Mathew Dodsworth Esqr son of John Dodsworth, Esqr of Thornton Watlas in Yorkshire.' Thus have I lost one of my best friends, a person for whom my father had the highest regard, as they were long acquainted vizt: from the year 1697, when they first met in the East Indies both very young, to the year 1756 when my dear father departed this life; during this long course of years they maintained a strict and constant friendship and correspondence, as may appear by the large number of letters from Mr Dodsworth to my father in my possession. Mr Dodsworth also when my father settled at Beverley in Yorkshire paid him several visits and staid some days at our house, when he made his northern tours; my father always said how much he was obliged to him, that he had been his best friend. Since my dear fathers death, Mr Dodsworth has been a kind friend both to my mother and self, and we have kept up a regular correspondence; the last letter I received from him is dated 16th December 1758 which came to hand 20th ditto and which I answered 22nd ditto. I wrote again to him February the 25th past, which was the last letter I ever wrote him. He was my Godfather. I have lost a good friend and wise adviser! I am surprised I have not a letter from Mr Stonestreet, about Mr Dodsworths decease. I find he has left the bulk of his fortune to Mr Dodsworth of Watlass eldest son. I had wrote a letter to Mr Stonestreet and desired he would purchase such stock for me as he thought proper with the £250, for which I inclosed him a bill; I also desired he would give my mothers and my compliments to Mr Dodsworth etc. When I saw in newspaper Mr Dodsworth was dead, I made addition to my letter.

Tuesday May 8   Received a letter from Mr Stonestreet. Poor Mr Dodsworth died 30th ultimate. This morning at 10 o'clock set out from Beverley for Cambridge. Dined at Hull. Crossed the Humber and lay at Brigg.

Wednesday May 9   Breakfasted at Spittle.[35] Dined at Lincoln. Lay at Coltsworth [Colsterworth].

Thursday May 10   Breakfasted at Stamford — Dined at Huntington, and arrived at Cambridge a little past 5 o'clock in evening. NB My Mother and I went in post chaises and Tom rode on my little sorrel mare. We went directly to our lodgings at Mrs Staines's a milliner in the Market Place.

Friday May 11   I dined in College, having put on my gown etc. In evening went to chapel and then to supper. Wrote to Mr Stonestreet.

Saturday May 12   Wrote to my aunt Peggy.

Sunday May 13   This day changed mourning for Princess of Orange. Drest — black full-trimmed with coloured buckles etc. Undrest — grey frock — coloured buckles. I was at St Mary's the University church this morning and afternoon.

Monday May 14   In afternoon I waited on Dr Ridlington the Law Professor,[36] who fixed on Friday forthnight for my keeping my exercise in the Law Schools, and recomended two books for my perusal on the questions.

Thursday May 17   I was at the oratorio Messiah, performed this evening in the Senate House for the benefit of Dr Randal Professor of Musick.[37] The principal singers were Miss Young, Master Soaper, Messrs Hudson, Champness and his brother who is a pensioner of our college. The instrumental part too very full and fine. I heard Messiah before at Foundling Hospital,[38] though this here was very grand, yet still that was rather finer.

Friday May 18   Received a letter from Mr Stonestreet. He has bought for me £500 more bank stock, at 112¼ per cent which cost with brokerage £561 17s 6d.

Tuesday May 22   I received the Holy Sacrament in our chapel. In evening Dr Ridlington came to desire I would put off keeping my exercise 'till Friday the 8th of June, as he wanted to go out of town. I consented to it.

Wednesday May 23   Received a letter from my aunt Peggy.

Thursday May 24   This evening after supper, the Vice Master Dr Walker, the Dean Dr Hooper, the Bursar Mr Whisson who is my tutor, Mr Meredith, Mr Newbourn,

Mr Peck and Mr Wickens, Fellows, all drank a glass of wine with me in our Combination.[39] I asked all the Fellows that were at supper but several were engaged.

Monday May 28   This evening I was at a concert in our hall for the benefit of Sigr Nofferri; Signora Mingotti sung 3 songs, and the principal instrumental parts were performed by the finest players in England vizd: Sigr Giardini — First violin; Facet — German flute; Vincent — Hautboy; Gordon —Violincello; Abel —Violino di Gamba, or 6 string bass.[40]

Tuesday May 29   In evening heard the speech by Mr Marsh in our Hall, and after supper went according to custom to the head lecturer Mr Powells to meet the Orator. Lord Torrington[41] (who is of our College and with whom I had some conversation yesterday at dinner) was there and great many gentlemen.

Wednesday May 30   This evening after supper I drank a glass of wine with the Vice Master etc in the Combination.

Saturday Jun 2   It is seven years this day since I was admitted of Trinity College, Cambridge.

Sunday Jun 3   I went out of mourning for Princess of Orange. This morning I received the Holy Sacrament in our chapel being Whitsunday. Dr Hooper the Dean preached. Received a letter from Mr Stonestreet; he has bought for me £634 5s Old South Sea annuitys which cost with brokerage £509 16s at 80¼ per cent. So he has now disposed of all the money I have remitted him being £2750.

Monday Jun 4   After dinner I drank a glass of wine with Mr Byng, one of Admiral Byngs[42] nephews (as is Lord Torrington) but this Mr Byng is cousin to my Lord, and brother to Mr George Byng to whom Admiral Byng left his house and best part of his estate. Mr John Byng the gentleman I was with, was in the ship with his uncle; but left the service after his misfortunes.

Tuesday Jun 5   In afternoon I carry'd my questions to Dr Ridlington the Professor of Law, and then to the Vice Chancellour, Dr Caryll Master of Jesus College,[43] and desired his leave to have the use of the Law School on Friday the 8th instant. He looked at my name wrote beneath my questions, and asked me, what countryman I was, I told him a Yorkshireman, he replied it was a Devonshire name, I told him our family came from thence;[44] he then said I was very wellcome to the School.

Wednesday Jun 6   Received a letter from aunt Peggy. I gave my questions to the Vice Chancellors man to paste up at the School.

Friday Jun 8   This day I kept my act in the Law Schools. The ceremony of which was as follows, vizt: At one o'clock in the afternoon our little bell in College began to ring, and soon after the great bell at St Marys, about a quarter past 1. The Vice Master Fellows and Fellow Commoners and I went into the Combination, where I treated them with sack wine and macaroons etc. Ten minutes before two o'clock the Senior Esqr Beadle Mr Borroughs with his mace walked down stairs, I following him with my cap off and a Bachelours of Arts hood hanging behind me. Vice Master and rest following in order. We then went to the top of our Hall steps where the Beadle making a bow turned round, and I did the same; We then marched down the steps, all the College following us according to their rank. Our little bell ceased as soon as we came out of the Combination. But St Marys great bell continued ringing till we arrived at the Schools. The Procession was as follows, vizt:

The Senior Esqr Beadle with his mace
    I with my cap off, wearing BA hood
    Vice Master Dr Walker.
    Mr Whisson my tutor — Mr Meredith
    Mr Preston Father of the College with his [?]
    Rest of the Fellows with Fellow Commoners
    Bachelours of Arts
    Pensioners
    Sizars[45]

When we arrived at the Schools the Beadle conducted me to the rostrum, upon which was laid the Corpus Juris Civilis, and then he went out and returned with the Professor, in his robes who seating himself in his chair over against me. The Father bid me begin, which I did reading my questions and then my thesis which having finished, the Professor read his arguments and we began to dispute, and about a quarter or more past 3 o'clock, he began to read his determination, which lasted near a quarter of an hour, and then we returned in same order to our college only went the back way, and walked up in order into the Combination, where I treated those that came back with me, with tea and coffee, cakes, wine etc and thus the ceremony concluded. NB The questions upon which we disputed were pasted up in the following form, vizt:
Quaestiones sic sese habent.
Consensus parentum in nuptis liberorum est necessarius.
Creditor, qui ejudem debiti, plura chirographa habeat, si unum reddiderit obligationem remississe non videtur.
Die veneris 8 June 1759 John Courtney Resp Trinity College

Saturday Jun 9   Wrote to aunt Peggy.

Sunday Jun 10   Today being Trinity Sunday we had a great feast in our Hall, as usual; I invited Mr Benson to dinner, we sat at the Deans table. Mr B chose it. After dinner went upon Bowling Green, and a large party of us sat drinking wine and cool tankard there sometime.

Friday Jun 15   Received a letter from aunt Peggy with a bill for £24 6s. This afternoon the Vice Master, Dean, Revd Mr Whisson my tutor, Mr Boroughs the Senior Esqr Beadle, and Revd Mr Place,[46] who lives near Thornton Watlass, all drank tea with me, at my lodgings. NB I have company or am out almost every day sometimes twice and even thrice a day.

Saturday Jun 16   Wrote to aunt Peggy.

Monday Jun 18   This day went and paid the Procter his fees for my degree Mr Willy of Christs College, paid Dr Ridlington, went to Revd Mr Hubbard of Emmanuel

College the Register; and subscribed to 3 articles (vide Excerpta and Statutis) paid Mr Hubbard; paid Mr Whisson my tutor, the Bursar, for my degree, to our College. My Grace passed in College this day.

Tuesday Jun 19   This afternoon, after Lord Palmerston[47] of Clare Hall had taken his degree my Grace was read for the 1st time, and I was present. After which putting on a Bachelour of Arts hood, Mr Preston the Father of our college conducted me and Mr Neat,[48] and the Father of Caius College Mr Ashley to the Capat, the Vice Chancellour excused us going home with him to ask his leave to proceed in our degree, as did Dr Ridlington the Professor and Mr [blank]. We went to Dr Plumtres Professor of Physick, to Mr [blank] of Bennett College, and to Dr Law Master of Peterhouse, who compose the Caput.[49]

Wednesday Jun 20   This day I was admitted to the Degree of Bachelour of Laws in the Senate House by the Vice Chancellour Dr Carryll, Master of Jesus College. Mr Neat of our College and Mr Ashley of Caius College took their degrees at same time. The ceremony was as follows vizt:

My Grace being again read the Professor of Law Dr Ridlington in his robes preceded by a Esqr Beadle (Mr Daws[?]) came down to the bottom of the Senate House, where Mr Neat, Mr Ashley and I stood, having Bachelours of Arts hoods on, he turned, and we followed him, when we came near the Vice Chancellours chair the Professor took hold of all our hands, (the Vice Chancellour sitting in his chair in his robes) and presented us, as men whom he knew to be of good learning etc after this short speech we went to the table and I took the oaths of allegiance and supremacy reading them up aloud; and then Messrs Neat and Ashley swore the same as I had done but did not read the oaths only the Procter said to them you swear the same as John Courtney has done. Then the Beadle going before us we marched round the Vice Chancellours chair, I going first as Senior bowing as went by the table where the Vice Chancellour stood. When I came opposite the Vice Chancellours chair I stopped, and he seated himself therein, and I kneeled down before him holding up my hands closed, when the Vice Chancellour putting his hands over mine, admitted me to the degree of Bachelour of Laws, by the authority assigned to him; in the name of the Father, Son and Holy Ghost. Laus Deo in Secula Seculorum. Amen.

I then went home to my lodgings put off my Harry Sophs gown[50] and velvet cap, and put on a Master of Arts gown and cloth cap, the gown Mr Whisson lent me, the cap, Mr Peck, and I gave their bedmakers my old one.

Thursday Jun 21   This afternoon my mother and I drank tea with Revd Mr Whisson, my late tutor, and we went up into the observatory I never was there before. After supping in the Hall tonight, I took my leave of Vice Master, Revd Mr Whisson, and all my friends, and desired Mr Whisson would cut out my name on the buttery boards. My degree cost me near fifty pounds. So now I have quitted Trinity College, Cambridge, after being a member of it for upwards of seven years, being admitted 22d May 1752 and have compleated my business. Laus Deo!

Friday Jun 22   This morning at seven o'clock my mother and I set out from Cambridge in the Fly. (Sent Tom on my sorrel mare into Yorkshire.) Breakfasted at [blank]. Dined at Epping, and got to London about 5 o'clock. Took lodgings in Featherston Buildings, Holbourn at Mrs Denhams. 25s per week. 3 rooms and two closets.

Saturday Jun 23   This morning went to the Prerogative Court of Canterbury, read over the original will of the late John Eaton Dodsworth Esqr. He has left rings to several but none to my mother nor me.[51]

Sunday Jun 24   This morning Mr Stonestreet, came to us, as I had wrote him a letter by penny post,[52] and he, my mother, Master Goulton and I went in a coach to Kensington, where we got into the chapel on paying something to one of the beefeaters at the door. Saw the King and Princess Amelia. His Majesty looks old, and rather faint and dull; but hope he may live some years longer. Chapel very small, no singing. Dr Young author of the Night Thoughts preached.[53] A gentleman next me at chapel said he believed he could get me and my company into the Presence Chamber, we went upstairs, and got by his means into an Anti Chamber but could not get into the Presence Chamber as his friend was not there at the door. However we saw the Prince of Wales and Prince Edward pass by us twice; and some of the nobility who also went to pay their court to his Majesty. The Prince of Wales is lusty, but good looking young man. Prince Edward has white hair and eyebrows. God bless the King and all the Royall Family!

Tuesday Jun 26   This evening was at Marybone Gardens[54] saw the Burletta a kind of mock opera there. Very pretty. Sigre Sarratina sang in it. Mr Stonestreet dined with us.

Wednesday Jun 27   Was at Ranelagh[55] this evening; Mr Beard, Miss Formantel and Mrs Bridges sang.

Thursday Jun 28   Was this evening at Drury Lane theatre saw the Careless Husband performed there for benefit of some distrest actors. Thin house. Mr Obrian, Mrs Pritchard and Miss Pritchard acted, whom I never saw before.[56]

Friday Jun 29   Mother and I dined with Mr Stonestreet at Islington, went with him and his sister to Sadlers Wells[57] in evening. Saw Miss Wilkinson dance on the wire etc etc very curious. Mr Andrews one of Mr Dodsworths executors told me today Mr D did not die worth more than £12000. Never was more surprised. Gave him sketch of my account.

Sunday Jul 1   Should have dined at Peter Wyche Esqr but could not as had toothache. Mrs Denham very civil woman very good lodgings.

Monday Jul 2   Bought ticket and chance at Hazards Office under Royal Exchange. My mother and I called to see Old Mary, poor Mr Dodsworths late maid. I called this morning at East India House. Left note for Mr Stonestreet at Jerusalem coffee house.[58]

Tuesday Jul 3   Breakfasted with Peter Wyche Esqr in Great Ormond Street. Mr Stonestreet gave me 16 bottles of arrack.[59] Paid me £15. He will receive my dividend tomorrow.

Wednesday Jul 4   Was at Vauxhall.[60] Mr Lowe, Mrs Vincent, and Miss Stevenson sang. NB This afternoon I called at Mr Hogarth's in Leicester Fields, enquired after my cousin Miss Bere but she was at Chiswick with Mr and Mrs Hogarth at their country house; I called a day or two ago before. However went in wrote a letter left it for her, and then saw Mr Hogarths pictures of the election entertainment etc from which the prints were taken, which he published last. I saw his prints too etc.[61] NB Mr Stonestreet dined with us on Tuesday the 3d and then we took leave of him, I having settled accounts with him.

Thursday Jul 5   This afternoon my mother and I stepped into St Andrews Church in Holbourn, where my late dear Father was christened; there were 2 children christening when we went in.[62]

Friday Jul 6   This morning at seven o'clock set out from London, dined at Biggleswade, drank tea at Bugden [Buckden], lay at Peterborough. Went today in post chaise 81 miles.

Saturday Jul 7   Breakfasted at Bourn[e]. Dined at Sleaford. Lay at Lincoln. Went today in the Fly. 56 miles.

Sunday Jul 8   Breakfasted at Spittle — dined at Barton — pleasant passage over Humber — could not get a chaise or coach in Hull 'till 9 o'clock at night. Got home to Beverley about half an hour past 10; Laus Deo!

Friday Jul 13   Wrote to Mr Siddall sent him a bill drawn by Mr Abraham Sperin, payable at sight for £8 17s. Being full for what I owed him vizd: five guineas borrowed of him at London; and his note £3 12s for cloth I bought of him for a suit of cloathes. Revd Mr Sykes sent a man with bill for £500, the sum which he pays me off, and seven pounds, ten shillings in cash interest on the same from 27th February last to this day. I sent a receipt by the man. Wrote to Revd Mr Ambrose Uvedale[63] and to John Heywood Esq.

Saturday Jul 14   Wrote to Mr Stonestreet dated tomorrow.

Sunday Jul 15   This morning I went to York on horseback, and my mother went in the stage coach, which on account of Hull races, traveled today. We lay at Mrs Gibsons.

Monday Jul 16   In morning set out in a return coach, and got to Har[r]ogate about noon, and lodge at the Salutation.

Wednesday Jul 18   Rode with Montagu Brook Esqr Revd Mr Cappea and Revd Mr Sandicroft two dissenting ministers, to Knaresborough. Walked about the ruins of the castle, and was entertained with a noble prospect from the hill. Saw St Roberts Chapel on the banks of the River Nid hewn out of the rock.[64]

Thursday Jul 19   Rode to Knaresborough and from thence to Ripley, having a most romantick country all the way; returned to Harogate in evening.

Saturday July 20   Took a ride to Plumpton Castle the seat of one of the Lascelles's,[65] from thence round by Knaresborough.

Wednesday Jul 25   Went to Follifoot the seat of Mr Collins an attorney a charming place, fine country, and romantick and beautiful situation. At Knaresborough saw St Roberts cave, a nasty dark hole in the rock, about a mile distant from his chapel. Here were lately found the bones of a man, who was murdered 15 years ago. I could not stand up streight in this place.

Monday Jul 30   This morning left Harogate in a post chaise. Got to York at noon; got accomadations at Mrs Gibsons with difficulty it being the Assizes.

Tuesday Jul 31   Left York in John Binnings return coach and got to Beverley before 4 o'clock afternoon. Found the following letters which had come while I was at Harogate, vizt. From Mathew Dodsworth Esqr the late J E D heir. Thomas Stonestreet Esqr. From Mr Siddall. From John Heywood Esqr. 4 letters.

Friday Aug 3   Received a letter from Revd Mr Ambrose Uvedale at Needham Market. He wants me to stand Godfather for the child of which his wife is now big.

Saturday Aug 4   Answered Revd Mr Uvedale's letter, desiring he would excuse me standing Godfather for his child. NB I left this letter with my aunt Peggy to put in post house as going to Scarbro' tomorrow, in a return chaise.

Sunday Aug 5   My mother and I with Tom my man, with my 2 horses, set out from Beverley at 8 o'clock, morning, and got to Scarbrough before 7 o'clock in evening. The town very full; took lodgings at Mr F Clarkes. 3 rooms at 9s per week each, 27s per week for lodging; small rooms. Have lodged at Mr F Clarkes before good many years since. Tom gave me a letter which came by post from Miss Bere my cousin, it was brought just after I was set off; he staying a little behind.

Tuesday Aug 7   I have subscribed to both the rooms,[66] and to the coffee house. Was at rooms last night, and danced.

Wednesday Aug 8   Subscribed to the spaw.[67]

Sunday Aug 12   I was at church; in morning the Bishop of Lincoln[68] preached a charity sermon. Very good preacher. This evening I drank tea at the Long Room. Mr Coppinger gave tea, and invited me among the rest.

Tuesday Aug 14   Danced with the great beauty Miss Knight, a Warwickshire lady. (Danced with her again on Thursday the 23d instant.)

Wednesday Aug 15   Uncle Featherston came to Scarbro. (NB He went away again on 23d instant.)

Friday Aug 24   Danced with Miss Taylor grandaughter to Bishop of Lincoln.

Saturday Aug 25   This day Mr Francis Clarke paid me in my forty pounds with two pounds, five shillings interest due on the same to this day; when I delivered him his brother Revd Mr John Clarkes note for the said £40, and gave him a receipt in full.

Sunday Aug 26   Was at church; heard Dr Fountayne Dean of York preach in morning and Mr Kerridge Bishop of Lincoln's nephew in afternoon. Lord Greville Montagu, son to the Duke of Manchester, with whom I became acquainted, said should be very glad to see me at Kimbolton,[69] or this winter, if went to Oxford hoped I would call to see him at Christ Church. I have danced eleven times at Scarborough this season.

Monday Aug 27   This morning at ten o'clock set out from Scarborough in Todds post chaise and got safe to Beverley at seven o'clock in evening. Laus Deo! Found a letter from Mr Stonestreet on my return home. Has bought me £450 more bank stock at 112½ per cent.

Sunday Sep 2   Answered Mr Stonestreets letters of 19th July and 21st August; and wrote answer to Mathew Dodsworths Esqrs letter of 15th July.

Wednesday Sep 5   Settled accounts with uncle. Ballance due to him £6 3s 2d.

Thursday Sep 6   This day I saw Mr Perrott go by our house in his coach. I have not seen him since the 23d of January last.

Thursday Sep 13   This afternoon Ben (who was my servant and now lives with Mr Perrott as his footman) came with his Master and Mistress compliments and desired to know how we did; this is the first interchange of civility and good will that has passed since the 23d of January. We returned our compliments etc, and that we should be very glad to see them when they came to town. I am glad they are not quite offended with that embarrassing days work.

Sunday Sep 16   Received a letter from J B Petre Esqr. Wrote to Mr Simpson (my taylor at London) by Mrs Raguenau, who is going there.

Tuesday Sep 25   This day I received copy of Decree in Chancery relating to Springs affair; inclosed in a cover from one Mr John Bennett. The cause was heard at the Rolls before the Right Honourable the Master of the Rolls on the 24th of May 1759. He decrees that all proper partys do join in such conveyance as shall be directed, and that the expences thereof be born by the plaintiff Weston.

Monday Oct 15   I sent for Dr Hunter[70] having an obstruction in my bowells etc with the yelow jaundice. NB I first sent to Dr Johnston,[71] but he was out of town.

Sunday Oct 28   Wrote to Mr Stonestreet, and to Mr Scot peruke maker.

Tuesday Oct 30   Having a day or two ago sent two hundred and fifty pounds by Mr Sykes's man to Hull, my uncle writing a letter at the same time to desire he would send a bill for the same; I this day received a bill.

St Mary's Church, Beverley. (From G Oliver, *History of Beverley*, 1829). This was the burial place of members of the Courtney and Featherstone families.

Thursday Nov 1   'Tis three years this night since my dear father died. For he died the 1st of November 1756 at little past 9 o'clock at night.

Tuesday Nov 6   'Tis three years this evening since my dear father was buried, in the quire of St Marys church in Beverley.

Thursday Nov 8   This day I gave Doctor Hunter four guineas for his attendance.

Friday Nov 9   Received an answer from Mr Stonestreet, also from Mr Scot the peruke maker.

Tuesday Nov 13   I paid my mother sixteen pounds fifteen shillings and fourpence halfpenny, which with what I paid on her account to my uncle yesterday makes up the whole sum I have borrowed of her. Being forty one pounds, twelve shillings. This day I also paid my mother her quarters annuity due the 20th of August last, being twenty five pounds.

Sunday Nov 18   Wrote to Mr Stonestreet.

Wednesday Nov 28   Paid my servant Thomas Routlidge his wage due Martinmass the 22d of this month.[72] NB He stays with me again on the same terms as before, only I am to give him a great coat which he is to take away if he stays two years.

Thursday Nov 29   Thanksgiving day.[73]

Sunday Dec 2   Received a letter from Mr Stonestreet; he has received the bill for £250 which I sent him this day was sevnight. NB Sent Mr Robinson of Buckton his receipts for his out rents and my mother received what she had paid by a man, by whom sent back the said receipts.

Thursday Dec 6   I was at the ball given by the officers of the Militia of Lord Downe's battalion, in this town.[74]

Friday Dec 7   Wrote to J B Petre Esqr and John Heywood Esqr at Trinity College, Cambridge.

Monday Dec 10   This morning went to Hull, dined at Mrs Collings's with uncle and aunt, who are at her house. Went to the assembly.

Tuesday Dec 11   Dined at Mrs Collings's. Went to the play, Frodshams benefit, spoke to Mr and Mrs Perrott, who were there; this is the first time I have spoke to them since the 23d January last. They were shy.

Wednesday Dec 12   At 12 o'clock at noon, set out from Hull and got to Beverley about a quarter past 1 o'clock in afternoon.

Sunday Dec 23   Wrote a letter to my cousin Nat Courtney[75] which sent to my aunt Mrs Featherston who will inclose it under cover to her aunt Mrs Harris, who will deliver it to him. This day received a letter from Mr Hazard; my ticket in the present state lottery no 18,278, was drawn a blank Thursday last the 20th instant.[76]

Monday Dec 31   Received half years interest of Mr Hewitt[77] due the 1st July last on my £400 at 4½ per cent per annum nine pounds. This morning I went to Hull and in the evening went to the assembly, danced with Miss Harrison, and so concluded the old year, (and begin the new,) for we danced 'till 2 o'clock in morning. NB Spoke to Mr and Mrs Perrott at the assembly.

Laus Deo!
End of the year 1759.

MDCCLX [1760]

Tuesday Jan 1   Begun this year at Hull at the assembly, where danced with Miss Harrison, (part of last night and part of this morning till 2 o'clock.) Went to the High Church at 10 o'clock, and heard an excellent sermon by Revd Mr Robinson the vicar, on religious resolutions.[78] About 1 o'clock left Hull and got to Beverley a little past 2 o'clock. Went to St Marys church to prayers at quarter past 3. Saw a woman about 25 christened.

Saturday Jan 5   Received a letter from Mr Richard Moor.

Monday Jan 7   This evening kept Twelfth Night at Mr Saunders; but did [sic] sup there.

Wednesday Jan 9   This evening we had a concert and after it a ball at our house, to which I invited some of the Militia officers. The couples were vizd: 1 Capt Burton-Miss Saunders; 2 Capt Morritt-Miss Raguenaue; 3 Capt Legard-Miss Waines; 4 Mr Montet-Miss Hewitt; 5 Master Ragenaue-Miss Jenny Legard; 6 Myself-Miss Marianne Raguenaue; 7 Master Raguenaue junior-Mrs Saunders. Capt Turbitt did not dance being lame. Treated them with negus, plumb cake, etc.

Friday Jan 11   Supped at Mr Goultons; and danced there.

Sunday Jan 13   Wrote to cousin Miss Julian Bere.

Monday Jan 14   This evening Mr Lister with his lady and daughter, Mr Goulton, his lady, son and daughter, Mrs Johnston and her two daughters (Revd Mr Johnston only drank tea with us) Doctor Hunter, Capt Peirson and his lady, and uncle and aunt Featherston all supped with us.

Saturday Jan 19   I wrote an answer to Mr Richard Moor's letter and sent it by Tweed the fisherman.

Monday Jan 21   Dined, drank tea and supped at my uncle Featherstons.

Tuesday Jan 22   This morning I went to Hull, called at Mr Joseph Thompson's saw a horse which he thinks will suit me, for carrying a portmanteau or double, 5 years old and strong made; its tail being cut lately, I can't have it home on trial for 2 or 3 days 'till Monday when I am to send for it. Called upon Mr Joseph Sykes told him if it was convenient I desired he would pay me in £300, being the half of what he has in his hands of my money; he said he would pay it me, but could not say it was convenient to do so at present. I told him then I would not have it by any means, but would rather borrow that sum 'till the time when he could conveniently pay it in. I desired he would fix a time and we agreed upon the 27th of April next which is the date of the notes. NB He desired I would put him in mind about a fortnight before that time, and I promised I would. So I must be forced to borrow £300 to buy stock with. After dining at Jobs I left Hull and got home at 4 o'clock in afternoon.

Thursday Jan 24   Mr Enter had a concert, a vast deal of company there, Militia officers, ladies etc. I was there. He cleared seven pounds, and his expenses were three pounds. After the concert was a ball.

Sunday Jan 27   Wrote to Thomas Stonestreet Esqr: desired he would buy me stock.

Monday Jan 28   Wrote to Revd Mr Sykes, desiring him to pay me in my £1000 at new Midsummer or sooner if convenient. Gave my letter to uncle Featherston who goes to Hull tomorrow. Mr Thompson wrote to uncle F that the horse I was to have was not well yet so can't send for it.

Tuesday Jan 29   I wrote a letter to the proprietors of the Musical Magazine[79] which I inclosed under a frank to Mr J Coote at the Kings Arms in Pater Noster Row London (a printer or bookseller) and signed it Eugenius. NB The 1st number of Musical Magazine is to be published in London on Friday next. This day I agreed to borrow one hundred pounds of Mrs Myers for 3 months, the interest to commence from this day. I am to give her notice when she is to bring the money.

Saturday Feb 2   This morning Mrs Myers brought me one hundred pounds being the property of Mrs Frances Johnson her sister; I received the said sum, and gave her my note for it witnessed by uncle Featherston; we agreed that I should keep it three months and pay at the rate of 4¼ per cent and I dated my note the 29th of January 1760. NB This is the first sum (except trifling ones of uncle and mother) that I ever borrowed. My mother lends me on this occasion £44. My uncle Featherston brought me a bill for forty pounds, which he lends me on this occasion, to buy stock with. My mother also lent me £41 18s to which I added £18 2s of my own cash, which made £60 cash and with the bill for 40 and Mrs Johnsons £100, I made up to the amount of two hundred pounds. At noon I went to Hull and called upon Revd Mr Sykes from whom I had received a note by my uncle Featherston this morning. Mr Sykes said that my uncle F agreed that he should pay my £1000 in (at any time without giving any notice or fixing any time) within the year, I answered, that my uncle told me he had given him a years notice, but not on such conditions he replied that my letter permitted him to pay it in at any time within the half year without fixing the time, I told him that my letter imply'd that he should mention the time of payment. We had great dispute, and Mr Sykes spoke with freedom enough both of my uncle and me; at last I found it would make a downright quarell if I did not in some measure agree to his terms, and upon account of my uncles friendship in the family I was unwilling to bring matters to extremities; wherefore at Mr Sykes's desire I wrote as below on the back of my last letter to him, and took a copy of the said writing for myself. Mr Mark Sykes behaved very meanly in this affair and has showed himself an artful cunning fellow, ready to take all advantages where he can, and in short proved himself a person no wise man would have any dealings with if he could help. I made a mistake in giving him only 5 months instead of 6 notice, in my letter, when I drove him out of his other holds he ran to this, but I told him it was a mistake and I would give him the full half year. Copy of memorandum left with Mr Sykes vizt: 'Mr Sykes is to give a months notice for any particular sum or sums he pays in betwixt this time and the 28th of July next, for which time vizt 28th July 1760 I have given Mr Sykes notice to pay me in the sum of one thousand pounds.' I went afterwards to Mr Yonge about the £1000, which I am to borrow, I told him I would come on Tuesday to take the money and the bond should be dated and interest commence Monday 4th February. From thence I went to Mr Pease's and got a bill for £160, which I had in my pocket, paying seven shillings premium or discount. Returned from Hull in evening and got home just before it was dark.

Sunday Feb 3   Received letter from Revd Mr Ambrose Uvedale.

Monday Feb 11   Supped at Mr Meeke's, his daughter (Jane's) christening. My mother stood proxy for Mrs Tufnell, Mrs Waines for Miss Thompson and Revd Mr Hancock for Mr George Tufnel. Miss Waines, Mr Grimston etc there.[80]

Tuesday Feb 12   Capt W Bethel[81] came to invite my mother and me to the ball given on Friday by the Colonel of the East Riding Militia, now here, Sir Digby Legard, Bart.[82]

Wednesday Feb 13   Received a card from Revd Mr Sykes vizt: 'Mr Sykes' compliments to Mr Courtney and aquaints him that he will pay in £200 upon the 11th of March next which is a months notice, or if it is more agreable to him, it is at his service on the 27th instant when the half year is due or any day sooner he pleases to appoint. Hull February the 11th 1760.'

Thursday Feb 14   Returned a card in answer to Revd Mr Sykes vizt: 'Mr Courtneys compliments to Revd Mr Sykes, and he will take the £200 the first time Mr Sykes has an opportunity of sending it by a safe hand, for he cannot conveniently come to Hull at this time his horse being very ill of the distemper now stirring.'

Friday Feb 15   I was at the ball given by Colonel Sir Digby Legard Bart, Colonel of the East Riding Militia, there was a very grand appearance, and about 24 couple danced; we had an elegant repast of sweetmeats, jellies, etc, etc, etc.

Saturday Feb 16   Received of Mr Goforth of Hull attorney at law two hundred pounds principal from Revd Mr Sykes and three pounds fifteen shillings interest on the same from 27th August 1759 to 16th February 1760. I gave a receipt to Mr Goforth.

Friday Feb 22   My birthday — I am twenty six years old. Praised be God! Uncle, aunt, Mrs Truby, Miss Appleton, Mr Hawdon, and Mr Enter dined with us, and all of them but the two last also drank tea and supped with us.[83]

Sunday Mar 2   Wrote to Mr Stonestreet.

Tuesday Mar 4   Received a letter from John Dodsworth Esqr of Thornton Watlass.

Friday Mar 7   Received a letter from Revd Mr Sykes writes me he propose to pay me in £100 the 11th of next month and £300 in May. Mr Robinson of Buckton supped with us he gave me £5 12s 4d to pay his outrents due the 28th April next.

Wednesday Mar 12   This morning my mother and I went to York and took lodgings at Mr Williamsons in Stonegate at 12s per week; we took a man and maid servant with us and I had my two horses at Mrs Gibsons in Lendall.

Friday Mar 14   Fast day.

Monday Mar 24   Received a letter from aunt Peggy at Beverley inclosing a letter from Mr Stonestreet with a power of attorney for receiving dividends etc in the bank annuities 1760, in which stock Mr Stonestreet writes me has purchased for me one thousand pounds capital, which cost £937 7s 8d.

Tuesday Mar 25   At the play sat next a young lady talked to her but did not know of good while after that it was Miss Newsham.[84]

Wednesday Apr 2   I rode to Tadcaster dined and drank tea with Mr and Mrs Clarke have not seen them for almost 8 years.[85]

Saturday Apr 5   This morning I wrote to Mr Stonestreet and returned him the power of attorney properly executed being witnessed by Dr Perrott[86] and Mr Horsefield last Monday when they drank tea with us.

Monday Apr 14   Received a letter from uncle and aunt Peggy inclosing a bill for twenty five pounds. Also a letter from Revd Mr Sykes to my uncle about paying in my money. Mr Myers paid me this day the amount of the said bill.

Thursday Apr 17   This morning mother and I left York and got to Beverley thank God; in the evening before 6 o'clock.

Monday Apr 21   This morning went to Hull, and danced with Miss Harrison, at the assembly. Lay at the Black Bull Samuel Leavens's, Job has given over business.

Monday Apr 28   Mr Robert Appleton[87] gave me a bill on my paying him three hundred pounds.

Tuesday Apr 29   Received a letter from Mr Peasegood. Also a letter from Mr Stonestreet. NB Yesterday paid Mr Robinsons out rent.

Thursday May 1   This morning went to Hull, Mr Peasegood Mr Joseph Syke's bookkeeper gave me a draught on Mr Pease and son, for £400 and paid me half years interest on the same (eight pounds) I delivered up Mr Sykes's two notes for £200 each. Mr Joseph Sykes has now only £200 of mine; half a years interest is due on the same. I received the cash for the same draught abovementioned of Messrs Pease and Son. Could not agree about bills so brought it home with me. Got to Beverley to dinner little past 2 o'clock.

Wednesday May 3   Paid Mr Popplewell £150 and he gave me a bill. Also this day paid Mr Michael Stavely Grocer in Beverley one hundred and four pounds, and he gave me two bills.

Saturday May 4   Wrote to Thomas Stonestreet Esqr and inclosed him 6 bills. Desired Mr Stonestreet would buy me one thousand pounds bank stock with the amount and the ballance he has in his hands.

Tuesday May 6   Wrote to Mr Stonestreet.

Wednesday May 7   This morning settled accounts with mother. NB Clear to this day. Went to Hull at 11 o'clock got a bill of Mr Pease for £90. Paid the premium. Got from Hull about quarter past 2 o'clock NB I have kept £46 out of principal paid me by Mr Joseph Sykes, in order towards paying mother, and expenses and Mr Stonestreets ballance due to me is about £66. So that he will have twenty pounds savings towards buying stock.

Saturday May 10   I dined with Sir Digby Legard and the rest of the officers of the East Riding Militia at Todds.[88]

Sunday May 11   This day my grandmother (Elizabeth Nelson)[89] died. I was with her after 5 o'clock yesterday evening and she was in good spirits and pretty well and we talked about severall things; she got up as I was informed this morning to stool and went to bed again between 5 and 6 o'clock without any help, and my aunt Peggy thought on looking at her sometime after, that she was asleep; so she did not go to wake her till about 12 o'clock at noon, when she found her cold and stiff; but laid on her side, with the clothes all tucked about her, and one of her hands held up to her cheek, looking as if she was asleep. So that she had expired probably without a groan or the least strugle. My mother and I were at church in the morning but were sent for between 12 and 1. I was out, my mother went, and I also went about 2 o'clock. I saw her as she was laid out at 3 o'clock. I never saw a corpse before. It was a great change, two and twenty hours before I had seen her walking about and chearful and had talked and laughed with her, and now in so short a time I saw her lifeless and laid out. She had an easy departure. May God of his infinite mercy fit and prepare us all for this great event, and I most heartily beseech him to make us a clean heart and that he would renew a right spirit within us, for Jesus Christ's sake. Amen.

Tuesday May 13   Wrote to Mr Stonestreet, inclosed him a bill for £90. Also inclosed him 1 lottery ticket, 4 shares and 7 chances in lottery 1759, desiring he would receive what might be due on the same. Mr Robinsons man called tonight, I gave him [blank].

Wednesday May 14   Alass! Alass! This evening between 6 and 7 o'clock the corpse of my grandmother was buried in St Marys churchyard on the right hand of the south door, near the remains of her first husband (Mr Featherston). My uncle and aunt Peggy were at the funeral; but mother and I did not go. God grant us his grace and favour that we may be always prepared for death. Amen.

Thursday May 15   Received 1 years interest of Mr Collings due 18th October last; and passed receipt for same £4. Received also 1 years interest of Mr Yates and passed receipt. This day went into mourning for my grandmother.

Friday 23 May   Received a letter from Mr Stonestreet.

Thursday May 29   This morning went to York. Got there in evening.

Friday May 30   Took Dr Dealtry's[90] opinion, advised Harogate water and gave a prescription, something to take 3 days before.

Saturday May 31   Called to see Mrs Grime, Mrs and Miss Newshome the latter plays and sings very well. Saw Mr Sterne, author of Tristram Shandy, this evening, as I was reading his sermons in booksellers shop.[91]

Sunday Jun 1   Mrs and Miss Newshome etc drank tea with us at Mrs Gibsons.

Monday Jun 2   Drank tea with Mrs Grimes Mrs and Miss Newshome.

Tuesday Jun 3   This day went from York at noon and got to Harogate about 2 o'clock.

Friday Jun 13   Wrote to aunt Peggy and inclosed a letter to Dr Hunter.

Sunday Jun 15   Received letter from aunt Peggy inclosing one from Mr Stonestreet with his account.

Tuesday Jun 17   Wrote to Mr Stonestreet inclosed copy of my account with my approval.

Tuesday Jun 24   Received letter from aunt Peggy.

Sunday Jun 29   Wrote to aunt Peggy again (for I wrote to her on Friday last). Received letter from Mr Stonestreet.

Monday Jun 30   Danced with one Miss Kent a Lincoln lady.

Thursday Jul 3   This afternoon at 2 o'clock left Harogate and got to York in evening called upon Dr Dealtry who gave me a prescription, an antiscorbutick.[92]

Friday Jul 4   Called at Dr Perrotts. Poor Mrs Dolly Perrott of Hull is dead.[93] I am very sorry for her. Poor Mrs De Ponthieu (that was Miss Sykes)[94] died last Sunday was sevnight. Sorry for her. Mr Stonestreet got to York this evening in stage, brought him to Mrs Gibsons.

Saturday Jul 5   This morning left York and got to Beverley in evening with Mr Stonestreet and my mother.

Sunday Jul 6   Wrote to Mr Andrews attorney at law.

Tuesday Jul 8   Received a letter from Revd Mr Uvedale.

Thursday Jul 17   This morning I went to Hull. Called at poor Mrs Dolly Perrotts house, seeing as I went by that her goods were selling up, nothing that I could buy. I got home about 3 o'clock in afternoon.

Saturday Jul 19   This morning Mr Stonestreet and I went to Hull on horseback, dined at Leavens's. Went up to the steeple of the High Church. Saw poor Mrs Dolly Perrotts grave, by the altar table. We got home before 8 o'clock in evening.

Thursday Jul 24   Gave Dr Hunter two guineas and asked him some questions of importance.

Monday Jul 28   Gave notice to Mr Collings, Mr Yates, Mr Hewitt, Mrs Tennison and Mr Joseph Sykes to pay in my monies in their hands.

Tuesday Jul 29   This morning I went to Buckton to pay a visit to Mr Robinson; Mr Stonestreet and my mother went also in a chaise, and we got to Buckton before 2 o'clock to dinner. I rode on horseback. Sir William and Lady Foulis and Master are at Buckton, Master a fine child.[95]

Saturday Aug 2   This morning I went with Sir William Foulis and his lady in their post chaise and four to Scarborough. Got there before 1 o'clock. Went with Sir William to Coffee House and Long Room. Dined at the Globe. Sir William and my Lady dined with Lady Rockingham. Left Scarbro' at 6 o'clock in evening and got to Buckton between 8 and 9 o'clock. There is but little company at Scarbro'. Very few who were there last year, especially of the ladies.

Tuesday Aug 5   This day at 2 o'clock in afternoon after dinner left Buckton and got to Beverley little past 7 o'clock in evening.

Thursday Aug 7   Went with Mr Stonestreet this afternoon to St Marys showed him where my dear father was buried.[96]

Friday Aug 8   Went to Hull with Mr Stonestreet this morning. Got back in evening between 7 and 8 o'clock.

Sunday Aug 11   Mr James Yates came and we agreed he should pay in my mony at Candlemass 2d February 1761.

Wednesday Aug 13   Mr Stonestreet desired that in case there should be a subscription made for Miss L---ds, I would subscribe for him as far as five guineas. Mr Stonestreet paid me this day the ballance of our account of 9th June 1760, for which I gave him a receipt. It is four pounds eighteen shillings and four pence. This evening about half an hour past 5 o'clock Mr Stonestreet went away in the Hull coach, and will go over the water — Humber — tomorrow morning, and take stage for London, which hopes to reach on Saturday evening.

Friday Aug 22   Received a letter from Mr Stonestreet, inclosing a bank post bill for thirty five pounds, being my East India dividend due Midsummer last and my dividend of bank annuities 1760. NB This is the first remittance Mr Stonestreet has ever made me. I answered Mr Stonestreets letter this evening.

Monday Aug 25   This day I indorsed the bank post bill gave it to my uncle and received the amount. Out of this paid my mother a quarter of her annuity due 20th of May last.

Sunday Sep 7   Received a letter from Mr Stonestreet.

Thursday Sep 18   This evening I was at a grand ball at Mr Saunders' which he gave on account of its being the anniversary of his wedding. We had a grand cold collation. We danced with some intermissions till 2 o'clock in the morning.

Saturday Sep 27   Mr Tennyson came and paid me in his wifes principal due to me and the interest thereon.

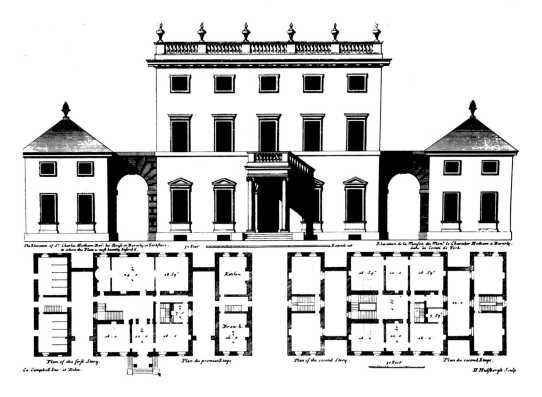

Hotham House, Eastgate, Beverley. John Courtney heard George Whitefield preach
in the yard here.

Saturday Oct 4   Wrote to Mr Joseph Thompson about a couple of horses by Mr
Ferraby.

Tuesday Oct 7   Let my uncle Featherston have the hundred pounds I received of Mr
Tennyson. I say Mrs Truby this morning took the said £100 for my uncle F for which
I am to have his note and he will pay me interest for the same.

Wednesday Oct 8   I heard Whitefield preach in Sir Charles Hothams court yard this
noon.[97] Poor discourse!

Tuesday Oct 21   Wrote to Mr Stonestreet.

Thursday Oct 23   Received 1 years interest by Mr Manby the attorney from Randalph
Hewitt Esq due 1st July £18. Gave Mr Manby a receipt.

Saturday Oct 25   This morning between 7 and 8 o'clock died our good and gracious
sovereign King George II of a kind of appoplexy, at Kensington, to the great grief of
all his good subjects, in the 34th year of his reign and 77th of his age. For account of his
death vide magazines etc.

Sunday Oct 26   King George III proclaimed at London.

Tuesday Oct 28   This day came the very bad news of the King's death (NB It was known by some last night when an express they say came to Hull, but I did not hear of it 'till this morning). I am very sorry. He was a good king and a good man. Sic transit gloria mundi! I received a letter from Mr Stonestreet today. I gave Mr Goulton a bill upon Mr Stonestreet for £30, payable to Mr Goulton 15 days after date and Mr Goulton paid me £30. Wrote to Mr Stonestreet.

Wednesday Oct 29   Paid my mother her quarters annuity due the 20th August last, out of the £30, Mr Goulton paid me (remains £5) also this day paid my mother £25 more, being quarter annuity which will be due the 20th of next month.

Saturday Nov 1   This night it is four years since my dear father died for he died 1st November 1756 about a quarter past 9 o'clock at night.

Sunday Nov 2   This afternoon King George III was proclaimed at Beverley. I saw the ceremony from Mr Randolph Hewitts window.[98] The Militia attended in the procession and after the proclamation was made fired 3 volleys. After which the bells rung. Pretty sight, yet something solemn! God save the King! I should have had my new mourning on for the King today but it was not ready, but as I am in mourning it did not so much signify.

Wednesday Nov 5   Wrote to Mr Joseph Thompson by Tom my servant who goes to morrow to Hull with 2 geldings I had on trial which dont suit me. This evening I hired one Thomas Lamb for my servant at 4 guineas a year with full livery and frock [?]. Half crown fasting penny.[99]

Thursday Nov 6   This evening 'tis four years since my dear father was buried; for he was buried the 6th November 1756!

Friday Nov 7   This day (yesterday being very rainy) Tom went to Hull with the two geldings; and returned about 2 o'clock with the black gelding and a letter from Mr Thompson, which vide.

Sunday Nov 9   This day I appeared at church in my new suit of deep mourning (with weepers[100] on) for the late King.

Tuesday Nov 11   This night King George II was buried in Westminster Abbey (vide magazines etc). At Beverley the bells at the Minster and St Marys tolled from 7 o'clock till 10. Very solemn!

Friday Nov 21   This evening we had a little concert at our house Mr Ragenaues family, etc with us.

Monday Nov 24   Paid my servant Thomas Routlidge his years wage due 22d instant: Old Martinmas £4 7s — for he got 13s in vails.[101] This according to agreement I was to make up five pounds. He goes away this evening and I gave him a written character as follows vizt: 'The bearer Thomas Routlidge was my servant two years vizt from Martinmass 1758 to ditto 1760 and was very honest sober and quiet. JC Beverley 24th November 1760.' He went away this afternoon.

Friday Nov 28   Today my new servant Thomas Lamb came.

Sunday Nov 30   Wrote to Revd Mr Whisson and also to Revd Mr Ambrose Uvedale.

Monday Dec 1   About 6 o'clock to night Mr George Tufnell who is a Major in the Westminster Militia with his brother Major Jolliff, Mr Waines etc came to our house, and Mr George Tufnel desired my interest against the general election I told him I had none, and could but wish him success. Soon after Mr Newton with young Mr Penniman came on the same account. They sat with me some time. I wished Mr Newton success and told him had no interest. He asked me to breakfast with him tomorrow, which I declined as I must have then gone about the town with them. My uncle has promised them.[102]

Tuesday Dec 2   This morning I heard that poor Mrs Clarke[103] died at York at 4 o'clock yesterday morning. An old acquaintance I am very sorry for her.

Wednesday Dec 3   At the assembly tonight Mr Newton asked me to dine with him tomorrow but I excused myself.

Saturday Dec 6   Received a letter from Mr Joseph Thompson.

Monday Dec 8   Mrs Meeke told my mother that poor Mrs Clarke was very chearful the day before she died, Mrs Ingram and Misses drank tea with her and she talked about fashions as usual, after supper she soon went to bed; and got up once or twice in the night complained she could not sleep (and she had not slept well for 3 nights before) she bid the maid give her a cup of the white mixture she used to take, which she did then she called for another cup of it saying that would make her sleep perhaps. As the maid was getting her to bed she said I think thou hast broken one of my ribs. Afterwards she called to the maid to turn her on her left side, saying then she should sleep perhaps, this being done, soon after she gave 3 great sighs and the maid going up to her found her dead. Poor Mr Clarke was in bed with her, they told him Mrs C desired he would go to another bed that she might get some sleep. So they got him to another bed. They have not told Mr Clarke of his wifes death. He often inquires for her, but such is his melancholy condition that by telling him a little story they can divert him from further enquiry. But one night he said he would not go to bed without his wife so they were obliged to put him to bed like a child. But this is too melancholy a scene to dwell on! She was buried they say on Wednesday last. Poor woman she has been long in a bad state of health, but her end was sudden at last. How certain may we be that there is a future state after this life, how confident may we be of the truth of that glorious revelation which assures us of it; this life how vain, the next how truly valuable, if we behave well in this! How vain the applause of men, how inestimable the testimony of a good conscience. In God alone is man's perfect happiness. Preserve me O God!

Wednesday Dec 10   I was at Mr Newton's ball, tonight, great deal of company.

Friday Dec 12   Received a letter from Revd Mr Whisson with my account and a bill for the ballance being £6 4s. This afternoon Mr Walker brought me a receipt for Mr Robinsons outrent 12 shillings which I paid him.

Saturday Dec 13   Betwixt last night and this morning (I believe about midnight) I was awaked by the ringing of the bells. I was much surprised; heard in the morning, it was on occasion of Hugh Bethel Esqr[104] declaring himself a candidate. But many people think it a frolick as he promised Mr G Tufnel (as Mr Tufnel says) that he would not stand. They rang the bells all day.

Sunday Dec 14   Received a letter from Revd Mr Ambrose Uvedale. This afternoon Hugh Bethell Esqr came with his brother and Mr William Gee and Mr Boynton to ask my interest.[105] I told him I had none. My uncle F was with me, and Mr Bethell asked him for his vote and interest, he replied he had been told that he said he would not stand a candidate, Mr B said with some little hesitation, that he had not said so. My uncle told him he would consider of it. 'Tis an odd affair. If Mr Bethell had declared himself a candidate some time ago he would have succeeded without doubt.

Monday Dec 15   Mr Bethell this morning has declared he declines standing candidate, as he found several of his friends were engaged, and consequently he should create disturbances in the town by persisting in his intention. This night Mr Tufnell gives his ball, to which I was invited, but I did not go, as my uncle is not for him, and though I wish him well, I have no interest.

Tuesday Dec 16   Mr De Montet told me that they waited last night half an hour at the ball thinking I would come to begin, and that Mr Tufnell enquired twice for me, and they were all surprised I was not there. I intend to tell them all the reason.

Wednesday Dec 17   This day Mrs Truby delivered me one hundred pounds in a purse sealed up, which she desired I would keep for my uncle till their return from Hull. I accordingly have put it up.

Thursday Dec 18   Paid Mrs Dickons[106] note from my suite of mourning, five pounds. Delivered her son Peter Mr Whissons bill for £6 4s and he gave me change.

Sunday Dec 21   Mr Munby attorney came to acquainte me that Mr Hewitt would if I agreed to it pay in my money about the 10th of January next to which I agreed.

Wednesday Dec 31
I put by a guinea to send to Nat; and six shillings and six pence for the poor. NB This year I shall have saved one hundred and thirty pounds, please God.

Laus Deo!
End of the Year 1760.

MDCCLXI [1761]

Thursday Jan 1   Begun this year at Beverley. Went to St Mary's, to prayers, in morning and afternoon.

Monday Jan 5   Wrote to Sir William Foulis Bart and sent it by coachman to meet him at Drif[f]ield.

Tuesday Jan 6   This afternoon Sir William Foulis and his lady came to Mrs Robinson, I called to see him there. This evening I was at Mr Saunders's, being twelfth night. We had a ball there; and cold chickens, ham and jellies with cakes, negus, wine etc. Did not break up till past 1 o'clock in morning.

Wednesday Jan 7   This morning Sir William Foulis and his lady and Mrs Robinson breakfasted with us and about 1 o'clock left Beverley to proceed on their journey to Bath. In evening I was at the assembly.

Thursday Jan 8   My uncle and aunt, Miss Parsons, and Mr Hawdon dined with us. I delivered uncle F his hundred pound. My uncle received of my mother £16 for a bill he gave her this day for that sum. This evening had a little concert at our house. Ten performers vizt: First fiddle — Mr Smith; Second Fiddles — Master Raguenaue, Master E Raguenau, Mr Enter; German Flutes — Mr Feanside, Mr Cox, Mr Tong; Violocello — Mr De Montet; Harpsichord, Thor Bass — J Courtney; Voice — Mr Raines. My uncle and Mr Pearson and Mr Groves drank tea with us.[107]

Friday Jan 9   This day I sent the black gelding back to Mr Joseph Thompson by my servant, which he took accordingly.

Sunday Jan 18   This day I heard that Richard Sykes Esqr died suddenly last night, he wrote 4 letters yesterday, 2 of which were to my uncle.[108] I imagine my £400, which the late Richard Sykes, Esqr had of mine will be paid in soon.

Thursday Jan 22   This morning my mother and I went to York in a post chaise and four, and got to Mr Howards (late Mrs Gibsons) in Lendal about 5 o'clock in evening.

Saturday Jan 24   This day went to our lodgings at Miss Hammonds a millener in Coney Street, for which pay 10 shillings a week only, if we stay above a forthnight.

Sunday Jan 25   This day I went into second mourning for his late Majesty King George II. Drest, black, full trimmed. Undrest, grey frock. Appeared at St Hellens in morning and Coney Street church in afternoon in light grey frock.

Wednesday Jan 28   This morning my mother and I called to see Mrs G---s [Grimes] and Mrs and Miss N--- [Newsome], Miss played and sung.[109]

Tuesday Feb 3   This afternoon Mrs M[ary] G[rime] Miss N[ewsome] and her mother, and Mrs A G--- [Anne Grime] and Mrs Mary Goulton drank tea with us. Miss N sung and played excessively well. She is a very fine girl in all respects. From this day I determined to try my fortune.

Thursday Feb 5   This morning I called at Mrs G---'s and carry'd Miss N--- some musick. In evening sat behind her at the play; treated her with sweetmeats; handed her out; the play was the Conscious Lovers; the farce Cheats of Scapin.

Friday Feb 6   I mett Miss N--- today but she held down her head and passed on the other side of the street.

Saturday Feb 7   This afternoon my mother and I drank tea at Mrs G---'s. Miss N played and sung and was very free and good humoured. All of them vastly civil. I was confirmed in my resolution.

Friday Feb 13   Fast day.

Saturday Feb 14   This night was at the play and saw for the first time the new entertainment of Harlequin Salamander, the Statue Scene, very well done by Fitzmaurice. I had a great deal of conversation with Mrs Sterne, Tristram Shandys wife.

Tuesday Feb 17   This afternoon we drank tea with Mrs A G---. Old Mrs G Mrs M G Mrs and Miss N--- were there. All very free and uncommonly civil. Miss N does not go to the assemblys yet.

Wednesday Feb 18   This day I heard of the death of my old Master the Revd Mr Clarke; he died at Scarborough some days ago. I am very sorry for him, though poor man! Life in his condition was not to be wished for. The last time I saw him was at Tadcaster the 2d of last April, when I dined and drank tea with Mrs Clarke and him, little thinking they would both be dead before that time twelve month. He was a most excellent schoolmaster, and his dilligence was equall to his learning, and he was a most worthy man; I shall ever reverence his memory.

Thursday Feb 19   This evening at the play I sat behind Miss N--- and treated her, and handed her out as before. The play was The Wonder or a Woman keeps a Secret, and farce, Miss in her Teens.[110] I dare say the young lady may begin to guess that I like her.

Friday Feb 20   Tonight I was at the concert Mr Coyles Benefit, danced with Miss N. Very full room.

Saturday Feb 21   This morning I went to Miss N---'s she played sung, and I played on harpsichord, and Miss P--- who was there sung and Miss N--- with her while I played, and I sang bass to them sometimes. In evening I was at Frodshams benefit Rival Queens, and The Chaplet, Mrs and Miss N sat in balcony opposite; full house, I could not get to them; but when all was over, I mett with them coming out, and handed Miss to the coach.

Sunday Feb 22   My birthday. I am twenty seven years old. Gods Holy name be praised! Miss Hammond, and her two apprentices dined with us; and Dr and Mrs and Miss Perrott and Mrs and Miss Ingram drank tea with us. Should have changed mourning for the late King today.

Monday Feb 23   I called this morning at Mrs G---s saw the old woman but Miss N--- was out. This day changed mourning for the late King, drest black full trimmed, coloured buckles, etc.

Tuesday Feb 24   This morning Mrs N---, and Mrs M G--- called to see my mother.

Wednesday Feb 25   This morning I went to Mrs G---s found Miss N--- at home; Miss P there again; I carry'd some musick. We played and sang as usual; about 1 o'clock Miss P went away; and soon after I spoke to Mrs M G and told her I had something to say to her and the other two ladies and asked them what time tomorrow I should wait upon them; she fixed betwixt 10 and 11. She did not seemed much surprised and was very civill as were they all.

Thursday Feb 26   This morning according to appointment I waited upon Mrs G---s and Mrs N--- and soon after told them that I loved Miss N--- and should be very happy in their consent; they all said they liked me very well, but that she was too young. I talked a great deal and argued the matter a long time, and we talked of various things in relation to this affair. At last they called the young lady down; and soon after left us together with little child Miss G--- in room and she went out now and then. Upon this I immediately made my declaration; they returned in about an hour and a half, and we talked about it a little. I came away upon the whole with hopes of success. I wrote to my uncle F tonight, desiring he would come over as I had some particular business with him. This is the first time I ever made my addresses to any one.

Friday Feb 27   This morning I waited upon Miss N--- again; was shown into the best parlour; saw Mrs G and Mrs N--- then Miss N--- came in; the old ladies went to church, I had an hours conversation with my sweet Miss N--- uninterupted, from which I hoped the affair in time might succeed. At last old Mrs G comes in a good deal fluttered, and told me she desired I would not make such frequent visits; for that her grandaughter was so young etc and that she could not permitt to come 'till they heard from Mr N--- her grandfather in London; and that she dared say he would not have her marry so young; we had a good deal of conversation; the old lady went out left us together again about a quarter of an hour; then Mrs N came in; Miss went out a little; I told Mrs N--- my fortune and expectations and she told me Miss N---'s, upon honour. I asked her leave to wait on Miss and at last obtained leave to come on Sunday to drink tea; Miss came in again, and soon after I took my leave, in good spirits.

Saturday Feb 28   This day received an answer from my uncle, he is not very well cannot come. Wrote to him to night hinting at the affair, and told him I would come to Beverley Monday or Tuesday.

Sunday Mar 1   This afternoon I drank tea at Mrs G---s. After tea Miss N--- going out; they told me they desired I would not think any more about Miss; for that they were sure it would never be to any purpose concluding with a long catalogue of my good qualities; a bad sign when we dont purchase 'tis common to praise what is offered us. I was thunderstruck. I told them I was going to Beverley in the morning they said I need not take the trouble. I said I would go. We all grew very stupid, at last I got up and said I am very bad company so will take my leave; saluted Miss N and came away.

Monday Mar 2 This morning I set out from York, on horseback got to Beverley between 3 and 4 o'clock in afternoon. Drank tea at my uncle F talked over the affair; he approved of what I had done.

Tuesday Mar 3 This morning my uncle came to me; we talked over the affair; he told me what he was worth etc, I wrote a foul copy[111] of what I should write to Mr N--- at London. Dined at my uncles. This afternoon destroyed my old will and made a new one.

Wednesday Mar 4 This morning at 10 o'clock set out from Beverley on horseback; got to York without dismounting about a quarter past 2 o'clock in afternoon.

Thursday Mar 5 This morning I waited on Mrs G---s and Mrs and Miss N---. When Miss was out read them copy of letter I intended writing Mr N they made no objection to it but said it would be no purpose; they gave me directions. I carryd Miss my Song of Innocence and Love, just printed, as also my Cantata, Temple of Flattery, in manuscript; she sang on intreaty some of them a little, while I played. This evening I sat behind Miss N--- and her mother at play; treated and handed Miss out as usual. The play was The Stratagem, entertainment, The Chaplet. NB In the morning I was desired not to come to the house till they had heard from Mr N---.

Saturday Mar 7 I wrote to Mr N--- inclosed it to Mr Stonestreet told him the affair desired he would deliver it to Mr N---.

Sunday Mar 8 This morning I went to St [blank] church where sat in a pew not far from Miss N--- and Mrs G---s but could not get to speak to them. Should have changed mourning today but could not.

Monday Mar 9 Tonight I was at the assembly in the Grand Room it being the Assize week. It was a very magnificent sight vast deal of company double set with ladies. I would not dance as Miss N--- was not there. This day I changed mourning for the late King, vizt drest, black full trimmed coloured buckles (white stockings) undrest, grey frock, ditto.

Tuesday Mar 10 This evening I was at the play; very full house I stood behind Miss N--- all the night; Mrs N--- sat next her. Play, Merope and Harlequin Skeleton. I handed Miss N to the coach and obtained permission of Mrs N--- to come and hear a tune to morrow. I was this morning at Castle to hear trials; never did before.

Wednesday Mar 11 This morning went to Miss N---s she played and sung; at last went out to walk; Mr and Mrs G of T--th--p[112] were there I spoke to him; he did not

York Castle, where the Assizes took place. Engraving by W Lindley, c1759.

say much except he should agree to what Mrs N and old Mr N intended. Mrs G and Mrs N told me there was no hopes for me.

Thursday Mar 12   Received letter from Mr Stonestreet. I was at the Castle to hear trials.

Friday Mar 13   I was at the concert in the Great Room; and danced with Miss Cayley.

Saturday Mar 14   This evening I sat before Miss N--- and Mrs M G at the play, and next Miss N--- during the entertainment treated her, and handed her out to the chariot. The play was The Funeral or Grief A la mode and Harlequin Salamander the entertainment. At night when I got home I found a letter from T N--- Esqr and one from Mr Stonestreet. Mr N--- was a civil refusal of my request.

Sunday Mar 15   This afternoon after church went to Mrs G---s. Miss N--- looked something fluttered; when she was out I talked with Mrs N--- and Mrs G---s told them I would wait upon Mr N--- when he came to Doncaster; they disswaded me from it. I told them I would wait a year or a year and an half for Miss N --- they said she would be much too young then; all would not do. I showed Mrs N---and Mrs M G Mr N--- letter. I told them I would wait upon them on the morrow to know their final determination.

Monday Mar 16   This morning I called at Mrs G ---'s the boy said they were all out. I told him I would wait upon them in afternoon. My mother called about noon and told them I would come and take my leave and drink tea with them in the afternoon. Accordingly, before 5 o'clock in afternoon I went to Mrs G ---'s, found them all set at work; they were civil, and we talked of indiferent matters. Miss N --- looked rather grave, said very little. After tea which Miss N--- made; I told them I was sorry they sent back the musick this morning it hurt me much; such a trifle as that I hoped they would have kept; Miss said she had a great deal of musick more than she played. Before 7 o'clock Miss going out I asked Mrs N--- if there was any hopes, she said no. Miss coming in, I soon after took her by the hand and holding it fast in mine, I told her with some confusion and in a good deal of concern, that I should have been very happy had I had success in the present affair, but as I was so unhappy as not to have any hopes left, I wished her most heartily and sincerely all possible happiness, and a husband, far richer, wiser, better and every way much, very much, more accomplished than me, and one who might have as sincere a love for her as I had. I protested that I had not to my knowledge said one untruth during the whole affair; the old ladies said they believed I had not; and they and Miss wished me the same good wishes; I said much more than I can write down; and wine being brought I drank Miss N--- health, and all their healths seperately and Miss N--- drank my health, as did they all. But before this Miss N--- played and sung one song; and then asked me to play; I sat down and played Ariadne and Soft Invader of my Soul. I told Miss N--- while I had hold of her hand that I would always be a sincere and fast friend to her throughout life; and should always have a high respect for her. I told Mrs N --- and Mrs G---s that I should always have a friendship and regard for them, and if I did not call at any time in my passing through York, it would not be any want of respect, but quite the contrary, and desired they would impute to the highness of my regard for Miss N ---. Soon after this namely about half an hour past seven o'clock I got up, saluted old Mrs G---, Mrs M G---; Mrs N--- Mrs A--- G--- and last of all Miss N--- wishing her the utmost happiness, and saying God bless you, then as fast as I could I hurried out making a very low bow; and being under great concern as they might perceive. Thus concluded this affair the first of this kind I was ever engaged in. I must own I cannot enough admire the sweet and prudent behaviour of my young lady, and I pray God to grant her all possible happiness here and hereafter. The old ladies too have been very civil and full of expressions of their great regard for me.

Tuesday Mar 17   My mother and I intended to have left York this morning and the chaise was at the door, Miss Perrott who was to go with mother in chaise to Beverley was come, I was just paying Mr Howard his bill for my horses, which were also brought to the door, (this was about 11 o'clock) when in come Mrs N--- and Mrs M G---. I never was more surprized in my life, as to see them of whom I had taken such a formal leave the night before; but I was much more astonished when they said we had better not go that day but put it off to another it was so late then; my mother asked me what I would do, I looked more like a fool I dare say I ever did in my life, I said I would do as she had a mind; Mr Howard seemed to take the hint; in short the chaise was sent back, Miss Perrott went away in a huff; and Mrs N--- and Mrs M G--- sat down. I was in such confusion, concern and surprize, that I said nothing, at last I went out and left my mother with them, and walked about in my own room in a condition that can much better be imagined than expressed; after some time I returned, my mother coming to call me, and telling me that Mrs N--- said she had no sleep all last night she was under such concern for me; and what a regard she had for me; but said nothing favourable when talked to about the matter in hand. So I went in to them as pale as death and in vast confusion; I stood with my back to the fire, and did not say 10 words. At last they took their leave and I saluted them and desired my compliments to Miss N--- and I wished her and them all happiness. Miss N--- said she hoped I would make myself easy. I was much more chagrined today than I was yesterday and heartily vexed. NB In morning before this happened I made an agreement with Haxby for a desk organ with 5 stops.[113]

Wednesday Mar 18   This morning about a quarter before 9 o'clock my mother and Miss Perrott got into post chaise, and at 9 I mounted my horse at the door of my lodgings. Left York and got to Beverley before 5 o'clock in evening. Thank God! (NB I had several letters from my uncle and aunt Peggy while I was at York and wrote now and then to them.)

Sunday Mar 22   This being Easter Sunday I received the Holy Sacrament at St Marys church.

Friday Mar 27   This day Michael Newton and George Tufnell Esqrs were elected Members for this borough; I saw them in their chairs.[114] I was at Mr Bowmans.[115] Mr Newton invited me some days ago to dine with him today but I sent him word I was engaged. Tonight Mr Tufnell sent to invite me to dine with him tomorrow, I sent word I was engaged.

Tuesday Mar 31   Tonight Mr Tufnell gave a ball; I was invited, but was not there.

Wednesday Apr 1   Mr Tufnell and his brother Major Jolliff, and Mr William Meeke were so complaisant as to call to see me today, I was at dinner, so they would not come in; but we shook hands, and I wished Mr Tufnel joy. I had a great cold he might hear by my voice, so he might not think it strange I was not at his ball last night.

Thursday Apr 2   Tonight Mr Newton gave his ball; I was invited but was not there having a cold. My mother was there.

Friday Apr 3   Received a letter from Mr Haxby.

Thursday Apr 9   Lent Mr Hawdon a guinea.

Friday Apr 10   This afternoon by the York waggon I received 3 cases weighing 40 stone, for which paid for carriage 13s 4d besides ls for portridge from the waggon to our house. I did not unpack the organ. Received letter from Haxby at same time.

Sunday Apr 12   This evening Mr Haxby came to our house.

Monday Apr 13   This morning Mr Haxby began to set up the organ.

Wednesday Apr 15   This evening Mr Haxby completed my desk organ; and afterwards he went with me to Mr Enters concert, where was a great deal of company. NB Mr Haxby tuned my harpsichord.

Thursday Apr 16   This day at 12 o'clock Mr Haxby went away; I set him as far as the top of Weighton hill. NB This morning I paid Mr Haxby 36 guineas for the organ and he gave me a receipt.

Sunday Apr 19   This day I went out of mourning for the late King, George the 2d.

Friday Apr 24   Received a letter from Mr Stonestreet.

Saturday Apr 25   This evening I was at a concert and ball at Mr Raguenau's, where had a supper. We danced 9 couples and did not come away 'till betwixt 1 and two o'clock in the morning, but gave over dancing, before 12. Two of Mr Baums nephews are at Mr Raguenaus, Mr Devishes.

Monday Apr 27   This morning I went myself to the Blue Bell[116] and paid Mr Robinsons out rent £5 12s 4d whch sum Mr Robinson sent me a little while ago for that purpose I got a receipt for the same. This morning I carried Mr Joseph Sykes's note for £200, to my uncles in order that Mr J Sykes may send me the amount in a bill.

Tuesday April 28   Answered Mr Stonestreets letter.

Friday May 1   This morning I went to Hull got a bill of Mr Joseph Sykes for Mrs Popple for £460 13s. I got from Hull betwixt 2 and 3 o'clock in afternoon, and delivered the above bill to Mrs Popple; my uncle F who was with me at her lodgings having first indorsed it. I have not been at Hull before today since the 8th of August last.

Saturday May 2   We had a little concert at our house this afternoon 8 performers. Mr Raguenau, Mr Bowman, Capt Raines, Mr Smith, Mr Hawdon, and my uncle drank tea with us.

Tuesday May 5   Wrote to cousin Miss Julian Bere, and to the Revd Mr Ambrose Uvedale.

Monday May 11   This day betwixt 12 and 1 o'clock I went to the Tiger, according to notice, to attend the meeting of the rest of the subscribers for building an assembly room towards which I subscribed £25 some days ago. There were about a dozen subscribers present. We agreed upon a committee of seven, of which number they would have had me to have been one; but I would not, as I knew nothing about building. Seven of the subscribers were chose for two years, and we agreed upon purchasing a piece of ground and the old buildings thereon in Norwood, of Mr Charles Witty for two hundred guineas and an article was drawn up accordingly and signed by Mr Witty, and by Warton Warton,[117] Hugh Bethell and some other subscribers. It was also agreed that we should pay to Mr Robert Appleton our treasurer a quarter part of our subscriptions on the 20th of June. We all dined at the Tiger, and afterwards drank success to the assembly room etc etc and I came away betwixt 6 and 7 o'clock in the evening.

Saturday May 17   Received a letter from Mr Stonestreet with a bank post bill for £101 12s 6d. Answered Mr Stonestreets letter today.

Friday May 22   This night I was at a ball or assembly given by Lieut Col Turner etc, of Col Duncombes battalion of North Riding Militia now here. I spoke to Col Turner, and asked him to come and see me, he promised he would. I told him he would find me in the old house; he said he remembered it.

Saturday May 23   Received a letter from Mr Robinson, he desires I would pay the entrance money for two horses he designs to start at the races here.[118]

Sunday May 24   Answered Mr Robinsons letter by a man who will go to Buckton tomorrow; told him I would pay the 8 guineas entrance as he desired.

Friday May 29   Mr Robinsons man Richard came and told me I need not pay the money for entering the horses as he had brought it, and should pay it.

Tuesday Jun 2   Beverley races begin to day.

Friday Jun 5   This day the races at Beverley ended. Received a letter from my cousin Miss Julian Bere.

Saturday Jun 6   This morning remarkable for the transit of Venus over the sun. I did not see it myself.

Monday Jun 8   This day my mother and I dined and drank tea at Rowley with Revd Mr Wakefield.[119]

Tuesday Jun 9   I dined and drank tea at Brantingham with Revd Mr Bowman;[120] Mr Goulton, Wakefield, Territt and Bowman with us.

Monday Jun 15   This evening I was at an assembly given by the officers.

Tuesday Jun 16   Received a letter from Revd Mr Uvedale. This morning as I was riding out saw a coach, standing on the side of a hill and some ladies got out of it, I galloped up to them and offered them my assistance, I found it was a gentlemans coach and six, and 3 ladies, two of whom had the title of Ladyship; one of the horses had fallen down and some of the traces were broke, and one of the ladies was holding the foremost horses. I dismounted and made my servant take hold of the horses. They came from Everingham and were they said going to Beverley. I handed them into the coach and wished them well there. They gave Tom two shillings. Wrote to Mann Horsefield Esqr.

Thursday Jun 18   This day Mr Haxby came and dined with us and then looked over the organ and tuned it, where necessary, by a little past 8 o'clock in the evening he finished what he had to do at it. After supper he sung us some very pretty songs, vastly well.

Friday Jun 19   At 6 o'clock this morning before I was up Mr Haxby went away. NB Today I paid Mrs Featherston the guinea which I owed her, which her aunt had paid to Nat.

Saturday Jun 20   Last night or rather this morning one of the windows of the back parlour was broke in a terrible manner the window shutter split, and bricks etc thrown into the room to a great distance. One of the best chamber windows was also broke.[121] My mother sent the bellman about this afternoon to cry a reward of 3 guineas to any one, who discovers the person or persons guilty of the above outrage; which appears to have been committed with great fury. This day settled accounts with my uncle Featherston and paid him his ballance £45 4s so we are now clear. My uncle paid me in £10, principal of my £100 Beverley and Hull Turnpike; also half years interest due 12th instant on £100. £2 10s. I have now only £90 in Beverley and Hull Turnpike. NB Left with uncle Yates and Ellerkers bond, in case Yates should pay in his £50, while I am absent, and sent my little escrutore with box of writings etc, to my uncle.

[At this point in the diary there is a draft, with many alterations, of a notice to be given to the bellman:

Whereas last night some malicious person or persons broke Mrs Courtneys windows split one of the window shutters and threw some large pieces of brick into two rooms of Mrs Courtneys House in Walkergate this is to give notice that whoever will inform Mr Featherston of the person or persons who committed the said outrage, so as that he or they may/shall (receive proper punishment) [crossed through]. The Informer shall thereupon be entitled to three guineas reward, to be paid by the said Mr Featherston and if more than one person was concerned in the aforesaid fact if one of them will discover his accomplice or accomplices, he shall receive the above reward and be pardoned.]

Monday Jun 22   This morning I set out on horseback from Beverley and got to York before 5 o'clock in evening. My mother called at Mrs G---s [Grimes] but I did not. She mett with them all, there was some company there; very civil and free. I sent my compliments to them, I was obliged against my will to pass by the house when I went with Mr Horsefield to Mr Yowards. My mother went in a post chaise to York, I went 3 or 4 miles with her in it.

Tuesday Jun 23   This morning left York and went to Green Hammerton in post chaise with my mother; from thence I went to Harogate on horseback; and got there before 2 o'clock, to dinner at the Salutation. Sir Septimus Robinson[122] and his brother William Robinson, Esqr were there, very sensible civil men. Sir Septimus is Gentleman Usher of the Black Rod.

Monday Jun 29   I had agreed with one Mr Foxlow for a roan horse 4 years old near 14 hands high for which I was to give him 6 guineas but on Mr Vevers desiring I would let him have it as he was very ill, and could not get a horse to suit him to ride, I out of compassion let him have it; but found afterwards he did not often ride it, but another horse he had lately got, so told him should be much obliged to him if he would let me

Walkergate House, Beverley, built c1770 on the site of the house where John Courtney
lived when writing the first two volumes of his diary.

have it but he would not. Went with Mrs Lister, Lady of [blank] Lister Esqr of Gisburn
Park a mighty agreable good woman and Mr Wardell etc to Plum[p]ton, very pretty
place, much improved since I saw it. NB Mr Frank Dodsworth and his lady were at
Harogate he was very complaisant. I heard him preach at chapel the 28th instant yesterday.
Very good preacher. I mett with Revd Mr Wells,[123] whom I have not seen these 9 years,
since I left school, he came to see me, we were in same seat at school.

Sunday Jul 5   This morning Mr Wells read prayers and preached, reads prayers sadly,
but preached a very good sermon. Lady Margaret Dalzell a Scotch lady is come to our
house, a very obliging polite old woman.[124]

Sunday Jul 12   Mr Dennis preached a very good sermon.

Monday Jul 13   This morning early my mother and I in a post chaise and a large party on horseback went to Studley,[125] which I had not seen before, walked all over the gardens etc, saw the house, chapel, dairy etc etc. Charming place; vastly grand walks. The house grandly furnished many fine pictures. We afterwards dined at the Park Gate, and then went to Rippon saw the Minster played a little on the organ, as did Miss Ethelston a young lady with us. We drank tea at Ripon; 'tis beautifully situated, but not so pretty a town as Beverley. We got back to Harogate before 8 o'clock in evening.

Tuesday Jul 14   This evening Lady Dalzell and my mother and a party of us went to G[reen] D[ragon]. I talked to Miss Yorks a little, and Lord Northesk[126] and I talked a good while together.

Saturday Jul 19   Mr Docwray preached a most excellent sermon, inculcating the Christian Duties of Charity and Universal Benevolence.

Monday Jul 20   This morning about 9 o'clock left Harogate (I on horseback mother in a chaise with one Miss Wright) having first taken leave of all our friends, who exprest themselves very kindly and seemed sorry to part with us. Before I came away Mr Robinson sent for me up into his room. I found him going to bed, and complaining of an aguish disorder, and desired I would get 2 ozs of powdered bark for him at Mr Jubbs, and gave me money to pay for it. I left my compliments to Sir Septimus, (who as well as his brother have been very civil). At one o'clock got to York, went to Mr Jubbs and bought the powder of bark and sent it with a letter to Sir Septimus Robinson with the post chaise boy. NB I gave them an invitation to come and see me and eat a bit of mutton, when they came our way and they said they would and Mr Robinson said if he came within 20 miles of Beverley he would come and see me. This afternoon I settled accounts with Mr Hinxman the bookseller I let him have Smollett for 2 pence a number without the cuts and Stachouses History of the Bible for a guinea and a half and Renandots Account of China for 2s 6d and the ballance of our account due to him was 17s and 2d which paid him.[127] I also changed some musick at Haxby and received 4s 6d ballance. My Mother called at Mrs G---s but they were all gone to T---p [Towthorpe]; Mrs Ann G she saw at Mrs Milwards and she told her they were gone to T.

Tuesday Jul 21   This morning betwixt 8 and 9 o'clock I left York, my mother went in the stage coach I on horseback, at Weighton, where we dined, called to see Mr Hudson's organ, which is a very fine one, 7 stops, it only cost him £25. Vastly cheap. He played very well upon it, as did also Master Allott and sung an Italian song very finely, I played a little upon it. I saw also an harpsichord of Mr Hudsons own making, not a very good one. I got very well, thank God to Beverley betwixt 3 and 4 o'clock in the afternoon.

Tuesday Jul 28   Wrote to my cousin Miss Julian Bere.

Saturday Aug 1   Wrote to Sir Robert Hildyard Bart.[128]

Monday Aug 3   This evening received a letter from Sir Robert Hildyard. Memorandum. My aunt Peggy paid to Mr Robert Appleton treasurer the 1st payment of my subscription towards building an assembly room I say she paid £6 5s which sum I left with her for that purpose when I went to Harogate. She paid said £6 5s last month.

Wednesday Aug 5   This morning at 8 o'clock set out from Beverley in a post chaise with my mother, dined at Foxholes and got to Scarborough at 5 o'clock in evening: took lodgings at Mr Chancellours next door to the new Long Room. In evening I went to Browns Long Room, saw the Duke of York[129] dance with Miss Clare Adams. He is grown much fatter, but dances very well.

Thursday Aug 6   In evening I danced at Cooks Long Room with Miss Caroline Houghton; the Duke danced again with Miss Clare Adams.

Friday Aug 7   This being a drest night there was a very fine show of ladies and gentlemen and upon the Duke's coming in every body stood up 'till he had taken his seat, he opened the ball with Lady Scarborough[130] and danced country dances with Mrs Chomley. He generally dances two dances down but never dances up, and always calls up the dances he dances being always at the top. I danced tonight. Received a letter from Mr Stonestreet.

Thursday Aug 13   Revd Mr Wind[131] dined and drank tea with us.

Sunday Aug 16   This afternoon heard Wainman who was some time ago curate at Beverley Minster preached the strangest sermon I ever heard; he said among many other odd things, that very few of the clergy would be saved. Poor man is mad!

Monday Aug 17   This morning the Duke of York was at the spaw, and 2 of his servants played on French horns and 2 on the hautboy all the time he was there. Nobody put off their hats when they meet him, but when he sat down in the shed the gentlemen therein pulled off their hats and sat with them off. It being given out that it was expected the gentlemen should wait upon him if I may so say, when they knew he was out, this morning Sir Brian Stapilton Bart[132] and I went to the Duke of Yorks lodgings and upon Sir Brians saying we were come to pay our compliments to his Royal Highness, the gentleman told us he would take our names down, and desired us to walk into the parlour, which we did and he brought us a quarter of a sheet of paper and pen and ink, and Sir Brian set down his name and then I set down mine, the gentleman assured us he would give it to the Duke on his return; and thus we performed this peice of ceremony.

Tuesday Aug 18   This day at 12 o'clock his Royal Highness the Duke of York left Scarborough in his own post chaise with Mrs Chomley, and had 4 or 5 old portmanteaus behind to my very great surprize, Mr Chomleys Mr Crofts etc coaches attended him. This evening my uncle F came to Scarborough.

Thursday Aug 20   This morning I breakfasted with Captain Blomberg, and his mother, and Mrs and Miss George, the latter I danced with last night. I knew her formerly at

Cambridge; she was younger daughter to late Dean of Lincoln Provost of Kings College.[133]

Saturday Aug 22   This morning before 9 o'clock I left Scarborough on horseback, my mother in post chaise. Dined at Driffield, and got well, thank God, to Beverley a little past 6 o'clock.

Thursday Aug 27   This morning Governor Dawson returned the visit I made him the other day.

Friday Sep 4   Mr Scot the barber from York called today when I was out left word that Mr Vevers desired him to acquaint me I might have the horse if I would, and that as he was about disposing of him, he thought proper to give me the first offer.

Sunday Sep 6   Wrote to Mr Scot, dont chuse to buy the horse.

Wednesday Sep 9   In the morning I saw Colonel Duncombe's battalion of North Riding Militia reviewed by General St Clair; and in evening I was [at] a ball given by Colonel Duncombe.

Thursday Sep 10   This afternoon Governor Dawson, a merchant of great eminence in London one Mr Wilson, Captain Smith, and Ensign Harding of Colonel Duncombes Militia now here, Ensign Smith of East Riding Militia, Mr Raguenau and his family, Mrs Dawson and Misses and Miss Belt drank tea with us, and we had a little concert, vizt: Voice — Miss Raguenau; First Fiddle — Mr Smith; Second — Master Raguenau; Violincello — Mr De Montet; Mandolina — Miss Marianne Raguenau; Harpsichord, Thor Bass — John Courtney.

Sunday Sep 13 Wrote to Mr Haxby. King George III was married to the Princess Charlotte of Meclenburg last Tuesday night the 8th instant. God Save King George and Queen Charlotte.

Saturday Sep 19   This afternoon I paid Mr Robert Appleton, treasurer, the second payment of my subscription to the assembly room, vizt £6 5s.

Tuesday Sep 22   This day being their Majesties King George and Queen Charlotte's coronation, the Militia in this town, vizt Col Duncombe's battalion, drew up in the Market Place and fired 3 vollies, there were some few bottles of wine brought into the Market Place, and the officers and one or two gentlemen drank the King and Queen's health, etc, 50 men or more discharging their musquets at every health. The Mayor gave a dinner to the Corporation, officers and a few gentlemen, and they drank twelve healths, there being a discharge of musquets after every health and peal of bells; in the evening were illuminations and an assembly; I was there; but strange to think of, no ball and a regiment here. Fine day! God Save King George and Queen Charlotte!

Wednesday Sep 23   This evening Mr Haxby came to set my organ to rights for the wood being shrunk or from some other cause the keys many of them stuck which is a fault he ought to be sure to mend or take the organ back again.

Thursday Sep 24   This morning Mr Haxby begun upon the organ and was all day at it. This afternoon Tom, my man, fell out of our mulberry tree as he was pulling mulberries, I was walking on gravel walk, just by, when he fell. He did not hurt himself much, falling on his back; the bough breaking was the occasion of his fall. I had him let blood.

Saturday Sep 26   Mr Haxby did not finish with the organ 'till near 5 o'clock this evening when he went away. He spoke to Aldermen, etc, about building the organ at the Minster, my uncle spoke to some of them about him.

Sunday Sep 27   This morning at St Mary's church I saw old Mr N--- [Newsome] and his nephew Mr D---. I thought it was them, and heard after Mr N had been in town. I saw him look at me.

Tuesday Sep 29   Wrote to Mr Stonestreet inclosing a letter of Miss Appletons to the Major therein, which she desires Mr S to put into the office at London.

Saturday Oct 3   NB This morning Mr Milner called and brought me a letter from Mr Robinson of Buckton.

Tuesday Oct 13   Received a letter from Mr Stonestreet.

Thursday Oct 15   This day dined with the officers of Col Duncombes battalion of North Riding Militia, on an invitation from Capt Smith whose son is also here, and in the afternoon Capt Smith and his son came to drink tea with me, but the former being ill went away.

Sunday Oct 25   This being his Majestys accession when he enters into the second year of his reign the bells rung etc. God send him a long and happy reign!

Tuesday Oct 27   Lady Margaret Dalzell dined with us today.

Sunday Nov 1   At ¼ past 9 o'clock it is five years ago since my dear father died, for he died 1st November 1756!

Friday Nov 6   'Tis five years ago this evening since my dear father was buried; for he was buried the 6th of November 1756!

Monday Nov 9   This is Lord Mayors day at London, the King, Queen and rest of the royal family are to dine with the Lord Mayor at Guildhall as is the custom for every King to do once in his reign. There will be a grand procession into the city.

Sunday Nov 15   Wrote to Mr Stonestreet about buying some stock for Mrs Truby.

Tuesday Nov 24   Paid my servant Thomas Lamb his years wage due Martinmas four guineas. NB Yesterday I agreed with a boy called Robert Kenningham to be my servant (till I can meet with a man) at 2 shillings per week if I keep him only 4 weeks but afterwards I am to give him only 1s 6d per week if I keep him longer. Tom went away in evening.

Thursday Nov 26   I hired a man servant who lived with Mr Greyburn[134] his name is William Constable; I am to give him six guineas a year wage, full livery, frock and hat, and he is to come Monday next.

Sunday Nov 29   Wrote to Mr Stonestreet, desiring he would buy with the amount of my last dividends which is £101 12s 6d old South Sea annuities for me.

Monday Nov 30   This evening my new man William Constable came, and Bob Kenningham went away.

Wednesday Dec 2   This afternoon Mr Mrs and Miss Waines, Mr and Mrs Saunders, Dr Hunter, etc being at our house I played a good deal to them upon the organ, with which they were much delighted.

Thursday Dec 3   This evening betwixt 4 and 5 o'clock poor Mr William Gee's corpse was brought to St Marys Church from Bristol, and interred in the quire of the same church. I went to see the ceremony along with two young Mr Constables whom I saw going. Mr Gee was an old acquaintance and schoolfellow, I have known him 20 years and we were in the same seat at school many years. He was in the 27th year of his age. Poor man I am very sorry for him!

Friday Dec 4   My new man William upon my asking him where he had been this morning gave me his fastenpenny again, and I found afterwards that Mr Greyburn had been persuading him back again, which is a very unjust and ungenteel behaviour.

Saturday Dec 5   William asked me this afternoon whether he was at liberty I told him, yes to be sure; he accordingly went away; but wanted to come again as he told them in kitchen, but I will have nothing to say to such a fickle unsettled fellow. In evening Bob Kenningham came again to look after my horses etc.

Sunday Dec 6   Received a letter from Mr Stonestreet.

Tuesday Dec 8   William came to me this morning and told me he was very sorry for what he had done, and begged I would take him again and that he would settle etc, he says that Mr Greyburn sent for him last Wednesday night, we had company so he did not go to speak to him till Thursday morning that Mr G offered to take him again and promised he would please him; I told William that Mr G had certainly used me very ill, and was more to blame than he; but that I could not think of taking him now, though I told him I forgave him, and advised him to settle etc and stay in his place a year however. He said Mr G had not yet hired him but he is at his house.

Thursday Dec 10   Memorandum. I agreed with Hop, barber to give him 30 shillings a year for shaving me and dressing my wiggs, and I am to be shaved 4 times a week whenever I chuse it, and I am to pay him quarterly. NB I commenced shaving with Hop on Tuesday the 1st of this month. NB On the 1st instant I discharged Mr Thomas

White as he told me in an uncivil manner that he must advance my price from one guinea to 30 shillings a year, and insisted I had not agreed to shave 3 times a week; but I showed him the agreement in my book which did not seem to satisfy him however I offered him 25 shillings per annum but he would not take it. As Hop is a poor man, I told him as soon as found he could dress my wigs, I would give him 30 shillings a year as above.

Monday Dec 14 This morning I went to Hull and got there before 1 o'clock in afternoon went to the George Inn. At night went to the assembly. I have not been at Hull assembly for upwards of a year and an half.

Tuesday Dec 15 This morning I called at Dr Sykes's told him I hoped he would pay in the £400, late lent to his brother in 3 months time, he according to custom said he could not promise to pay it in 3 nor 20 months, that his brother did not leave effects in personals sufficient to pay, I had a good deal of talk with him but could make nothing of him so came away. Strange man! I dined and I had tea at old Mrs Collings with uncle and aunt then went to the play. Afterwards went to my inn, and went into the room where the Beverley ladies and gentlemen were, (who came to see play and go back tonight) and supped with them. Mr Thomas Constable[135] staid all night.

Wednesday Dec 16 This morning about half hour past 10 o'clock, Mr Thomas Constable and I left Hull, and got to Beverley a little past 12 o'clock at noon.

Thursday Dec 17 I went this day to Mr Robert Appletons and paid the third part of my subscription for building the assembly room £6 5s to Mr W Ellis, junior his clerk who gave me a receipt for the same. This evening I was at a private ball at Miss Hewitts went at 4 o'clock afternoon drank tea then began to dance and had queens cakes and negus, and broke up at 9 o'clock.

Friday Dec 18 This evening I was at a private ball at Miss Goultons went to drink tea at 4, and broke up at 9 o'clock as last night. We had queens cakes, biskets, rum punch and mead negus.

Monday Dec 21 NB I put by £6 5s for the last payment of my subscription for the new Assembly Rooms, that it may be ready when called for.

Tuesday Dec 22 I settled accounts with my mother.

Tuesday Dec 29 Wrote to Revd Mr Ambrose Uvedale.

Thursday Dec 31 I put by a guinea to send Nat, some silver for the poor etc. NB This year I have saved one hundred pounds, and besides, twenty five pounds subscribed to the new Assembly Room, for which £25 I dont expect to receive great interest, so that in all (reckoning this £25 subs) I have saved this year one hundred and twenty five pounds.

Laus Deo!
End of the year 1761.

MDCCLXII [1762]

Friday Jan 1   Begun this year at Beverley, and was at prayers at St Mary's in morning and afternoon. Received a letter from Mr Stonestreet. He has bought me £125 old South Sea annuities at 7 per cent.

Monday Jan 4   Received of my uncle Featherston £2 5s being half a years interest on my £90, Beverley and Hull Turnpike. NB This day war was declared against Spain at London (as heard afterwards).

Tuesday Jan 5   This day I agreed with Peter Hornby, who formerly lived with Mr Greyburn, to take him, as my servant on trial for two months, for which time I am to give him one pound four shillings, (without a livery,) and if at the end of the said 2 months, I find him suitable and think fit to keep him, I am to give him 5 guineas a year, a full livery, hat, and fustian[136] frock from that time. The man is about 24 years of age.

Friday Jan 8   Received a letter from Messrs Hinxman, Todd and Sootheran, booksellers.[137]

Saturday Jan 9   This day my new servant Peter Hornby came, and I dismissed Bob Kenningham, paying him 7s 6d for 5 weeks he has been with me.

Wednesday Jan 13   This afternoon war was declared here at Beverley against Spain I was to see the ceremony at Mr Randolph Hewitt. God send us good success, and good peace sooner than we can now expect! NB I remember seeing war declared against Spain the last time, which is 22 years ago, and this is the fourth time I have seen war declared, vizt twice against Spain and twice against France.

Saturday Jan 16   Received a letter from Revd Dr Sykes, inclosing a bill for £140, in part of payment of principal £400, due from late Richard Sykes Esqr. I was surprized to see this, but it is like all his doings, he pretends to make it a great favour, unaccountable man. He thinks he does me a favour by paying me in my money in what sums and at what times he chuses. But however on my uncles account I took the said bill, and also 18s 6d interest and gave a receipt for the same. Vide also the doctors smooth letter. Revd Mr Territt dined with us today.

Monday Jan 18   This being the day appointed to be kept for the Queens birthday, we had an assembly at night.

Thursday Jan 21   This evening drank tea and supped at Revd Mr Johnstons, where I drank more than have done a long time, or I believe ever did, I walked home, but was very sick when I got home and was obliged to be helped to bed.

Friday Jan 22   This evening Dr Cotes and Mr Jacombe came to talk with me about establishing a weekly concert for 6 nights, the proposals are each gentleman pay 1s 6d or 2s, each night present or absent, and they may bring what ladies they please gratis. I am to talk with Mr Hawdon about it.

Saturday Jan 23   Having seen Dr Perrott going towards Hull last Wednesday evening I was much afraid that Mr Perrott was very ill, Mrs Johnston told my mother he was t'other day; this morning I asked Ferraby, who gave me the melancholly account, that Dr Perrott had sat up with him all last night, the beggining of which he was better, but at five o'clock this morning he changed for the worse, and that his life was not expected. I feel a concern not to be described. It is three years this very day since I was in Mr Perrotts house, I was too much affected to even go there again, though sorry I did not call last time I was at Hull! I have not been in Mr Perrotts house since 23d January 1759.

Sunday Jan 24   Received a letter from Mr Stonestreet.

Monday Jan 25   This day I heard the melancholly account that poor Mr Perrott died yesterday; some people say that the badness of his circumstances broke his heart, but Mrs Perrott (some time ago when my uncle and aunt were at Hull) told my aunt that Mr Perrotts foot which used to break every two years, not breaking was the occasion of his illness. Whatever be the occasion of his death, one thing is very certain that the world has lost a most worthy man and myself a person for whom I had a very great value and esteem. He was a man, whose great benevolence, Christian charity in forgiveness of injuries, piety etc were heightend by a chearful open behaviour which joined with the gracefulness of his person (notwithstanding his misfortune in his foot) and the advantages of a good countenance inspired every one who conversed with him with infinite pleasure. But what signify words, he was an amiable and good man!

Wednesday Jan 27   We had Revd Mr Johnston, with his wife and 2 daughters, Mr Goulton his wife and daughter, Lady Margaret Dalzell, Dr Hunter, my uncle and aunt Featherston and Miss Parsons to dine with us.

Thursday Jan 28   I hear Mr Perrott was buried at Hessle either on Tuesday or yesterday. I am very much concerned at his death!

Sunday Jan 31   Mrs Robinson informing us that Mr Robinson was extremely ill and had no advice; I wrote to him today to desire he would let me send him Dr Hunter or some other physician, and that I would come and stay with him if he chose it, till Sir William Foulis could come to him. I shall send my man over to Buckton with this letter early tomorrow morning. This afternoon I drank tea at Miss Appletons, we talked about poor Mr Perrotts affairs, she says they are she fears very bad, but hopes Mrs Perrott will have something left of her jointure, I hope she will with all my heart! Poor Miss Harrison[138] will get nothing then however 'tis plain, but am glad Mrs Dolly Perrott left her a fortune. I am sincerely sorry for the distresses of all these worthy people, they touch me to the quick! I am very sorry I did not call at poor Mr Perrotts, last time I was at Hull, that I might once again have seen him and shaked hands with him! I had not seen him of a long time. I saw Mrs Perrott when I was at Hull and enquired after him. Poor man!

Monday Feb 1   This morning early my servant Peter went to Buckton with my letter to Mr Robinson. This day dined, drank tea and supped at my uncles.

Tuesday Feb 2   This afternoon Peter returned with a letter from Mr Robinson.

Friday Feb 5   Mrs Featherston gave me a receipt for Nats guinea which I sent him.

Saturday Feb 6   This morning betwixt 9 and 10 o'clock I set out on horseback for York, dined at Barnby Moor[139] and got to York little after 4 o'clock in afternoon, to Howards. Went to the play Frodshams benefit.

Sunday Feb 7   Went in morning to St Martins church in Micklegate in afternoon to Belfreys.[140] Drank tea at Mrs Milwards in St Andrewgate. Called at Dr Perrotts this morning. Not at home.

Monday Feb 8   In the evening was at the assembly. Danced with Miss Fanny Morritt. Saw Capt C who they say in York makes his addresses to Miss N.[141] A good smart man. NB This morning breakfasted at Mrs Mary Goultons.

Tuesday Feb 9   This morning I went to Mr Bacon Morritts to see my partner, the eldest Miss Morritt showed me a room which is hung round with her own work, consisting of landscapes, fruitpeices, etc all of needlework so vastly fine that at a very little distance I took it for very choice painting, all in fine proportion, and charming colours, they are all in gilt frames.[142] They are as great curiositys as any thing I ever saw. I dined at Mann Horsefields, Esqr. I spoke to him about my money, told him I thought I should have 5 per cent as could make more now than 5¼ in the stocks that my uncle was of same oppinion, he gave me a letter to my uncle, wherein he says he has mentioned it, and seemed willing to give me 5 per cent. I drank tea at Mrs Ingrams afterwards went to the play. NB This evening I sent my man with a note to Mrs Grimes and Mrs Newsome and Miss and desired to know how they did and if they had any commands to Beverley I proposed going tomorrow; they sent word they were all very well, should have been glad to see me, and wished me a good journey. I sent a note to same effect to Dr Mrs and Miss Perrott, and received a note with same answer. I should have wished to have had some talk with Dr Perrott about poor Mr Perrotts affairs but Miss Perrott is just recovered of a fever, so thought better not to call. NB I have not called at Mrs G---s [Grimes] nor seen anything of them or Miss N[ewsome].

Wednesday Feb 10   This morning betwixt 9 and 10 I left York on horseback, found it very bad riding, being an hard frost and ice all the way. Dined at Weighton, and got well thank God, to Beverley betwixt 5 and 6 in the evening.

Saturday Feb 13   NB Some time ago I subscribed to a concert proposed to me by Dr Cotes and Mr Jacomb, to pay 12 shillings for 6 nights to carry what ladies you chuse gratis to be at the assembly room, in nature of a private concert, Dr Cotes will play on violincello, and Mr Jacomb on harpsichord and sing, some other gentlemen will play and Hawdon and others to be hired to assist.

Sunday Feb 14   Poor Mr Perrott has died in a vast deal of debt they say; he left Miss Harrison £2000 by his will but fear she will be little better for that.

Wednesday Feb 17   Tonight at the assembly Dr Cotes pressed me very much to lend my harpsichord to the concert but told him I had made a resolution not to lend it some years ago. He seemed not pleased.

Thursday Feb 18   This morning I revived the old and good custom of going to see my partners, which I had not done at Beverley (nor at Hull) sometime. But this morning went to see Miss Smelt my last nights partner. She played and sang extremely well to my great entertainment.

Friday Feb 19   We had our first private concert at the assembly room, (26 subscribers) I carried Lady Margaret Dalzell and my mother gave them tickets on a card. After the concert we had a dance. This day received a letter from Mr Thomas Haxby of York, with a design for the organ for Beverley Minster, in a tin case.[143]

Saturday Feb 20   This morning went to Mr Waines talked to him about the organ, and in the afternoon sent him the design which he will show to the Corporation at a meeting. Heard that Miss N[ewsome] is soon to be married to Capt C[ooke].

Monday Feb 22   My birthday; I am twenty eight years old, praised be God my preserver! My uncle and aunt Featherston, Mrs Truby and Miss Parsons, Miss Appleton and Mr Enter all dined, drank tea, and supped with us except Mr Enter who went away after dinner.

Tuesday Feb 23   This afternoon, according to notice sent me yesterday I attended at a meeting of the subscribers to the private concert, when it was resolved that the officers of the West Riding Militia, who are coming to this town to morrow, shall be invited to the concert on Friday next and afterwards may subscribe 8 shillings for the remaining 4 nights; it was also agreed that the tickets given to the ladies should express the night, second third and so on. Then 5 of the subscribers were chosen as a committee to manage all matters relating to the concert of which number I was one. The committee are vizt Mr Raguenau; Mr Constable; Dr Cotes; Dr Hunter; John Courtney.

Wednesday Feb 24   This day at noon a battalion of the West Riding Militia commanded by Lieut Col Lister, late Finch, late Lord Downes came here. Major Myers is the commanding officer, who was an old schoolfellow of mine, he was 2 seats below me. This batallion was at Beverley several months about 2 years ago.

Tuesday Mar 2   This afternoon I went to see Major Myers and drank tea with him and his lady. Capt Cooke drank tea there I asked him to come and see me with the Major.

Wednesday Mar 3   This evening I danced with Mrs Myers the Majors Lady at the assembly; she as well as the Major are old acquaintance of mine.

Thursday Mar 4   This morning I acquainted my mother of the particular regard I had for Miss S---t [Smelt]; she seemed to like her very well.

Friday Mar 5   This morning my mother changed her oppinion in regard to yesterdays affair. Received a letter or note from Dr Sykes; he will pay in my money the 17th.

Saturday Mar 6   Major Myers and Capt Cooke, made me a visit this morning. Mr Enter sent me a letter that he gave up the subscription, etc vide the letter, being surprised I went to see him found him very ill of a sore throat talked a good deal about his behaviour to some people his playing at the concert etc. I called afterwards at Mr Raguenaus, who has received letter to same purport, I explained this matter as well as I could to him, he said he should give him the same when he made a concert, very generous and kind!

Monday Mar 8 Heard to day that old Mr N[ewsome] is dead; tempora mutantur, — I wish his grandaughter very happy with Capt C[ooke]. Had this event happened last year it might have been very different, I am not mercenary though, so dont regrett it did not. NB The 7th instant I hired Thomas Campelman who was Mr Ellerkers[144] whipper, I am to give him four pounds a year wage and a full livery and frock, and a hatt. He has not, tis pity, had the small pox. He is about 20 years of age.

Thursday Mar 11 This day Thomas Campelman my new servant came.

Friday Mar 12 Received a letter from Mr Peirson.

Saturday Mar 13 This afternoon I carry'd Miss Smelt a country dance I had composed, having the other night at the assembly agreed to compose the tune if she would the figure to which she consented, I say carried her the dance (the first music I ever composed) and staid and drank tea with her and 3 more young ladies with her played over the tune on her spinnett she and rest [of] ladies danced and she composed a figure to the tune, which she danced with the rest; she gives the name of the Whim to the dance.

Wednesday Mar 17 This morning the Revd Dr Sykes's servant brought me two hundred and sixty pounds being the principal and three pounds five shillings interest. So now Revd Dr Sykes has paid in all the debt due from the late Richard Sykes Esq.

Sunday Mar 21 My mother received a letter from Lady Mary Dalzell in which she inclosed me a rebus.[145] I wrote to Mr Thomas Haxby.

Monday Mar 22 Wrote to Mr Yates at Hull send letter by uncle F tomorrow.

Tuesday Mar 23 This day I made my will, having destroyed my old one some days ago.

Friday Mar 26 Received a letter from Mr Haxby with a catalogue of the late Revd Mr Clarkes (my late worthy masters) library.

Monday Mar 29 This evening a catalogue of Mr Clarkes library was brought me, which the person who brought it said Mr Luban brought (from York) [crossed through] for me. I suppose Mr F Clarke has ordered them to send me one, as his brother was my master, for whom he knew I had a very great respect. Mr Barry of Hull[146] last Wednesday morning fell upon his sword and was found dead. The cause of this terrible action is not yet clearly known. But thought to be lunacy.

above: Beverley Assembly Rooms, Norwood, in centre. Built in 1762–3 to the designs of John Carr. Demolished in 1935.

N.° A 7
PROPRIETOR
To the
BEVERLEY
Affembly Rooms,
1763.

Warton Warton Esq.

left: A ticket for the Beverley Assembly Rooms, printed on the back of a playing card. (East Riding of Yorkshire Council Archives and Records Service.) This ticket is made out to Warton Warton who lived in Newbegin House, where John Courtney spent most of his married life.

Thursday Apr 1 Paid to Mr Appleton the last payment of my subscription money towards building the new assembly rooms at Beverley. Vide Mr Appletons receipt. I have now paid my whole subscription of five and twenty pounds.

Friday Apr 2   This morning heard to my great surprise and concern that poor Mrs Meeke died last night; she was better yesterday Mrs Waines says, and very chearful. I am extremely sorry for her, she was a good natured inoffensive woman, and will be I fear an irreparable loss to her family. God preserve them and comfort them

Sunday Apr 4   Received a letter from Mr Stonestreet.

Monday Apr 5   We had a sort of musical rout, several fine airs of the oratorio of the Messiah were sung by Mr Jacomb, and Mr Hodgson from Newcastle and accompany'd by Mr Hawdon on the organ, and other sacred musick fit for this week was also performed; Miss Raguenau and Miss H Waines also sung the anthem to the full organ (I playing) and they sung some songs too, as did Mr Jacomb to the harpsichord. Major Myers his lady, Capt Cooke, Dr Cotes and his sister, Mr Raguenaus family, Mr Waines ditto, Dr Hunter, Mr William Meeke, Mr Jacomb, Mr and Mrs Saunders etc we were in all I believe 25.

Tuesday Apr 6   I wrote to Mr Hotham at York for several books out of the late Revd Mr Clarke's library, the sale of which begins to morrow.

Friday Apr 9   Received by carrier books out of sale of Revd Mr Clarkes library etc, to the amount of £3 2s carriage ls total £3 3s.

Sunday Apr 11   Received a letter from Mr Stonestreet with a letter of attorney for my uncle Featherston.

Tuesday Apr 13   This morning a little past 5 o'clock my mother and I left Beverley in a post chaise (and aunt Peggy went with us as far as Hull), got to Hull before 7. (NB I have not been at Hull before since Mr Perrotts death.) Crossed the water, fine passage, dined at Spittle, and got to Lincoln before 5 o'clock in evening. I calld to see Miss Caroline Houghton, and drank tea with Revd Mr Hewthwaite, afterwards went to the assembly, mett with Revd Mr Palmer a college acquaintance of my year, and knew the queen of the assembly and 3 or 4 ladies more, I would not dance, never was at Lincoln assembly before. NB 'Twas the up hill assembly.[147]

Wednesday Apr 14   Dined at Colesworth [Colsterworth], lay at Stilton; tasted stilton cheese for the first time I believe.

Thursday Apr 15   Set out this morning at half an hour past four, and got to breakfast at Bugden [Buckden] at 6; dined at Barnet, and got to London about 5 o'clock and at last took lodgings at one Mrs Powells in Cecil Street in the Strand; parlour and 2 lodging rooms on the second floor at 28 shillings a week. NB as was inquiring at Mrs Denhams our old lodgings I saw Revd Mr Neat passing by whom I knew very well at college, and who took his degree along with me, he came up to me and said very civilly and kindly, that if my mother could meet with any accomodation, he had a bed at my service at his house in Gloster Street.

Saturday Apr 17   Called this morning at Peter Wyche's Esqr in Great Ormond Street he has been ill and is not well recovered. Mett with Revd Mr Neat and went in with him to his aunts house in same street very grand, many fine pictures, saw a little girl of Mr Neats a charming child, can just talk; he has been married above 2 years and his wife was lately delivered of a boy, he went with me to his house in Gloster Street. In the evening I was at Drury Lane theatre, 'twas one of Garricks own benefits, King Lear, and Intriguing Chambermaid; Garrick in Lear, and Mrs Cibber in Cordelia were inimitable; Mrs Clive was excellent in the part of the chambermaid; prodigous full house.[148]

Sunday Apr 18   I went with Vincent Matthias Esqr Undertreasurer to the Queen to St James's Chapel, and got with difficulty into the organ loft; I had the pleasure of seeing the King and Queen and Prince William, Prince Henry, and Lady Augusta; the Queen is not handsome, little and pale, but seems chearful and agreable. The King looks vastly well handsomer than he was when Prince of Wales, Dr Pyle[149] preached. In the afternoon drank tea with Mr Matthias, their room commands a noble prospect of the Thames the cities of London and Westminster, the bridges etc.

Monday Apr 19   Mr Stonestreet, my mother and self drank tea at Mr Hogarth's with my cousin Miss Bere; Mr Hogarth is a plain man showed and explained the election pictures to us, talks much against the French. NB Mr Stonestreet came today to our lodgings after dinner. Talked about my affair about Miss N[ewsome] last year etc.

Tuesday Apr 20   Mr Stonestreet dined with us. I was at Drury Lane theatre, saw the Alchymist and the Enchanter, (Mrs Vincents Benefit, who sang several songs). Garrick played Abel Drugger, Mrs Pritchard, Doll Common, Miss Nancy Dawson, etc danced.

Wednesday Apr 21   I was at the oratorio of Judas Maccabeus (Frazi's Benefit) at the Great Room[150] in Dean Street Soho, twas very grand but the Messiah is finer, Frazi, Miss Young, Beard and Champness etc, etc, sung; and Stanley played a concerto on the organ; very fine!

Sunday Apr 24   I went to the exhibition of the paintings, etc, at Society of Arts etc, Great Room in the Strand;[151] some good pictures; saw Chevalier Taylor there.[152]

Sunday Apr 25   I was at court at St James's; one Mr Duke a young Templar[153] an acquaintance of Mrs Popples went with me, we went there in chairs, I was drest in my new suit with sword etc. I had a full view of their Majesties, who both went round the ring to make their compliments etc. Her Majesty seemed very merry; agreable easy behaviour. The Prince of Meclenburg was there, plain man, very black and swarthy. Prince William, Prince Henry and Lady Augusta were also there; Princess Augusta vastly like the King, handsome lady, rather too fat. The Dutch ambassador was at court, a portly man, Lady Sarah Lenox was there too, a good fine looking woman. God save King George III and Queen Charlotte! When court was over we walked through the park and took a coach at Spring Garden Gate and returned to my lodgings, and Mr Duke dined with us; after dinner we walked into Somerset Gardens. Fine prospect from thence. Mrs Hogarth Miss Bere and Mr Duke drank tea with us.

Monday Apr 26   Dined at Islington with Mr Stonestreet, went with him and his sister to Sadlers Wells; saw Mathews dance on the wire. Miss Wilkinson played on the musical glasses; pretty enough. The tumblers and Mathews surprisingly expert and active. Went to see the sign painters exhibition in Bow Street Covent Garden. Whimsical.

Tuesday Apr 27   This morning went with Mrs Popple to the rehearsal of the musick for the benefit of the Westminster Infirmary at St Margarets Westminster, a most elegant church, which was repaired and beautify'd at the expence of the House of Commons; there were I dare say an hundred performers Beard, Champness, Baildon Cox etc sung; near 40 voices I believe; Handells Te Deum, The Grand Chorus in the Messiah for the Lord God omnipotent reigneth. The Anthem of Dr Boyce's[154] for their Majesties Nuptials, and the Coronation Anthem were performed, and it was vastly grand, there being all sorts of instruments. Dr Boyce beat time in the front. Dined and drank tea at Mrs Popples.

Wednesday Apr 28   Was at Ranelagh; Miss Bere went with us. Heard Miss Brent sing — fine voice and manner — Miss Thomas, Signor Tenducci, and Mr Hudson sang very well. NB This morning I drest in my new frock and went to Lord Robert Manners in Grosvenor Square, he was gone to the House of Commons; his gentleman Mr Smith told me his lordship would be found at home any morning betwixt 10 and 11. I then went and paid a visit to Mr Mollineaux in Bury Street an old schoolfellow, who is now one of the gentlemen ushers to the Queen, sat near an hour with him; he reccomended one Mr David Adamson in Pall Mall opposite St James's as a peruke maker, I called there and he took measure of my head for a drest bag wig.

Thursday Apr 29   Was at Drury Lane theatre, where was acted by their Majesties command, The Provok'd Wife, with the Farmers Return from London (a new interlude wrote by Garrick) and the pantomime of the Genii. Sir John Brute by Garrick and the Farmer also by that excellent actor, Lady Brute by Mrs Cibber. Their Majesties, Prince William and Prince Henry and the Prince of Mecklenburg were there, the boxes for their Majesties and the Royal Family were lined with crimson velvet laced with broad gold lace, the chairs for the King and Queen the same, a grand canopy of the same and crown over the Kings box, the other not quite so grand; the King was drest very fine, cloth of gold diamond buttons etc the Queen had on her diamond stomacher;[155] vastly blazing. There was great clapping. The house looked very grand. A little girl about 6 years old danced so vastly fine that I was much surprised. Mr Stonestreet dined and went to the play with us. The scenes in the Genii very splendid.

Monday May 3   Master Smelt and Master R Raguenau drank tea with us. There being a kind of epidemical cold and disorder stirring in London at present, so that the greatest part of the inhabitants are ill, and my mother and self not being well, I determined not go round Bury, Cambridge etc as I intended, but to go streight to Beverley.[156]

Tuesday May 4   This morning I went in a chair to Lord Robert Manners's, and after waiting above two hours in his gentlemans room his lordship came down to me, I gave my uncle F compliments, he asked me to dinner; I excused myself, he talked very free and was mighty complaisant, desired to know where I was that he might wait upon me, I told him I should be sorry if I was out when his lordship did me that honour, and that I went out of town on Thursday, he said he hoped should see me when I came to London, and so I came away. Mr Stonestreet dined with us, he and I settled accounts he and Miss Bere drank tea with us and he took his leave. I wrote to aunt Peggy to acquaint her we were coming home.

Wednesday May 5   Miss Bere called this evening and took her leave. I called at Walshs musick shop was before at Johnson Oswalds, Rutherfords etc, etc.

Thursday May 6   This morning betwixt 8 and 9 left London (in a post chaise) dined at Biggleswade, lay at Bugden [Buckden].

Friday May 7   Breakfasted at Stilton, dined at Colesworth [Colsterworth], lay at Lincoln.

Saturday May 8   Dined at Brig[g], drank tea at Barton, post chaise from Brig[g] broke down forced to stay 'till another came for us. Crossed the Humber in a boat that was Lord Stairs's they say, not the least sick, got to Hull a little before 9 o'clock, lay at the George, which is a very good inn, very civil, reasonable people.

Sunday May 9   Left Hull before 10 o'clock this morning and got safe thank God to Beverley betwixt 11 and 12.

Saturday May 15   The late Mr Perrotts goods are to be sold by auction on Tuesday next at Hull. Poor man! I heard this afternoon that poor Dr Perrott died (yesterday) of an appoplectic fit, I am very sorry for him.

Sunday May 16   Wrote to Mr Stonestreet and Miss Bere.

Tuesday May 18   Mr Hawdon and William Sigston[157] dined with us. Mrs Perrott left Hull today, I heard and came through Beverley in her own coach for last time I suppose, she is gone to her brother Mr Cooks at Garton.

Wednesday May 19   M S [Miss Smelt?] I hear goes to L on Monday next! Pulcerrima! NB Let Tom have 6 shillings and he had 6s when we were at London, that is 12s must be deducted when his wage is due.

Friday May 21   I read in the Whitehall Evening Post today an account of the death of Lord Courtney, who was advanced to the peerage not a month ago, when I was in London; he died at his House in Grosvenor Square: last Sunday after being ill about a week of a pleuretic fever, and has left one son in the 20th year of his age and four daughters. The newswriters say twas a task above their abilities to give the character of this nobleman, and then proceed to an account of the family of Courtenay, they say he was descended from one of the first families in all Europe, and that branch which is in France is next to the Crown of that kingdom, in failure of the present reigning family of Bourbon. This Lord Courtenay, of Powderham Castle in Devonshire was the head of our family, and if the attainder of one of his ancestors, (as the papers say) had been taken of, he would have been the First Earl in England, Scotland, or Ireland. Virtus est vera nobilitas![158]

Tuesday Jun 8   This day Beverley races begin.

Friday Jun 11   This day the races ended; I had toothache all the week so could not go to the field or assemblies. Received a letter from my cousin Miss Julian Bere.

Thursday Jun 24   Went with Mr Mrs and Miss Waines's the Johnston family etc to Bainton to dine with Revd Mr Territt.

Saturday Jun 26   This day I sent my black mare to grass at Tickton to John Frankland at 1s per week.

Sunday Jun 27   Wrote to Mr Dearlove at the Salutation in Harogate.

Friday Jul 2   Received an answer from Mr Dearlove.

Monday Jul 5   This morning about 9 o'clock set out from Beverley on horseback (my mother in the stage) I dined at Barnby Moor and got to York about 3 o'clock in afternoon and went to the Bowling Green.

Tuesday Jul 6   This morning at 9 o'clock left York and got to the Salutation at Harogate about 1 o'clock. The Earl of Huntingdon at this house.[159]

Wednesday Jul 7   This morning I went to the Queens Head saw and spoke to Mrs and Miss N[ewsome] whom I had not seen since took my leave 16th March 1761. I saw Mrs M[ary] G[rime] at Bowling Green on Monday she told me they were at Harogate; I talked about indiferent subjects they told me they left Harogate this day. This night Lord Huntingdon and good many of us played at Commerce.[160]

Thursday Jul 15   This morning Lord Huntingdon and I had a long conversation about our ailments; he is a very agreable affable man, and very sensible. I have sent compliments to Miss Smelt, Miss Harrison and Miss Wharram by some or other of their acquaintance whom I have seen here at Harogate.

Monday Jul 26   This morning at half hour past 9 left Harogate on horseback; (my mother and Capt Smith in a post chaise) I got to York about 2 o'clock. My mother and I called together at Mrs G---s but they were out, but met afterwards in evening with Miss N stopped and talked sometime about indiferent matters. At night they sent to invite us to breakfast tomorrow. My mother sent word she was going in the stage early tomorrow morning. I went to the assembly to night, ('tis the Assize week) and danced with Miss Clare Adams.

Tuesday Jul 27   This morning about ½ hour past 9 o'clock I left York and dined at Barnby Moor, afterwards got two very great showers, and got well, thank God, to Beverley betwixt 4 and 5 o'clock in afternoon. Found a letter from Mr Stonestreet which here, by the post on Friday last.

Friday Jul 30   Wrote to Mr Stonestreet, and directed to him in Dorsetshire. I received twenty seven pounds this day of Mr Goulton.

Monday Aug 9   This morning betwixt 8 and 9 set out from Beverley, dined at Foxholes and got to Scarborough betwixt 3 and 4 o'clock in evening. Lodge at the same place I did last year. NB I went on horseback taking my servant with me.

Tuesday Aug 10   I breakfasted at the Coffee House, dined at Browns Room, paid 8 shillings ordinary and extraordinary, drank clarett. Mett Miss N this morning saw her and talked to her again at the Rooms.

Wednesday Aug 11   I danced this evening with Miss N. I dined today at Blacksmith Arms at the ordinary.[161]

Thursday Aug 12   I dined at New Inn at the ordinary.

Friday Aug 13   I dined with Mr Allen. Drank old hock.

Sunday Aug 15   Dined with Mr Clarke; Mr Errington gave public tea at Rooms I was there.

Wednesday Aug 18   This evening 86 of us gave a grand ball and supper to the ladies each of us subscribing 2 guineas each on the joyful occasion of the birth of a prince; we danced and drank tea at Cookes Room and then went and supped at the other Room, at 3 tables the length of the room and one cross at the top, we had clarett, hock and madeira; it was a very magnificent sight when we were all at supper. We had musick played all the time; the King and Queen's health was drank, and then we gave 3 huzzas,[162] then the Prince, the Princess Dowager and all the royal family and many other loyal toasts. God save the King was sung by Mr Adolphus and we all joined in chorus, as we did in Hearts of Oak, etc. After supper we danced one dance. The stewards were the Earl of Kelly, Sir George M Metham[163] and Mr Adolphus. I danced with Miss Molly Woolaston of London.

Saturday Aug 21   This morning we gave a publick breakfast with the remainder of our money, and dance after it, I danced with Miss Preston. The musick played all the time we were at breakfast.

Sunday Aug 27   I drank tea this evening at the Rooms with Lady Heathcote, a private sett.

Monday Aug 23   This morning before 10 o'clock I sett out on horseback for Beverley. Mr Wharton of Hatfield overtook me we rode on together, and I dined at Driffield with Mr Robert Burton, Mrs Burton, and Mr and Mrs Wharton and got to Beverley, thank God, before 7 o'clock. I breakfasted every morning at the Coffee House at Scarborough. Dined generally at an ordinary, and danced every night so had a pretty generall acquaintance; I had a plate of cold meat at night after came from the Rooms sent me from the New Globe, where had my horses, most time at grass. This Scarborough journey cost me in all £15.

Tuesday Aug 24   Received a letter from Mr Stonestreet, with a bank post bill.

Friday Sep 10   Wrote to my cousin Miss Julian Bere, Mr David Adamson, perukemaker in Pall Mall, and Mr Haxby, and also to Lady Margaret Dalzell inclosed under frank to Mr Haxby.

Sunday Sep 26   Received an answer from Lady Margaret Dalzell.

Wednesday Sep 29   Received my new wig from London.

Saturday Oct 9   Mrs Young Mr and Miss Wakefield and Mr Meeke dined and drank tea with us; Mr Wakefield is ill or he would have been with us.

Sunday Oct 10   Received a letter from Mr Stonestreet, dated 2d instant, must have been kept here or at London, or else a mistake.

Tuesday Oct 12   I was at ball at Mr Meekes this evening, we danced 9 couples, and broke up about 1 o'clock next morning.

Saturday Oct 16   Paid John Frankland for grass for two of my horses at Tickton at l shilling each per week; paid him one pound four shillings.

Thursday Oct 21   Sir Robert Hildyard, and his son and two daughters[164] with Mr Waines my uncle Miss Raguenau and Miss Goulton drank tea with us, we played on the organ and harpsichord and danced a little. NB I danced with Miss Hildyard at the assembly last night. The East Riding Militia came to town today. Very pretty to see them come in.

Monday Oct 25   Kings accession. The officers of Militia gave a ball to night I was there danced with Miss Kitty Hildyard.

Monday Nov 1   Tonight 'tis six years since my dear father died, for he died Monday 1st November about ½ past 9 o'clock at night.

Tuesday Nov 2   I paid Mr Robinson's outrent to Mr John Boss. I received a letter from Mr Stonestreet. NB Desired Mr Stonestreet to pay Adamson for my wig.

Thursday Nov 4   Mr Peirson of Stokesley; and young Mr Goulton breakfasted with me. This morning the Lincolnshire Militia commanded by Col Wellby arived here; being sent for to quiet some disturbance that had happened among our Militia men about giving up their cloaths, Sir George Savile[165] also came, from York. In afternoon I went to pay a visit to Mr Constables, played at whist which have not done many years.

Saturday Nov 6   This evening it is 6 years since my dear father was burried; for he was burried Saturday the 6th of November 1756, betwixt 4 and 5 o'clock in evening alass!

Sunday Nov 7   Received a letter (directed to the Revd Mr John Courtney) from my coz [cousin] John Courtney, Nats eldest son, he says he is going to be married.

Friday Nov 12   Answered c[ousin] John Courtney's letter.

Monday Nov 15   Heard this morning that poor Miss Biddy Johnston[166] died last night. She was at Mr Enter's Concert on Wednesday night last (I treated Mrs and Miss Johnstons as usual) and she danced and seemed very well and I talked to her once or twice. I heard she was very ill on Friday or Saturday. Imagine it was a pleurisy. Very sudden and shocking. God preserve us and fit us for death before it comes.

Tuesday Nov 23   Received a letter from Mr Stonestreet — he has paid Mr Adamson peruke maker in Pallmall for my wig £1 11s 6d. This afternoon I was at a meeeting of all the subscribers to the 6 concerts (there are now 30 subscribers) they chose me one of the comittee for managing the same. The comittee are vizt: Mr Raguenau; J Courtney; Capt Smith; Capt Gilchrist (Adjutant to East Riding Militia) and Mr J Johnston — our treasurer. Agreed that tickets should be in usual form.

Thursday Nov 25   This evening we had our first subscription concert and I paid my subscription 12s to Mrs Yates. After the concert we gave a ball to the ladies (as did last winter). NB This afternoon Mr Dalacourt[167] came to desire I would give my vote to his wifes being made mistress of the new Assembly Room; I told him, I imagined Mrs Yates would not stand again, and so then I would vote for Mrs Dalacourt please God I live. In evening Mrs Sally Webster, Mr Bowmans maid came to ask my vote, she being also a candidate; I was gone to the concert but they told her I was engaged to Mrs Dalacourt.[168]

Friday Dec 3   Wrote to Vincent Mathias Esqr.

Wednesday Dec 8   Received a letter from Revd H Wilson desiring my interest with Mayor and Aldermen for an exhibition for his nephew.[169]

Saturday Dec 18   I paid my mother her quarter annunity. Paid Ferraby's bill £1 13s 4d.

Tuesday Dec 21   I paid Mrs Dickons bill.

Thursday Dec 23   This day the East Riding Militia commanded by Sir Digby Legard were disbanded here at Beverley.

Friday Dec 31   This day I answered Revd Mr Henry Wilsons letter, and told him that my application to the Corporation of Beverley in order to obtain an exhibition for his nephew had been unsuccessful; as by the wills of the donors they could be given to no one but a freemans son born in the town of Beverley. This year I have saved one hundred and twenty pounds, and spent the same sum.

Laus Deo!
End of the Year 1762
Finis

[end of volume 1]

MDCCLXIII [1763]

Saturday Jan 1 Began this year at Beverley. I went to prayers at St Mary's morning and afternoon.

Sunday Jan 2 Received a letter from Mr Saunders and one from Mrs Saunders.

Monday Jan 3 This morning at about 9 o'clock, my mother and I set out from Beverley in a post chaise and four horses, dined at Barnby Moor House and got to York before 4 o'clock in evening and lay at Mr Howards inn in Lendall.

Wednesday Jan 5 We got to the lodgings we took yesterday at Mr Carpenters in Davygate.

Friday Jan 14 At the concert I danced with Miss Molly Thompson.[170]

Tuesday Jan 18 This being day kept for the Queens birthday I was at the assembly in the Grand Room, and danced. Received a letter from uncle Featherston.

Thursday Jan 27 Received a letter from aunt Peggy, as did afterwards and answered though not always here mentioned.

Friday Jan 28 Danced again (tonight) with Miss Molly Thompson.

Wednesday Feb 9 This morning I waited upon Mr and Mrs T and made my offers for their daughter Miss Molly T. They seemed very well pleased, said she was too young but they would consider of it; I told him my fortune and expectations and he said he had no material objections but thanked me for taking notice of his daughter and then went with me into another room to his two daughters, but the Dean coming to see him just after the ladies and I went into the other room again, and when he returned I addressed myself to the young lady and told her the regard I had for her; she made no answer, but I thought seemed not at all displeased; and after some little time I took my leave.

Thursday Feb 10 This morning I again waited upon Mr T and we being left alone he told me, that, he was sorry to inform me that his daughter could not think of marrying and that she had cry'd to him half an hour and desired him to give me no encouragement; I repeated again and again that perhaps on better acquaintance she might entertain a more favourable oppinion of me; but he replied that she could not think of it and that he could not force her; I assured him that if she was the finest richest and best woman in England I would not have her hand without her heart. He said as for his part he had no objection to me and had urged it as strongly to her as he could and that it was to no purpose for me to give myself any further trouble about the affair.

Monday Feb 14 At the assembly I spoke to Miss Molly T she was shy.

Tuesday Feb 22 My birthday. I am now, thank God for his mercy, twenty nine years old. Miss Hammond and Revd Mr Atkinson dined with us; and Mrs Mary Goulton,

Mr Perrott, Master and Miss Perrott and Mrs Milward drank tea with us. Received a letter from Mr Stonestreet with a particular inquiry therein.

Thursday Feb 24 Wrote an answer to Mr Stonestreet, gave him a full and particular answer to his question.

Sunday Feb 27 Dr Hunter dined with us.

Wednesday Mar 2 Received a letter from aunt Peggy with a copy of a note from Lord Clive[171] desiring my vote and interest at the election of directors of the East India Company on 13th April next, and desiring an answer.

Thursday Mar 3 Wrote to Mr Thomas Stonestreet about Lord Clives note.

Saturday Mar 5 This afternoon saw the Judge come into town, accompany'd by Mr Langley the High Sheriff and many gentlemen etc, etc. Drank tea at Mrs Thorpes.

Sunday Mar 6 I was at the Minster heard the Assize sermon and a new Te Deum composed by Revd Mr Bridges of York. The High Sherif was most magnificently drest in pompadour[172] and gold.

Monday Mar 7 I was at the assembly in the Great Room and danced with Miss Medcalfe.

Wednesday Mar 9 In morning I was at Castle to hear causes tried. This afternoon I went to the card meeting, and spoke aside to Mr T[hompson] asked him if he could give me any encouragement; he laid his hand upon my shoulder and said, Mr Courtney I wish I could I asure you, but she can't think of it, and gave me a final answer. Thus I have entirely concluded this affair.

Thursday Mar 10 This morning before 9 o'clock I went to the Castle sat not far from the Judge Sir Edward Clive[173] and heard the trial of Mr Park for murder, twas brought in manslaughter several other felons were tried, among the rest one Eli Longbotham for stealing a cow. This afternoon Mrs G —s all of them and Mrs and Miss N[ewsome] drank tea with us, and from the young ladies behaviour to me as well as the civility of the old ones, I could not help thinking that the match with Capt C[ooke] was quite off, notwithstanding I had heard about 6 weeks since that the writings were signed, and also had been a dupe to their civilities and show of love once before.

Friday Mar 11 This morning I was at the Castle sat next the High Sheriff; heard one William Bell tried for the murder of his fellow servant, he was found guilty and condemned to be hanged on Monday next and his body to be dissected; I saw also sentence of death pronounced on Eli Longbotham for stealing a cow and Mathew Fisher for stealing 5 sheep. (These two were afterwards reprieved.) I never saw sentence of death pronounced on a criminal before. Terrible. Park and two others were burnt in the hand. I was tonight at the concert in Great Room and most prodigious full it was 50 couples.

Saturday Mar 12   This morning I went to the Castle and heard causes tried. I sat very near the Judge. My mother went at my desire to Mrs N — s and asked if the match betwixt her and Capt C was quite off. She told her it was not. So no more could be said. Thus I was a dupe to their nonsensical behaviour.

Monday Mar 14   I was at the assembly in the Grand Room; the Judge was there to see us dance minuets.

Tuesday Mar 15   I drank tea at the Coffee [House], I went there almost every day. Very agreable, and good company.

Wednesday Mar 16   This morning a little past 10 o'clock I left York on horseback (my mother and maid in a post chaise). Dined at Weighton, and got well, thank God to Beverley about 5 o'clock in evening.

Monday Mar 21   I brought my accounts from my old book to a new one.

Tuesday Mar 22   Peace was proclaimed in London.[174]

Wednesday Mar 23   Settled accounts with my uncle Featherston; ballance due to me £4 11s. I repaid afterwards Mrs Featherston a guinea I ordered Nat in the late hard frost.

Wednesday Mar 30   This afternoon peace was proclaimed here at Beverley. I saw it proclaimed, and was upon the cross. God send it an happy and lasting peace! There were no acclamations of joy, no wine upon the cross, no shouting — all a dumb shew.

Tuesday Apr 5   Received a letter from Mr Stonestreet. Answered said letter. Wrote to Mr Percival.

Tuesday Apr 12   Received a letter from John Croft Esqr.

Friday Apr 15   Answered Mr John Croft's letter.

Monday Apr 18   Received of aunt Featherston Mr Horsefields half years interest due 14th instant £22 10s.

Tuesday Apr 19   Paid my mother £14 10s which, with what she owes me, makes up £25 her quarters annuity due the 20th of February last.

Monday Apr 25   I paid Mr Robinsons outrent; he left me money for it when he was here. This afternoon Mr Appleton's clerk came to me with a mortgage deed, whereby the assembly room would be mortgaged for £50. About 8 or 9 of the subscribers had signed it; but I told him I would neither sign the mortgage nor give them any more money. By the list of subscribers it appears that the sum of one thousand pounds is raised to build the assembly room etc.

Tuesday Apr 26   Received a letter from Thomas Stonestreet Esqr and one from John Croft Esqr. Wrote to John Robinson Esqr.

Tuesday Apr 29   Answered Mr John Crofts letter.

Sunday May 1   Answered Mr Stonestreets letter.

Thursday May 5   Thanksgiving day for the Peace. The bells did not ring, and no rejoicings made here, only one Mrs Legatt an old woman illuminated her windows.

Sunday May 8   Wrote to Mr David Adamson peruke maker in Pall Mall opposite St James London.

Sunday May 15   Received a letter from Mr Stonestreet with a bank post bill for £99 17s 4d. Answered said letter this day.

Wednesday May 25   This evening our new assembly rooms[175] were opened by a ball given by the officers of the East Riding Militia. Sir Griffith Boynton[176] opened it with Lady Legard. There was a very splendid appearance of ladies and gentlemen, and the rooms were also very elegant as well as the entertainment. I danced with Miss Thornton of Hull.[177]

Tuesday May 30   Received a letter from Mr Stonestreet; he proposes being at Beverley on Sunday morning at noon.

Saturday Jun 4   The Kings birthday. The Corporation gave a ball in the new assembly rooms to the officers of the Militia, and the ladies and gentlemen of the town and neighbourhood. I was there and danced with Miss Hannah Waines of this town.

Sunday Jun 5   This evening betwixt 5 and 6 o'clock Mr Stonestreet arrived well at our house.

Friday Jun 10   This day I received my ticket as a proprietor to the new assembly rooms, together with a printed paper of rules for the same.

Tuesday Jun 14   Received a letter from Mr Haxby desiring I would write my opinion about the organ I bought of him; I answered his letter commending the organ. This day Beverley races begin; Mr Stonestreet and I went upon the stand; and I was at the assembly at night and danced with Miss Raguenau.

Friday Jun 17   This day the races end, I was at the assembly and danced every night.

Thursday Jun 30   My aunt Featherston paid me the amount of the bank post bill, which I delivered and indorsed to my uncle. I paid my mother her quarters annuity due 20th of May last £25. Deducted for tea paid Blakiston £3 12s 8.

Tuesday Jul 5   My aunt Featherston paid me £2 being the half years interest of Beverley and Hull Turnpike due 23d past.

Wednesday Jul 6   I settled accounts with Thomas Stonestreet Esqr we are clear.

RULES for *Beverley* Affembly - Rooms, 1763.

THAT the Meeting be made up of fuch Gentlemen and Ladies, as fhall Subfcribe on the following Terms.

EACH Proprietor to the Rooms to have a Ticket for the Seafon, on the original Contract.

	£.	s.	d.
Each Subfcriber for the whole Year, Card-Meetings, and Races included,	1	1	0
For the Race Week,	0	7	6
For every fingle Night,	0	2	6

THAT the Subfcription be open'd, the firft Night in the Race Week.

THAT the Affemblies begin on the King's Coronation in every Year, and continue every other Wednefday for Twelve Nights, unlefs the Committee for the Time being, alter the Night, on Account of a publick Rejoicing, or other particular Occafion.

THAT no Proprietor fhall Transfer his Ticket to any Perfon, unlefs for the whole Seafon.

THAT a new Committee be chofen on the Monday preceding the King's Coronation in every future Year : The faid Committee to order and direct all ordinary and extraordinary Expences, Ornaments, and Repairs, but fhall not lay out in Ornaments or Repairs, a Sum exceeding Ten Pounds without leave from a Majority of the Proprietors, then prefent to be had at a publick Meeting, (on three Days Notice at the leaft) to be given them by the Committee for that purpofe.

THAT the Committee confift of Three of the Proprietors, to be chofen by Ballot by the reft of the Proprietors ; and that one of the Three be chofen Treafurer.

THAT the Treafurer's Lady, or any other Lady he appoints, fhall be Manager or Miftrefs of the Ceremonies.

THAT Mrs. *Sarah Webfter*, (who hath been appointed for that purpofe) do fupply the Company with Tea, Coffee, Chocolate, Negus, &c. and provide proper Perfons to wait on the Company, clean the Rooms, carry out Tickets, invite Company on particular Occafions, and do other neceffary Bufinefs belonging to the Affembly : Alfo to provide Two proper Perfons, for all which fhe is to be paid Seven Pounds a Year.

THAT fhe be allow'd 2 s. 6 d. per Ounce for Tea, 1 s. an Ounce for Coffee, 2 d. a Difh for Chocolate, (fhe finding Sugar, Milk, and Toaft,) for Wine made into Negus or Cool-Tankard 1 s. 6 d. per Pint, Ditto into Bifhop 1 s. 9 d. a Pint, Madeira Negus 2 s. a

Pint, and for Cards 2 s. 6 d. a Pack : That the Perfons who Order any of thefe Things, be Accountable to her for the Value.

THAT in cafe of the Death or Removal of the faid Mrs. *Webfter*, another Perfon fhall be chofen to fucceed her, by a Majority of Proprietors prefent at a publick Meeting to be held in the Rooms on ten Days Notice, to be given by the Committee for the Time being, each Proprietor to give a Vote for every Share he fhall be Poffeffed of.

THAT the Candles be Lighted at Seven o'Clock, and that no more Candles be allowed or admitted to be Lighted up that Night.

THAT the Mufic be paid as follows, the Hautboy 3 s. 6 d. and the others 2 s. 6 d. each Night, and that none of the Muficians leave the Room above Half an Hour, on Forfeiture of their Pay for that Night.

THAT if any of the Luftres or other Furniture be broken, the Perfon or Perfons breaking the fame fhall pay the Damages.

THAT the Servants be not allow'd to come into the outer Room, without being fent for.

THAT the Hackney Coachmen take their Turns in carrying Company and not croud near the Door, and for avoiding Confufion and Accidents, the Coaches with Company are to go and come by *Hengate*, and the empty-ones by *Walker-gate*. It is defired that Gentlemen will order their Coachmen to conform to this Rule.

THAT any Perfon or Perfons, (not Proprietors) defiring the Rooms for a private Ball, fhall pay to the Treafurer for the Time being, Four Guineas for the Ufe of the Rooms, and be anfwerable for, and Pay, all Damages.

THAT Card Meetings be allowed in the Rooms once a Week, each Perfon (not a Subfcriber) to pay 6 d. a Night for the ufe of the Rooms over and above what is paid for Tea, &c.

THAT any Perfon or Perfons defiring the Ufe of the Rooms for a Concert, fhall pay to the Treafurer for the Time being One Guinea for the Ufe of the Rooms, clean the fame, and be anfwerable for, and pay all Damages.

THAT Mrs. *Webfter* aforefaid, do collect the Subfcription and Nightly Payments, pay the fame to the Treafurer for the Time being, and find Candles both for the Card Meetings, and the Card Tables, on the Affembly Nights ; and alfo Fires for all the Rooms.

HULL: Printed by J. RAWSON & Son, in *Lowgate*, where Copper-Plate Printing is neatly done.

Rules for the Beverley Assembly Rooms, 1763. (East Riding of Yorkshire Council Archives and Records Service.)

Thursday Jul 14   This morning pretty early I set out from Beverley on horseback, and my mother and Mr Stonestreet in a post chaise, and got to Buckton betwixt 12 and 1 o'clock at noon. In the way thither my mother told Mr S she should be glad of a match betwixt me and his niece Miss A[178] if we liked one another, he said that he likewise should approve of it, and would talk about it with my uncle F.

Sunday Jul 17   At noon received a letter from my uncle Featherston acquainting me that Dr Clarke was dead, and that he had wrote to Lord Robert Manners, about the chaplainship of the Garrison at Hull for me, and that he would also enquire about the advowson sinecure that Dr Clarke had in Essex, worth near £300 a year; desiring me to come home to morrow. If I had been at home should have desired my uncle not to write about chaplainship.

Monday Jul 18   This morning about 10 o'clock left Buckton and dined at Brans Burton [Brandesburton], and I being on horseback got home to Beverley about 6 o'clock in evening but my mother and Mr Stonestreet did not get home till 8 being in a postchaise. My uncle Featherston came and we talked about Mr S niece, and Mr S appointed to morrow morning for further discourse on that subject.

Tuesday Jul 19   This morning my uncle, Mr S, my mother, and I all talked about the match, I gave him a sketch of what I was worth, and my uncle showed him his rental, and told him what he should do for me, Mr S acquainted us with Miss A's fortune, and chances, and we were all perfectly satisfy'd with these matters on both sides. Mr S will write about it to her father in Dorsetshire, and some way is to be contrived for me to meet her at Salisbury, Shaftesbury or some where thereabouts; I told him that I knew many pretty ladies whom still I could not like to marry, and hoped therefore that he would not take it amiss in case I did not like his niece, as I should not if she disliked me; he said he should not to be sure, that mutual love was very necessary to happiness in a married state.

Wednesday Jul 20   My uncle has had a letter from Mrs Clarke who says if the sinecure is to be disposed of as to her part my uncle shall have the first refusal.

Thursday Jul 21   Mr S showed me a copy of a letter he will write to Revd Mr A the young ladys father. My uncle Featherston went to Scarbro', this morning.

Friday Jul 22   My aunt Featherston brought me a letter she received this morning from Lord Robert Manners, acquainting my uncle the chaplainship of Hull Garrison was disposed of, that he had recomended Mr Robinson the Vicar of Hull before he received my uncles letter. I am glad of it, for I should scarce have accepted of it.

Monday Aug 1   Mr Stonestreet gave me a bank post bill on paying him cash for the same.

Thursday Aug 4   As Mr Stonestreet and I were returning from taking an airing on horseback this morning, just as we were trotting on the York Road in Westwood Mr Stonestreet got a very bad fall from my old sorrell mare by its stumbling and falling on its knees occasioned by stooping its head to catch the flies; I heard the noise looked back and saw him fall; thank God he luckily fell upon the beaten part of the road and though he pitched on his head received no hurt; many large sharp stones lay in the road which might have fractured his scull had he fallen on them.

Saturday Aug 6   This day I heard that Mrs S--- was dead.[179]

Tuesday Aug 16   This morning Mr Stonestreet received an answer from Mr A--- [Archer] the purport of which in regard to what he would give her was not to the satisfaction of my mother and uncle, nor indeed of Mr Stonestreet himself, and as to me I can say nothing not having seen her.

Thursday Aug 18   This morning before 8 o'clock Mr Stonestreet and my mother in a post chaise and I on horseback set out for Hull; we got there before 10. I went on board the vessel with Mr Stonestreet and staid a few minutes and then wished him a good passage over the Humber, and a pleasant journey to London, thanking him for all favours. Left Hull betwixt 5 and 6 in evening and met Miss S--- in Mr C---s post chaise coming to Hull.[180] We got home about 7 o'clock. I have not been at Hull since my return from London 9th May last year.

Saturday Aug 20   Paid Mrs Dickons bill. Paid my mother a quarters annuity due this day £25. Received a letter from Revd Mr Harry Wilson, by his nephew this day though dated 8th last month.

Friday Aug 26   Received a letter from Mr Stonestreet.

Saturday Aug 27   This afternoon Ned Wynne[181] my old schoolfellow youngest son to Sir Rowland Wynne Bart called to see me; have not seen him since I left school, eleven years ago.

Sunday Aug 28   Answered Mr Stonestreets letter.

Monday Aug 29   At 8 o'clock set out from Beverley on horseback, and my mother and uncle in a post chaise and four. Dined at Barnby Moor and got to York about 4 in afternoon.

Tuesday Aug 30   At 9 o'clock in morning left York and got to Harogate before 1 o'clock afternoon. Fixed our quarters at the New Inn. The company there all strangers.

Monday Sep 12   About 10 o'clock in morning set out from Harogate (taking leave of all the company who were very civil and agreable). I rode on horseback and mother and uncle in post chaise; we dined with Mann Horsefield Esqr at his seat at Thorp Green. I lost myself in going thither and rode about in a marshy moor for near half an hour, in the rain. Got to York betwixt 6 and 7 in evening, where soon after arived my aunt Featherston according to agreement, she being to stay sometime there with my uncle, who will take Dr Dealtrys advice.

Tuesday Sep 13   About 10 o'clock this morning I left York (I on horseback and my mother in a return coach and six). Dined at Weighton and got well to Beverley, thank God, before 5 in evening.

Friday Sep 16   Received a letter from Mr Stonestreet. Wrote to Richard Bagshaw Esqr.

Saturday Sep 17   Mr Bagshaw came to town tonight and sent for me to Robert Norris's the Blue Bell; I sat with him above an hour.

Sunday Sep 18   Mr Bagshaw breakfasted with us, I went with him to the Minster, and after service there to the assembly rooms etc, he supped with us. Goes away tomorrow.

Monday Sep 19   I was at a meeting at the assembly rooms this afternoon when Mr Gee, Mr Boynton and Mr J Johnston were chosen to be the committee for the ensuing year. Mr Gee to be the treasurer. Some new orders and regulations were likewise made. Vide the rules.

Tuesday Sep 20   Received a letter from aunt Featherston. Answered it. Wrote to Mrs Wormley and inclosed her at my aunt Featherstons desire the bank post bill for ten pounds which I had of Mr Stonestreet. Received today by the carrier Mr Stonestreets kind present of a gallon of Errindy oyl.[182]

Friday Sep 23   Received a letter from Mr Stonestreet.

Friday Sep 30   Received a letter from Mrs Margaret Wormeley.

Monday Oct 3   Mr Robinson gave me £6 4s 8d to pay his outrents the 1st or 2d of November next.

Friday Oct 7   Received a letter from Mr Stonestreet; Mr A the young ladys father is quite averse to the proposed match and would not give the fortune expected. So all is intirely over, and am glad of it not having seen the lady (whom indeed should not have married though if had not liked) and other circumstances not making me very desirous of the match. Vide Mr S's letter. I wrote a long answer to it by the post this night. I also wrote a few lines to Mr Stonestreet by Master Robarts (who sets out for London tomorrow by sea, and is going soon to the East Indies) desiring Mr Stonestreet would give him his advice and do him any service he could etc.

Thursday Oct 13   My mother and I after dinner had a long conference about Miss S---t [Smelt] she gave her free consent that I should apply to her and her uncle; and said she would speak to my uncle F about it; and she thought he would not be against it. I hope there is no foundation for the report of her being going to be married to Mr C[on]st[a]ble. I heartily wish I may have good success (if God pleases) and that I may obtain her for a wife.

Monday Oct 17   I wrote a letter to Mr Paul Canham and gave it to Mrs Featherston to carry to Hull to morrow. This evening I was at a ball at Mr Saunders.

Tuesday Oct 18   Received a leter from Mr Stonestreet, with a bank post bill.

Friday Oct 21   I left the said bill with my mother and indorsed it to my uncle Featherston who will send for it today. I received also of Mrs Featherston 6 guineas all but a shilling for my black filly which I sold to Paul Canham. In afternoon I went to Hull with a large party of ladies and gentlemen in two coaches; drank tea at Harrys Coffee House went to the play, and then had a handsome supper and got home to Beverley about half an hour past 1 o'clock Saturday morning.

Saturday Oct 22   My mother spoke to my uncle tonight about Miss S---, he approves of it. We had not much talk. I hope (please God) it will have good success.

Thursday Oct 27   This day I settled accounts with uncle Featherston.

Friday Oct 28   Received a letter from Mr Stonestreet. My uncle today disapproves of Miss S---t as having too small a fortune — I guess from what quarter the wind blows.

Saturday Oct 29   I was at a meeting of the trustees, proprietors etc of [sic — at?] the Tyger about branching out the turnpike road (betwixt Hull and Beverley) to the town of Cottingham; I think 'tis hard the inhabitants of Cottingham should pay as much for two miles as others for nine; but whether the proposed scheme is proper or not I can't pretend to determine?

Monday Oct 31   I dined with the Mayor Mr Bowman.

Tuesday Nov 1   'Tis seven years now this day since my dear father died. For he died on the 1st November 1756 about a quarter past 9 o'clock at night. Alass! Alass!

Wednesday Nov 2   NB Yesterday I paid Mr Robinsons outrent. This day Mr Alderman Hoggard[183] called to desire my vote and interest to succeed my uncle Featherston (who is going to resign) as surveyor to the Beverley and Hull turnpike road — I told him I would talk with my uncle and would not engage my vote to any other without acquainting him and that I wished him good success.

Saturday Nov 5   This afternoon at my uncles desire I wrote nine letters to Messrs Cayley, Watson, Maisters etc etc proprietors of the Beverley and Hull Turnpike, which my uncle signed, and will send his man to Hull with to morrow. The purport of them is to desire that he may wait upon them at Hull on Tuesday next, to have the money he has paid them off indorsed upon their securities; I promised him (please God) to go with him to Hull for that purpose. Mr Robarts called today — he says Mr Stonestreet is glad he has it in his power to recommend his son (as Master is going to Bombay) and promised he would do it. Mr Robarts was very thankful to me for the letter I wrote Mr Stonestreet in his favour.

Sunday Nov 6   It is seven years this evening since my dear father was buried. For he was buried in the quire of St Marys church about 5 o'clock in the evening on the 6th November 1756. Alass! Alass! It was in the Whitehall Evening Post today that on Tuesday died Peter Wyche Esqr in Great Ormond Street; now I read in same paper on

Tuesday that he died the Wednesday before. If he died on Tuesday, he died on the same day my dear father died 7 years before. So that Mr Wyche survived my father just seven years.

Tuesday Nov 8   This morning at 9 o'clock I set out with my uncle Featherston in a post chaise for Hull (my aunt Peggy went in the coach to stay sometime); we went to lawyer Cayley's and rest of proprietors to have their securities indorsed as uncle desired. We returned home in evening. NB My aunt Peggy left with me cash £15 1s 6d and her turnpike security.

Wednesday Nov 9   Delivered uncle Featherston my aunt Peggys turnpike security and received of him a note instead thereof for £80 at 5 per cent dated 23d June, to pay her on demand.

Tuesday Nov 15   This morning I went to Hull on horseback, my mother and uncle in stagecoach; my uncle and I went to the Guildhall to a meeting of the trustees of the turnpike from Beverley to Hull. There were very warm debates on account of the petition for a branch to Cottingham, Mr Wilberforce[184] spoke very strongly against and very warmly; he spoke extremely well, but rather too hastily, Mr Watson, Mr Ellerker and Mr Beatniff were the chief speakers for the branch. It was carried by a large majority in favour of the petition. I being only a proprietor and no trustee had no vote. I got home about 6 o'clock in evening.

Friday Nov 18   This morning I went to Hull on horseback and my uncle in the coach. After some disputing etc settled matters at lawyer Cayleys with Mr Watson in regard to his taking my uncles 7 turnpike securities. We dined at old Mrs Colling's. I got home about 5 o'clock.

Monday Nov 21   I paid my mother a quarter of years annuity.

Wednesday Nov 23   NB This day vails[185] to servants in the county of York are abolished. This morning I hired James Wilson (who lived servant to Revd Mr Tomlinson one year) I am to give him 5 pounds a year the first year (and six pounds the second year if he stays) a full livery, which Martin leaves, a frock and a pair of buckskin breeches, if he stays two years he is to take the breeches away with him as likewise the great coat; otherwise he leaves them both. I gave him half a crown fasten penny. I paid Martin Rilay four pounds ten shillings his wage to 2d December 1763. Three quarters of a year; he left his livery coat and waistcoat. Out of the £4 10s he paid his mistress £[?] she laid down for boots. This day at noon James Wilson my new man came.

Thursday Nov 24   Martin Rilay my late servant went away early this morning.

Wednesday Nov 30   This day I destroyed my will and made a new one and Mr John Tong junior, Mr Courtail, and Mr Christopher Elliott were witnesses to it.

Thursday Dec 1   I was at a ball this evening at Miss Goultons.

Saturday Dec 10   I was at a private ball at Miss Johnstons this evening.

Sunday Dec 11   The three Master Metcalfes and Mr Enter dined and drank tea with us.

Wednesday Dec 14   I was at a private ball at Mr Constables this evening.

Friday Dec 16   I was at a private ball at Miss Ragueneaus this evening.

Wednesday Dec 21   This evening I gave (at our house) a private ball to severall young ladies and gentlemen of this town, I did not take out a partner myself 'till all the gentlemen had got theirs. We broke up at eleven o'clock at night. The couples were as follows vizt: 1 Mr Constable-Miss Ragueneau; 2 Capt Peirson-Miss Goulton; 3 Capt Legard-Miss Peirson; 4 Mr Thomas Constable-Miss H Waines; 5 Capt Maynard-Miss Legard; 6 Mr S[--?] Maynard-Miss Cotes; 7 Capt Ward-Miss Waines; 8 Mr Jacomb-Miss Constable; 9 Myself-Miss Johnston; 10 Miss M Ragueneau-Miss Best; 11 Miss Hewitt-Miss S Goulton. I danced a dance or two with a Miss Cockerill a little girl with Miss Best, and also with Miss Hewitt, Miss S Goulton and Miss Marianne Ragueneau. NB Dr Cotes, Capt Hudson and Miss Ward were invited but did not come.

Friday Dec 23   I wrote to Mr Wind of New Inn at Harogate.

Monday Dec 26   I was at a private ball at Miss Peirson's this evening.

Tuesday Dec 27   Wrote to Mr Robinson of Buckton.

Friday Dec 30   My uncle much worse with his complaint in his foot sent for Atkinson again and Dr Hunter.

Saturday Dec 31   My poor uncle Featherston very ill, in afternoon I sent for Dr Chambers,[186] and he came in evening and Dr Hunter too, and Atkinson, Walker and they consulted together. They think him in very great danger. God almighty preserve him. Praised be God for all his mercies. Amen.

MDCCLXIV [1764]

Sunday Jan 1   I wrote to Mr Yoward. My uncle Featherston much worse; small hopes! I left him this evening betwixt 7 and 8 o'clock, I asked him in afternoon if he lay easy and he said, yes thank God I lay easy; this I believe were the last sensible words he said to me.

Monday Jan 2   This night betwixt 9 and 10 clock my dear uncle departed this life; I did not see him all day as he was dying and insensible. He died very easy and quiet, almost insensible of pain towards the last. God comfort us, and fit us all for this inevitable event. My dear uncle Featherston died of a mortification in his foot, wanting about 2 months of 64 years of age. Alass! Alass!

Tuesday Jan 3   We were most of the day at my aunt Featherstons. Received a letter from Mr Wind of New Inn at Harogate.

No 48 North Bar Without, Beverley, the house where John Courtney was born in 1734.
The house was built for his uncle, Ralph Featherstone.

Wednesday Jan 4   This evening betwixt 4 and 5 o'clock my dear uncle was buried in the quire of St Marys church close by the remains of my late dear father on the right hand side. I and my aunt, and Neddy Blanchard[187] and my aunt Peggy attended his corpse to the grave; when the coffin was quite let down as heard after it was two feet under water. Alass! Alass! NB He was buried in same manner as my father was.

Thursday Jan 5   This morning I read my late dear uncles will, at my aunts; she, my mother, aunt Peggy and Neddy Blanchard being present. My mother and aunt Peggy are executrixes, and he has left me the closes subject to pay Mrs Featherston annuity; so that I don't get much myself; my uncle lately often told me he would alter this will of which he showed me a sketch at Harogate; but he never did and I could not think of mentioning it to him in his last illness. I reverence his memory for his kind intentions, and am not discontent with this will.

Friday Jan 6   Received a letter from Mr Yoward.

Saturday Jan 7   Wrote to Mr Gylby of Hull.

Sunday Jan 8   This afternoon I went to St Marys church and appeared in my deep mourning for my late dear uncle, my mother and aunt Peggy did the same. I received a letter from Mr Stonestreet inclosing a bank book bill for £33 18s 6d being my ballance. NB All but 5 shillings of this is due to the executrixes of my late uncle Featherston. I answered Mr Stonestreets letter, and acquainted him with my uncles death. I wrote to Mr Yoward also today.

Tuesday Jan 10   By post came a letter from Mrs Wormley to my late uncle. I answered it.

Monday Jan 16   Paid some of land tax for some of the closes.

Tuesday Jan 17   Received a letter from Mr Stonestreet. Answered it, inclosed to him a copy of my late uncles will and codicill. Received a letter from Mrs Wormley.

Sunday Jan 22   My aunt Featherston, Mrs Truby and Miss Parsons dined, drank tea and supped with us. (First time of being at our house since my uncles death.)

Monday Jan 23   This morning my aunt Featherston and I went in a post chaise to Hull — I went to Mr Cayleys and took his opinion on my late uncles will, etc etc. I was with him near two hours. Vide his written opinion. I left a copy of the will with him, and also Mr Robarts assignment of 2 securities of Hedon Turnpike to draw a fresh one to rectify a mistake, and gave him some other directions etc. My aunt and I dined at old Mrs Colling's, and got home about 5 o clock in evening. 'Tis almost an entire sea from Beverley to near Hull. Surprising innundations.

Tuesday Jan 24   This morning I went to my aunt Featherstons and looked over and received sundry deeds, securities etc. We were in the room, where my dear uncle died, which still smells of the fomentations.[188] I went this morning to see the graves of my late dear father and uncle covered and stones laid down.[189]

Wednesday Jan 25   This morning received the rest of the securities etc. In afternoon I received G Duncans rent for my close (late my dear uncles) in Butt Lane.[190] I went again to see the graves the stones were laid, some gravell (which Corporation owed my uncle) being first put under them.

Thursday Jan 26   This morning William Parkinson gave me notice to quit my two closes (late my uncles) on Newbegin next to Westwood[191] at Candlemass next unless I would abate his rent, which I refused to do and accordingly accepted of his notice. Mr Easton (late Mr Nelsons[192] clerk) tells me that a steward not being yet appointed for the court, the surrender to be made by a[unt] Margaret may be made by the copyholders, and be valid immediately, but cannot be presented till there be a court; also that my mother must be found heir in court of that copyhold estate at Newland[193] which is sold (though not conveyed) to one J Kirby, and that then my mother must surrender the same and convey the freehold part to said J Kirby, and he thereupon must give a mortgage of the whole purchase according to the agreement in Mr Kirby late Mr Nelsons clerks hands for the £600, remaining unpaid.

Friday Jan 27   Received a letter from Mr Stonestreet. William Parker gave a note to executrixes of my late uncle, for £27 17s which he owed.

Saturday Jan 28   I gave the bellman the following to cry in the market today: To be let to enter at Old Candlemass next two closes in Newbegin next to Westwood now tenanted by William Parkinson gardener enquire of Mr Courtney.

Sunday Jan 29   Received a letter from Mr Nathaniel Andrews attorney at law with a requisition for the proving of my uncles will; which requisition I inclosed in a letter I wrote to Mr R Mackley Proctor in York.[194]

Monday Jan 30   This morning my mother, aunt Peggy and I went to Hull in a post chaise — I went to Mr Cayleys — but was not long there left some writings etc with him. We got from Hull about 5 o'clock in evening.

Wednesday Feb 1   I gave the bellman the following addition to the paper he cry'd before vizt: Likewise to be let to enter on immediately a very good stable with six standings and with a chamber over it. Enquire likewise of Mr Courtney.

Thursday Feb 2   I attended a meeting at the Tyger, they chose Mr Hoggard surveyor and treasurer of the Hull and Beverley Turnpike in the room of my late dear uncle Featherston. They desired I would show them the books about a dismission of a clerk some years ago I accordingly brought them; and they ordered me to attend this day sev'night to have accounts examined and ballance paid to new treasurer. Then they proceeded about road to York, from whence came an alderman and the town clerk, who acquainted us that the City of York would oppose our petition if we did not consent to have a bar no nearer than Kecsby[Kexby]; it was put to the vote whether the petition should go on notwithstanding and carryd in the affirmative by a very large majority. I voted for the carrying it on; but we seemed unanimous in not consenting to have the barr at Kecksby.[195] Mr Grimston was chairman. Mrs Goulton told us tonight that Miss Newsome and Captain Cooke were married.

Friday Feb 3   Received a letter from Mr Mackley Proctor at York inclosing the requisition a commission to Revd Mr Johnston and Mr Ward to swear the executrixes and a certificate of the same paid said postage.

Saturday Feb 4   This afternoon a messenger of the House of Commons came to us and gave me, my mother, aunt Peggy and aunt Featherston orders to lay the books etc relating to Beverley and Hull Turnpike before a committee of the House on Tuesday the 14th of this month. I wrote to Mr Cayley sent letter by my servant, who returned with an answer.

Sunday Feb 5   My mother and I went to Hull to Mr Cayleys he is of opinion; need not go to London; but send books. I wrote accordingly to Sir George Savile chairman of committee.

Monday Feb 6   Resolved to go to London by advice of Mr Goulton etc.

Tuesday Feb 7   I let Parkinsons closes to Mr Saunders. I wrote to Sir George Savile.

Wednesday Feb 8   This morning my mother aunt Peggy, aunt Featherston and myself set out for London. Laid at York. Thursday at Castleton, Friday at Stamford, Saturday at Welwyn and [blank].

Sunday Feb 12　We got safe thank God to London about one o'clock. Took lodgings at Mrs Haines [?] in Greek Street Soho.

Monday Feb 13　I waited upon Sir George Savile, and talked with him; he was very civil and polite.

Tuesday Feb 14　I went to the House of Commons to the committee and authenticated the books; in evening was at opera of Leucippo.

Wednesay Feb 15　Mr Stonestreet dined with us. I went to the bank got a bank bill accepted.

Sunday Feb 19　I was at St James's Chapel; saw the King and Queen etc there. Drank tea at my cousin Miss Beres at Mr Hogarths.

Monday Feb 20　I was at committee at House of Commons.

Tuesday Feb 21　I was in gallery at House of Commons to hear the debates. Sir John Phillips made a motion for regulating Secretary of States Office. This was first time I heard debates here.

Wednesday Feb 22　My birthday — I am now thirty years old thank God. Mr Stonestreet, my cousin Miss Bere, and Miss Jenny Legard drank tea with us. I was at committee at House of Commons 'till near 5 o'clock. Gave evidence about state of Hull and York roads.

Thursday Feb 23　I was in Prince of Wales's drawing room at St James's. Saw Prince of Wales and Prince Frederic. The under governess said turn about Prince of Wales say your ta[196] to that gentleman, he begins to talk. Fine children.

Saturday Feb 26　I was at court in the drawing room. Very splendid court, I saw King and Queen very fairly and Prince William and Prince Henry; many ambassadors there. I went by myself.

Monday Feb 27　I was at the general court at East India House called upon Mr Stonestreet at Jerusalem Coffee House. I was at East India House 6 or 7 hours. Great debates but no voting.

Tuesday Feb 28　We dined and drank tea at Mr Tufnells. We had grand dinner and silver plate, and clarett. Mrs Tufnell (who was Miss Meeke) looks vastly well.

Wednesday Feb 29　I was at committee at House [of] Commons, I gave a clause to Mr Poynta one of clerks whom I am acquaint with about passing accounts to be put in new bills.

Thursday Mar 1　I was at East India House at general court.

Friday Mar 2   I was in gallery at House of Commons; Sir George Savile made the report. I heard debate about Cyder Bill. Velters Cornwall made a curious speech.

Sunday Mar 4   We went to the Magdalen Chapel in Mrs Allens coach; we had dined there. Mr Dodd made a fine sermon.[197]

Monday Mar 5   Dined with Mr Stonestreet at Islington.

Wednesday Mar 7   Dined and drank tea at Mrs Wyches. Grand dinner, as came passed by an house in flames.

Thursday Mar 8   I was at the Ridotto,[198] and danced with Miss Hawkesworth, never was at Riddotto before. Staid 'till near 6 o'clock. Went along with Miss Allen Miss Hawkesworth Mrs Woolfe etc.

Friday Mar 9   I was at oratorio Allegro ill Penseroso at Covent Garden. King and Queen, Prince of Wales and Prince Henry there.

Sunday Mar 11   I was at Foundling Hospital chapel in morning.

Tuesday Mar 13   This day we all went to the bank, mother and aunt Margaret. Transferred £500 4 per cent bank annuities. I called at Change, and just stepped into Change Alley. I was at a concert at Mrs Cornellys Great Room at Carlisle House in Soho Square. Miss Carters benefit. Vastly elegant room.[199]

Wednesday Mar 14   I was at oratorio at Covent Garden[200] Deborah. King and Queen and 3 princes there.

Thursday Mar 15   I was at British Museum, saw all curiosities, very extraordinary; Mr Harper one of librarians vastly civil; he being my acquaintance got me in though had no tickett but there was a vacancy.[201] Mett with good company. Young Mr Smelt Mrs Popple and Miss Bere drank tea with us.

Friday Mar 16   I was at museum again with mother and aunts. I was at House of Commons in gallery to hear debates. Mr Stonestreet dined with us. NB Sir George Savile and many members with whom I conversed were extremely civil and free.

Saturday Mar 17   We left London in stage and got to Cambridge in evening to Black Bull. NB I can't insert a hundredth part of transactions etc at London.

Sunday Mar 18   We were at St Marys morning and afternoon. I dined in the hall at Trinity College, and afterwards went up with Mr Whisson who was formerly my tutor, and several other Fellows of the College into Combination Room to drink a glass of wine. At night we went to our chapel.

Monday Mar 19   Left Cambridge this morning. Lay at Colesworth [Colsterworth].

Tuesday Mar 20   Lay at Brigg.

Wednesday Mar 21   We got to Beverley, thank God, this evening about 6 o'clock. I called at Mr Cayleys in my way through Hull. The particulars of my transactions at London I can't recapitulate.

Sunday Mar 25   Wrote to Mr Stonestreet.

Monday Mar 26   I went to Hull this morning. Called at Mr Cayleys. Returned in evening.

Tuesday Mar 27   Revd Mr Johnston his wife and daughter, Miss Hayward, Mrs Truby, Mrs Featherston and Miss Parsons drank tea with us.

Friday Mar 30   I wrote to Mrs Wormley sent her accounts and 2 bills.

Sunday Apr 1   A great eclipse of the sun. I saw the whole, very plain. I wrote to Mr Neate, and my cousin Bere.

Tuesday Apr 3   Mother both aunts and I all went to Hull in coach to Mr Cayleys and Mr Beatniffes. Got home in evening.

Wednesday Apr 4   I registered probate of my uncles will at office in this town.

Thursday Apr 5   This morning I went with my late uncles late servant Richard Wallis to look at my closes, beginning at Newbegin but did not go to see them all.

Sunday Apr 8   This morning about 10 o'clock I set out on horseback from Beverley and got to York without baiting betwixt 3 and 4 o'clock in afternoon.

Monday Apr 9   This morning I went to Mr Mackley the Proctor about my uncles will being proved.   At night I went to the assembly.

Tuesday Apr 10   This morning at eleven o'clock I set out from York together with my servant on horseback dined at Easingwold where left my portmanteau and we went to Sessay to the Revd Mr Kitchingmans,[202] where I staid all night, and opened the business I came upon to him; and had the happiness of finding Miss Smelt well etc. I undertook this journey with the consent and approbation of my mother and aunt Margaret.

Wednesday Apr 11   This morning I made a declaration of my affections to Miss Smelt, and hope she may be inclined in time to comply with my desires, and give me her hand and heart in marriage. I had much conversation on this subject with Mr and Mrs Kitchingman (the latter aunt to Miss Smelt) and also Mrs Betty Smelt (another aunt). They all approve it, but leave it to Mr Smelt her uncle and her own inclinations. Miss Smelt behaved on the occasion in the most prudent and sweet engaging manner. I was most kindly, hospitably and politely entertained by the whole family.

Thursday Apr 12   This morning after breakfast I had a second interview with my dear Miss Smelt, and explained my mind more fully, she behaved very prudently and sweetly. I took my leave of her and the good family and left Sessay about 11 o'clock;

Miss Smelt is to go to her uncles in about a forthnights time, when she will talk over this matter with him and he will write to me about it. I called at Easingwold took my portmanteau and got to York through the worst roads I ever saw; the water was out in one place and being a bad bottom my horse sometimes got in holes almost up to the neck. After this on the turnpike I was up several times in stiff clay and mudd up to the horses belly and expected to have been dismounted or laid fast, but at last, thank God I got to York about 3 o'clock in afternoon.

Saturday Apr 14 This morning at quarter before ten o'clock I left York and got to Beverley (without baiting) 10 minutes before two o'clock in afternoon; having rode it (32 miles) in 4 hours and five minutes, and through very bad roads. I found letters from Mr Cayley and Mr Andrews, also drafts of release and settlement of uncles affairs.

Monday Apr 16 I read over and observed the drafts and then read them over before mother, aunt Margaret, and Mrs Featherston and Mrs Truby.

Tuesday Apr 17 This morning I went to Hull on horseback, found out John Maud got a description of the 4 closes George Thompson has. Called at Mr Wadmans to enquire for writings of cottage etc at Anlaby, he was out. Called about several jobbs. Went to Mr Cayleys, I found he knew of my late expedition, he asked me if I had gone on to Leases.[203] I dined with him, talked with Miss Cayley; drank Miss S's health after dinner; Dolly was there.[204] I called at Baxbys about surrender of Newland estate. I got to Beverley before 6 o'clock in evening.

Friday Apr 20 Received letters from Mr Stonestreet Mr Cayley and cousin Miss Bere; also from Mr Mackley Proctor at York with probate of uncles will. I answered Mr Cayleys letter.

Sunday Apr 22 (Easter Sunday) This day I went into second mourning for my late dear uncle Featherston, and was at St Marys morning and afternoon in my light grey frock suit made at London.

Tuesday Apr 24 This morning I went to Hull, called at Mr Cayleys, and at Newland on John Kirkbys, etc. I got home to dinner.

Wednesday Apr 25 This day I went to the court held at the Hall Garth to have my aunt Featherston surrender of a part of the copyhold at Stork to my aunt Margaret for her life and after her death to me, delivered in at court; I paid half a guinea (Jury 7s 6d Steward 2s Bailiff 1s). This was the first copyhold court I ever attended.[205] At night I was at the assembly in my full trimmed black suit.

Thursday Apr 26 This morning I went to the court at Cottingham to get my mother found heir of estate at Newland left her by my late uncle, I carryd the probate of his will with me. Mrs Dickons gave me amount of bank post bill for £59 4s.

Friday Apr 28 This day I received a letter from Miss Smelt. I answered it and likewise wrote to Rev Mr Kitc[h]ingman under cover. Likewise a letter from Mr Andrews answered it.

Tuesday May 1   Received a letter from Miss S with a final answer.

Friday May 4   Received a letter from Leonard Smelt Esqr[206] and one from Revd Mr Kitchingman. Answered letter.

Saturday May 5   Received a letter from Cornelius Cayley Esqr answered it by Ferraby.

Monday May 7   This day Mr Cayley his daughter and Miss Dolly Smelt all came dined and drank tea with us, but before dinner we settled all my late uncle Featherston's affairs, and Mrs Featherston Mrs Truby, my mother, and aunt Margaret executed the necessary writings; the former gave the executrixes a release, and they all four joined in a conveyance of lease and release or settlement (for particulars, see the same). My mother gave up to me all lands she is intitled to by my uncles will, and by descent, and my Aunt Margaret gave me Stork after her death, and the lands she is intitled to by descent she gave me immediately all but little Mantram [Mantholme] which is to go along with Stork. A memorial was registered here at the office.[207] The executrixes gave Mrs Featherston and Mrs Truby a release with memorandum annexed. Mr Cayley and I had a little talk about a late affair. I told him it was all over, which he knew before I believe.

Thursday May 10   This morning mother and I went in a postchaise to Anlaby to see my cottage there, which wants repairing. We got home to dinner.

Friday May 11   Received a letter from Mr Smelt. Wrote to Revd Mr Neate, and to Nat.

Saturday May 12   Received a letter this morning from Mr Cayley.

Monday May 14   The East Riding Militia commanded by Lieut Col Hassell[208] came to town to excerise for a month.

Tuesday May 15   This morning I went to Hull called at Mr Cayleys among other things. I talked with him about a late affair. Told him I had given up all thoughts of pursuing it, and desired him to give my respect to Mr Smelt, and acquaint him with my resolution. I told him some of my reasons and he could not help owning they had some weight. I expressed at the same time the grateful sense I had of the kind partiality of the family in my favour and the pleasure it would always give me to see them at Beverley, desiring he would present my respects to the lady, whom I should be always glad to serve as a friend. I called at Dr Sykes etc etc and got home about 4 o'clock in afternoon.

Wednesday May 16   Mr Bowman called upon me — he said Mr Metcalf[209] when in town, desired him to speak to me about a late affair, how glad he should be to meet me at Leases, and how much all the family wished for the match. I told Mr Bowman my resolutions on that head, expressing likewise my scuse of their kindness. Mr B said Mr M told him that it was owing to some letters Miss S had received which gave her an ill impression, he said that probably the motive of those letters arose from envy. On this I observed that impressions were sometimes not be removed, but assured him I had dropt all thoughts of carrying on that affair.

Friday May 18   Received a letter from Mr Haxby. Answered it.

Saturday May 19   Mr Hargrave, the dancing master[210] dined with us, he has not been at our house these 12 or 14 years I believe.

Sunday May 20   Received a letter from Mr Stonestreet with a bank post bill.

Monday May 28   This morning I went to Hull and attended the first meeting, since late Act, of the trustees for the Hull and Beverley Turnpike; I carry'd the books of account of my late uncle Featherston's the late treasurer, which were examined, a mistake of £6 in 1754 to prejudice of proprietors and an overcharge, as they termed it of £1 1s for lunar insted of calendar months being allowed, I paid the ballance £227 10s 1d by their order to the new treasurer Mr John Hoggard, and received a receipt in full of all money due from the executrixes of the late treasurer to the trustees of said turnpike, which receipt was signed by 6 trustees, vizt Cornelius Cayley Christopher Scott, E M Ellerker, Francis Bei[l]by, Samuel Watson junior and Thomas Wakefield. I acquainted the trustees with the order myself, my mother and 2 aunts had received from the House of Commons, and desired that our expences might be considered, what I left to themselves. I was desired to withdraw, while they debated about this point, and in about ten minutes was called in and acquainted me that they had agreed to allow us fifty guineas; this was what I had told them the journey up and down (without expenses at London) cost us. I told them very well — upon which they made an order that such a sum should be paid us, and inserted in the Bill of Charges of procuring the new Act. So it will be paid when they have raised the money for expence of Act and making new branch.[211] NB The whole expence of procuring the Act comes to £889, odd money! Mr Wilberforce was for having me pay the interest due to proprietors not only to 23d December last but also to 23d June; I told him as to the latter I absolutely would not do it. However it was at last agreed that Mr Hoggard should pay the interest of both half years — I had some warm debates with one or two of the trustees. I dined with them at Cross Keys where meeting was, and returned home in evening got to Beverley about 6 or 7 o'clock.   NB Mr Hoggard paid me my half year's interest on Hull and Beverley Turnpike due 23d December last. I gave the books up to Mr Hoggard. Mr Cayley asked me to drink tea with him. I told him I was expected home — he said nothing about my late affair.

Thursday May 31   This evening the gentlemen of Beverley gave a ball to the officers of the Militia, the ladys etc. I was a subscriber towards it, and was there.

Saturday Jun 2   I was at a meeting (the first) about the turnpike road from Beverley to Kexby Bridge. I was one of the trustees gave my vote for Mr Keld to be clerk, Mr Staveley of Pocklington was the other candidate. Mr Keld got it. I voted again for Mr Keld to be treasurer; he had 27 to Mr Staveley 33 votes. So last was chose. I voted that there should be a bar betwixt Beverley and Weighton and then came away.

Sunday Jun 3   This afternoon Mr Daniel Draper whom I have not seen upwards of twenty years came to see me, he has been many years in East Indies, is married and has 3 children. His house at Bombay stands on the very spot where my father's house stood. He is going to Scarbro' proposes to return to India next March.[212]

BEVERLEY RACES.

ON Tuesday the 14th of *June*, 1763, will be Run for, on *Beverley-Westwood*, in the *East-Riding* of the County of YORK, FIFTY POUNDS, (given by MICHAEL ARCHER NEWTON, Esq; and Friends) by any Horse, Mare, or Gelding, that never won that Value, Matches excepted; Five-year Olds, to carry eight Stone; Six-year Olds, eight Stone nine Pounds; and Aged, nine Stone two Pounds; to run Heats, four Miles each Heat. Certificates to be produced of their Age from the Breeder at Entrance.

On Wednesday the 15th, FIFTY POUNDS, by Horses, &c. Give-and-take, that never won that Value, Matches excepted; fourteen Hands, aged, to carry nine Stone; allowing seven Pounds for every Year under seven; higher or lower, Weight in Proportion; to run Heats, four Miles each Heat. Certificates of their Age to be produced from the Breeder at Entrance.

On Thursday the 16th, a Subscription Plate, by Horses, &c. that never won the Value of Five Pounds, Matches excepted; to carry Weight for age, to run Heats, four Miles each. To enter on Monday the 13th, between the Hours of Four and Eight in the Evening.

On Friday the 17th, the LADIES Plate of FIFTY POUNDS, by Horses, &c. four Years old this Grass, that never won that Value, Matches excepted; to carry nine Stone, to run Heats two Miles each Heat. Certificates of their Age to be produced from the Breeder at Entrance.

The Owner of every Horse, &c. shall subscribe and pay, on or before the Day of Entrance, Three Guineas towards the next Year's Plates, and one Guinea Entrance to go to the second-best Horse for Stakes.

The Horses for the above Plates to be shewn, entered and measured at ROBERT NORRIS's, at the *Blue Bell*, on Thursday the 9th of *June*, between the Hours of Four and Eight in the Evening.——Three Running-Horses (to be judg'd so by the Subscribers) to enter and start for each Plate, or no Race.——All Horses, &c. shall be agreeable, and run according to such Articles as shall be produced to them at the Time of their Entrance.——The Horses, &c. to stand at the Houses of such Inn-holders only as have subscribed and paid Two Guineas to the above Plates, on or before the 21st of *May*, and who have assisted in collecting the Subscription for the said Plates; and not above four Horses to stand at one House, the Horses, &c. belonging to the Founders and Inhabitants of *Beverley* only excepted.

Pursuant to an Order of the Mayor, Aldermen, and Pasture-Masters, no Person shall break the Ground, to sell Ale and Wine in *Beverley-Westwood* aforesaid, but such Wine-Seller as have subscribed and paid Half a Guinea, and such Ale-Seller Five Shillings to the above Plates; and every Person to take Care to level the Ground as they found it.

A MAIN of COCKS to be fought every Morning during the Races, between the Gentlemen of *Hull*, and the Gentlemen of the *East-Riding*, for four Guineas a Battle, and Forty the Main. An ASSEMBLY every Night during the Races, at the New Assembly-Room.

Notice of Beverley Races, 1763. (East Riding of Yorkshire Archives and Records Service.)

Monday Jun 4   Mr Draper dined and drank tea with me, and this being the Kings birthday he and I went to the assembly together. I was out of mourning tonight. Mr Draper is one of my oldest acquaintance.

Tuesday Jun 5   This day I went to Mrs Dickons gave her my bank post bill for £102 7s and she gave me £65 1s 6d in cash and £37 5s 6s in a bill she drew for me. I then went to the Tyger and gave to Mr Yoward and his brother in law, Mr Gylby Mr Horsefield's account and paid to the latter the ballance being £65 1s 6d due from the executrixes. I paid my my mother her ¼ annuity due 20 May last, £25.

Tuesday Jun 12   Received letter from Revd Mr Neate. Beverley races begin today.

Thursday Jun 14   This day I destroyed my will, and made a new one which Mr Robarts, Mr Clubley, and Mr Christopher Elliott witnessed.

Friday Jun 15   Beverley races end. I was three days upon the stand in the race ground, and danced every night at the assembly. Mr Draper dined with us today.

Sunday Jun 17 Mr Draper was back again to Scarbro' yesterday, I believe.

Tuesday Jun 19   My mother and aunt Peggy in a post chaise and I and a servant on horseback set out early in the morning from Beverley, crossed Humber, dined at Spittle and lay at Lincoln. 50 miles.

Wednesday Jun 20   Dined at Newark, got to Nottingham in evening.

Thursday Jun 21   Saw the castle, from the terrace finest prospect I ever saw. Went to Mortimers Hole a vast cavern in the rock on which castle is situated. I observed the house M Tallard resided in when a prisoner.[213]

Friday Jun 22   Saw the cellar of White Lion Inn 60 steps under ground in the solid rock and a most prodigous length, going all under the street. We saw likewise several houses cut in rock with gardens on the top of them and only a chimney appearing. This is a fine situated town, and beautiful market place.

Saturday Jun 23 Dined at Loughborough, lay at Leicester.

Monday Jun 25   Left Leicester early in morning. Breakfasted at village called Kipworth [Kibworth], dined at Bricksworth [Brixworth] another village and got to the George at Northampton about 5 o'clock in evening. I [got] wett through in a violent rain.

Tuesday Jun 26   I went with Sir John Robinson's son[214] whom I knew at college and dined with nobility and gentry of the county at Peacock Inn[215] Boughton Fair being the time when they dine together in this manner every year. Lord and Lady Northampton, Lord and Lady Sussex and many ladies and gentlemen were there; after dinner I went with gentlemen into another room, where we drank claret, and in evening we had a dance, and a cold colation. I danced.

Wednesday Jun 28   About 5 o'clock in evening left Northampton and lay at Wellinborough 10 miles off.

Friday Jun 29   Tasted the mineral water, and at 5 o'clock evening left W and got 10 miles further to Thrapston.

Saturday Jun 30   Went to see Drayton a fine old seat of Lady Betty Germains;[216] dined at Oundle a pretty situated town; lay at Norman Cross.

Sunday Jul 1   Breakfasted at Wheatsheaf, went to church at Huntingdon lay at Cambridge, but did not go to T[rinity] College nor call to see anybody.

Monday Jul 2   Dined at Kennett and got to Bury St Edmunds to Angel Inn about 5 o'clock in evening. It is above 11 years since I was here.

Tuesday Jul 3   Called at Mrs Perkins where we formerly lodged. Drank tea at Mr Lestranges who is yet living.

Thursday Jul 5   This morning early left Bury breakfasted at [blank] called at Stowmarket at Uvedales at Needham [Market], and got to dinner at Ipswich. Took very neat lodgings at one Mrs Kerridge's a mantua maker[217] in Cross Keys Street. Tis a very pleasant town.

Saturday Jul 7   This morning about 7 o'clock we embarked on board a wherry and went down the fine river or arm of the sea to Harwich, dined there and returned in evening. 24 miles there and back. We sat so near the water that we could touch it with our hand when we pleased. Coming back the wind being against us we were obliged to tack all way.

Thursday Jul 10   The races began today. I went to the assembly but did not dance. Grand appearance.

Wednesday Jul 11   I was at public breakfast; and at the assembly at night and danced.

Friday Jul 13   Early in morning left Ipswich, and got to dinner at Bury. In evening I went to the assembly but there was so little company, they could not make a dance.

Saturday Jul 14   Early left Bury, breakfasted at Newmarket, dined at Cambridge and lay at Huntingdon.

Sunday Jul 15   Morning being rainy did not set out till after dinner went to Norman Cross and thence to Oundle.

Monday Jul 16   I went to Mr Creeds garden where saw the aloes that is going to flower.[218]

Tuesday Jul 17   This morning left Oundle, breakfasted at Wandsworth [Wansford] dined at Colesworth [Colsterworth]. Lay at Grantham.

Wednesday Jul 18   Breakfasted at Bingham and got to Nottingham to dinner.

Thursday Jul 19   Early in morning left Nottingham, called to see Sir George Savile at Rufford [Abbey], he showed me improvements he was making in that fine place, dined at Palethrope [Perlethorpe]. Lay at Blythe.

Friday Jul 20   Dined at Doncaster, lay at Ferrybridge.

Saturday Jul 21   Breakfasted at Aberford, where dined 13 years ago when I was going to Wakefield School, dined at Wetherby and got well, thank God, to Harogate about 4 o'clock in afternoon. No room at New Inn nor Salutation so got in at Queens Head. Vastly full of company.

Wednesday Aug 8   This morning mother and Miss Sinclair in a chaise, and I and Revd Mr Sinclair[219] and our servants on horseback left Harogate and got to York to dinner.

Thursday Aug 9   Breakfasted at Whitwell, dined at [blank] and got to Scarb[o]rough to Mr Listers in Beast Market in evening. I went to Cooks Room.

Friday Aug 10   I went to Long Room and danced; this place not so gay and agreable as Harogate this year.

Thursday Aug 16   This morning left Scarb[o]rough, dined at Malton, at the Talbot, and got to York in evening. I was wet through 7 miles before I got there.

Friday Aug 17   In morning left York and got back to Harogate in evening.

Saturday Aug 18   There was a dance and I danced with one Miss Eyles.

Monday Aug 27   My mother and I took a post chaise and went to see the ribbon manufacture at Harwood, Lord Chief Justice Gascoigne's tomb in Harwood church, Mr Lascelles house or rather palace at Gauthorpe and then dined with Revd Mr Metcalf.[220] They said nothing about a late affair. I was glad of it.

Sunday Sep 2   This day before dinner arrived the son and two daughters of Mr S---n of Newcastle,[221] one of them a widdow; Mr and Mrs S had expected them some day, and I waited with impatience to see the young lady, whom I was told was very pretty, and the father and mother were become very intimate with my mother and self, Mr and Mrs O-d [Ord] another daughter of theirs were here a day or two ago. I knew him at college, as I did the widdows late husband Mr I-r-n. I had a good deal of conversation with the young lady this evening, and began to admire her.

Monday Sep 3   I was at the ball at the Green Dragon and danced with Miss S---n and found her a most amiable and accomplished woman. She made an entire conquest of my heart.

Wednesday Sep 5   I was at the ball at Marquis of Granby and danced again with Miss S---n, to whom I now show myself attached. I rode out this morning with her and Mrs I to Plumpton and Knaresborough; they rode single.

Friday Sep 7   Ball at our house. I asked Miss S and her sister but they won't dance any more here as they drink the water. I was forced to dance however with a stranger by Mr S---n.

Saturday Sep 8   I went to Plumpton with Mr S family. I rode with Miss and young Mr S all on horseback.

Sunday Sep 9   This afternoon I acquainted Mr S---n with my love for his daughter and he said he would speak to his wife and tell her and sound her inclinations. I told him fortune he made no material objections.

Monday Sep 10   This morning Mr S---n told me his daughter said it was not agreable; I had a good deal of conversation with him. I went to ball at D [Dragon] with Miss S but did not dance.

Tuesday Sep 11   I spoke having about two minutes opportunity to Miss S---n she gave me no encouragement. I made Mr Crowle my confident tonight, for he had found out my liking for her. He gave me his advice.

Wednesday Sep 12   I was at ball at Marquis of Granby but did not dance as Miss S---n did not. I am almost always by her. I spoke to Mrs I-r-n about my love for her sister tother day.

Friday Sep 14   Ball at our house. I did not dance. Miss S---n very shy.

Saturday Sep 15   I had very little conversation with Miss S---n all day. I spoke to young Mr S---n about my passion for his sister.

Sunday Sep 16   Having yesterday resolved to leave Harogate today I took an opportunity twice of speaking to Miss S---n she replied much as before. I had some conversation with her mother for first time about the subject of my love; she said she was afraid she could give me no hopes she thought not. At church time I handed my dear Miss S---n into the coach, as usual, and took my leave of her and the other ladies and then Mr S---n and I had a long conversation, and he gave me leave to write to him and said if his daughter gave any hints that she might have liked me better, had she known me better, or anything of that sort, that he would acquaint me. I thanked him kindly for this kindness and it being about 12 o'clock at noon, I took my leave of him and left Harogate, I and servant on horseback and mother and Miss Nelson in a postchaise, we dined at G[reen] Hammerton and lay at York.

Tuesday Sep 18   This morning left York, dined at Weighton and got well thank God to Beverley about 5 o'clock in evening after an absence of a quarter of a year, and making a tour of seven hundred and ten miles. All of which but 40 miles in post chaise and 30 by water, I travelled on horseback. We saw several fine seats and remarkable things in the course of our tour. I found a letter from Mr Stonestreet.

Sunday Sep 23   This day I went out of mourning for my late dear uncle Featherston. I wrote to Mr S---n.

Tuesday Sep 25   I wrote to Mr Stonestreet.

Wednesday Sep 26   Revd Mr Myers and his mother dined with us.

Tuesday Oct 2   Received an answer from Mr S---n which puts an end to all my expectations in regard to a late affair.   Received a letter from Mr Stonestreet the bank have raised their dividend for the half year due 10th October to £2 10s — and hope to continue it. If so the interest will be 5 per cent per annum instead of 4½.

Wednesday Oct 3   This morning my mother, aunt Peggy and I went in a postchaise to Anlaby to look at my cottage lately rebuilt there; and also to Hessle to see my cottage there. We got back to dinner at 3 o'clock in afternoon.

Thursday Oct 4   In morning my mother and aunt Peggy in a postchaise and I on horseback went to Hull, I called at Mr Baxby the attorney, he says that it is high time things were settled about the Newland estate and that if Kirby delays I must get a copy of the article and tell him if he refuses to comply, we shall enter upon the land and receive the rents. But he says I must be careful in signing the convenant which will require consideration (shall therefore get Mr Cayley to peruse it before 'tis signed). I called at Mr George Thompson, he was out but I spoke to his wife and son told them what was due on my closes at Summergangs,[222] and that I hoped to see Mr Thompson at Beverley very soon. I called at Mr Thorleys and got late Coulson now Stevensons house Blue Boar and Horns[223] ensured, on which executrixes have a mortgage. Made some other calls and we got home about 5 o'clock in evening.

Sunday Oct 7   Wrote to my cousin Miss Bere.

Friday Oct 12   Wrote to Capt Hare.

Saturday Oct 13   I paid John Taylor twenty one pounds for rebuilding my cottage at Anlaby. My mother surrendered the copyhold land at Newland and Hullbank to Robert Kirby brother to John Kirby at said John Kirby's desire as per writing on back of the article. This is to be delivered into court at Cottingham next Monday. He is to resurrender it to me and also to make a mortgage of freehold for money yet upon it.

Sunday Oct 14   Wrote to Mr Stonestreet.

Tuesday Oct 16   Wrote to Revd Mr Sinclair. Paid aunt Featherston her half years annuity £50 due 10th instant.

Friday Oct 19   Wrote to Mr Stonestreet and for my mother to Mrs Popple and inclosed the rings for them both; sent the letter and mourning rings by Mrs Betty Constable.

Thursday Oct 25   This day I hired Richard Wallis, who sometime ago lived with my late uncle Featherston and since with Mr Warton. I am to give him nine pounds a year wage, full livery and a pair of buckskin breeches which last he is not to take away with him except he stays two years without my leave. The assemblys begun tonight (the Kings accession). I was there, and opened the ball with Mrs Saunders.

Sunday Oct 28   Received a letter from Capt Hare.

Thursday Nov 1   'Tis eight years this night since my dear father died; for he died the 1st November 1756, about a quarter past 9 o'clock at night. Alass!

Sunday Nov 4   Received a letter from Mr Stonestreet.

Tuesday Nov 6   'Tis 8 years this evening since my dear father was burried; for he was burried the 6th of November 1756, betwixt 4 and 5 o'clock in evening. Alass!

Wednesday Nov 7   This morning Mr Iveson[224] called to desire I would give up some writings now in my possession belonging to Mrs Clarke and Mr and Mrs Tennyson; I told him I would consult Mr Cayley about it tomorrow. He brought me a letter from Mr Tennyson.

Thursday Nov 8   This morning I went to Hull, called at Mrs Wormleys to show her writings I was about giving up, she looked at them and said they did not concern her she was obliged to me notwithstanding. I then went to Mr Cayleys; he looked at them and gave me his opinion I might give them up, but said he would consider more about it, before Mr Iveson called for them tomorrow, who when he takes them is to give a receipt for them. I took Mr Cayleys opinion also on the draft of conveyance of land at Newland and the mortgage of it; I would say I left the draft with Mr Cayley for his opinion. I asked him a question or two besides, not very material and gave him a guinea. I called at Mr Thorley about the insuring my late uncle's houses. I likewise called at Mr George Thompsons he told me he would either come tomorrow or Saturday sevnight to settle accounts with me etc. I called at Mr Kirkbys and Mr Baxby's attorneys at law but they were both out of town. I got home to dinner about a quarter past 3 o'clock in afternoon.

Friday Nov 9   Wrote to Mr Stonestreet, and inclosed a letter of Mr Robarts his to his son, which Mr Stonestreet will forward.

Saturday Nov 10   This morning I received a letter from Mr Cayley inclosing a draft of conveyance and mortgage, in which he has made several alterations; he also inclosed me Mr Tennysons's letter with Mr Iveson's receipt for the writings belonging to Mrs Clarke and Mr and Mrs Tennyson which Mr Cayley writes me delivered him.

Sunday Nov 11   Received a letter from Revd Mr Sinclair. He is my very good friend.

Friday Nov 16   Mr Hargrave and Mr George Thompson supped with me. The latter paid me twenty one pounds 16 shillings in part of rent due to me.

Saturday Nov 17   This afternoon my mother conveyed the freehold part of the estate at Newland to me and Robert Kirby; that is to me only by way of mortgage (see the deed). My mother John Kirby myself and Robert Kirby executed this deed. Afterwards Robert Kirby surrendered the copyhold (formerly surrendered to him by my mother) to me, by way of security for £540, which with £60 secured by the above mentioned mortgage of the freehold part makes £600 the sum yet remaining unpaid for the estate sold to John Kirby and by his direction conveyed to Robert his brother so that I now must carry this said £600 to my book of acounts my mother and aunt Margaret having previously to this given up their right in the same to me. NB The surrender is to be delivered in to court at Cottingham the court after next; that is at Michaelmas next.

Sunday Nov 18   Received a letter from Mr Stonestreet who has ... paid £3 3s to Mr Adamson for two bag wigs for me. Answered Mr Stonestreets letter. This day I dined with the Mayor, Mr Hoggard.

Saturday Nov 24   This day I paid James Wilson my servant his wage, five pounds and he left his great coat and buckskin breeches as agreed. I gave him a written character as follows vizt: 'James Wilson was my servant one year, he understands looking after horses pretty well — can wait at table and was very honest and sober. J C November 24th 1764. Beverley.' He went away this day after dinner; and my new man Richard Wallis came in the evening.

Thursday Nov 29   I wrote to Mr Kirkby attorney at law at Hull.

Saturday Dec 1   Wrote to Mr Thorley to insure my house malt kiln and stable without North Bar also Mrs Featherston's and aunt Margarets houses etc.[225]

Sunday Dec 2   Wrote to Revd Mr Sinclair.

Monday Dec 3   Received from Mr Kirkby attorney at law fifty guineas being allowance of Commissioners of Beverley and Hull Turnpike for journey to London, pursuant of an order of honourable House of Commons of John Courtney, Elizabeth Courtney, Margaret and Ann Featherston. I gave a receipt for the same.

Saturday Dec 8   Paid aunt Featherston her ballance. I finished the deeds etc with Robert Kirby. Paid Mr Easton the attorney his bill. I paid £4 10s, and Robert Kirby 13s 8d.

Sunday Dec 9   Received a letter from Revd Mr Sinclair.

Monday Dec 10   In morning before 9 o'clock my mother and self in a post chaise and four servants on horseback set out from Beverley, dined at Barnby Moor, and got to York before 4 o'clock in evening. Mother and I this morning mett Miss M[olly] Thompson did not know her till past. She looked confused. I have not see her before since I made my addresses to her.

Thursday Dec 13   In morning early left York, dined at Ferribridge, lay at Doncaster.

Friday Dec 14   Dined at Blyth; lay at Worksop, a neat little town.

Saturday Dec 15   Dined at Mansfield, a good old town; and got to Nottingham, to Blackmoors Head. I sent a letter to Mr Sinclair and received his answer. There was a great flood.

Sunday Dec 16   Mr Sinclair came about noon and we all set out on foot and with great difficulty, some part of the way going in a boat and some too being carried on mens backs we got to his house being 3 miles.[226] 'Tis a sweet situation, and commands a delightful prospect of Nottingham Castle and the town etc with the River Trent gliding through the beautiful meadows, and is as picturesk a scene as I ever saw.

Monday Dec 17   This morning about 10 o'clock Revd Mr Sinclair and I in one post chaise and Miss Sinclair and my mother in another set out from Wilford with my servant on horseback; dined at Loughborough, lay at Leicester.

Tuesday Dec 18   In morning set out as before from Leicester, got a snack at Hinckley, tollerable market town, lay at Coventry. Which seems a pretty large old city, not a very handsome one. I never was in Warwickshire before. Terrible road today from Hinckley we were in great danger and bad drivers too.

Wednesday Dec 19   Early in morning we left Coventry, breakfasted at a village called Castle Bromwich, where we left Miss Sinclair and my mother and went on to Birmingham 6 miles farther. Got there to dinner at the Hen and Chicken Inn. Before 5 o'clock Mr Sinclair went to Mr Peake's soon after they sent to me. I went and found Mr Carver there. We all went to his house, where found a good deal of company. The two young gentlemen came in, and at last Miss Carver came in and made tea, we saluted her. Afterward we paid our compliments to Mrs Carver in another room. We supped with them and were very genteely treated with great civility.

Thursday Dec 20   Breakfasted with Mr Peake; after which young Mr C went with us to Mr Baskervilles to see his printing office and tray painting manufacture,[227] Mrs Baskerville very civilly showed us these things herself; then he conducted us to Mr Taylors and his son went about with us to see his famous button etc etc manufactures. We there saw about 300 people at work, greatest part women, we saw the process of gilding, enamelling etc, the gilt brass buttons go through 14 or 15 hands; 'tis surprizing how quick they do them. From thence we went to a famous maker of rings there we saw the making of rings of a farthing, halfpenny and penny apeice which were sent abroad to Germany, America etc in very large quantities for Mr Carver told me that his father had had £700 worth of these rings in one year of this man. We went to see the church too. Birmingham is a very large, well-built populous town with some fine squares and looks something like London. We dined at Mr Carvers. I went home to dress, they sent the chariot for me, we drank tea and so went to the concert, which was in the assembly room. After the musick there was a ball and I danced with Miss Carver, and was carried home as was Mr Sinclair in their chariot.

Friday Dec 21   We breakfasted at Mr Carvers; dined, drank tea and supped at Mr Peakes; Mr Mrs and Miss C were there but the ladies went away before supper.

Saturday Dec 22   We breakfasted at Mr Carvers; Mr Sinclair was obliged to leave Birmingham today, but I thought of staying. Accordingly after breakfast he took leave; and we came away; Mr C shook me by the hand at door. Before breakfast, I was beginning to speak to him about the young lady, but he stopped me short with concern, by saying he would talk to Mr Sinclair on that subject. As soon as we got into our inn, Mr S told me that Mr C had acquainted him, that he had a great opinion and regard for me, but that his daughter was averse to my proposal, and he desired I would not put myself to the trouble of taking a formal leave. I immediately got every thing ready and left for Birmingham in about an hours time with Mr Sinclair at 12 o'clock at noon, and got to Castle Bromwich to dinner, after which he and I in one chaise and Miss Sinclair and my mother in another set out and got to Coventry just before it was quite dark. Miss Carver was tall, seemed about 22 years old, of a dark complexion, black eyes and hair, and was very accomplished and sensible. She played extremely well on the harpischord. Her fortune likewise was large.

Monday Dec 23   Left Coventry in morning, dined at Hin[c]kley. Lay at Leicester.

Monday Dec 24   Left Leicester in morning got snack at Loughborough and arrived at Wilford about 3 o'clock to dinner.

Tuesday Dec 25   Being Christmas day, we went to church. Mr Sinclair read prayers and preached a very good sermon, we received the Holy Sacrament which he administered. We were at prayers again in afternoon.

Wednesday Dec 26   In morning betwixt 11 and 12, my mother and I left Wilford with our servant crossed the ferry, got into a post chaise, passed through Nottingham without stopping and got to Mansfield about 3 o'clock to dinner, staid there all night.

Thursday Dec 27   In morning left Mansfield, went through Worksop, dined at Blythe, lay at Doncaster.

Friday Dec 28   Dined at Ferribridge. Lay at Tadcaster.

Saturday Dec 29   Got to York to breakfast betwixt 9 and 10 o'clock; in afternoon went to lodgings at Mr Goulletts, jeweller in Blake Street, at a guinea a week.

Monday Dec 31   I received a letter from Henry Carver Esqr inclosed in one to my mother from Miss Sinclair. He very genteely apologizes for our abrupt parting. 'Tis a very kind and handsome letter. I answered it. I was at the assembly tonight and danced. Praised be God. Amen!

MDCCLXV [1765]

Tuesday Jan 1   I wrote to Revd Mr Sinclair. I went to prayers at Coney Street church in morning, and to the Minster in afternoon.

Wednesday Jan 2   'Tis a year today since my uncle Featherston died!

Thursday Jan 3   This evening the new theatre at York was opened, with the comedy of the Provoked Husband, and Lying Valet, for Mr Baker, the proprietors benefit. 'Tis a large handsome house. It was not very full, so rather cold.[228]

Sunday Jan 6   Called to see Mr and Mrs Sterne (late Miss Waines) they were married Tuesday came here Wednesday.[229]

Tuesday Jan 8   This morning I mett with some ladies of my acquaintance walking with whom was one Miss B H[230] whom I thought rather pretty than otherwise.

Tuesday Jan 15   I saw and talked with same young lady at play, she and an elder sister were with Miss C-n-tt[231] again.

Friday Jan 18   Kept as Queens birthday. Concert and ball in Great Assembly Room: Coyles benefit. I danced with the bride Mrs Sterne being her first appearance in publick. Talked with Miss B H but thought many others prettier.

Sunday Jan 20   Walked with Miss C-s-tts and Miss B H etc.

Saturday Jan 26   This morning I mett Miss Th-mp-n[232] at the turn of a street. I spoke to her for the first time since I had made my tender almost 2 years ago. I walked with her a little way till she went into a milleners shop. She was very civil and free, and looked most charmingly.

Sunday Jan 27   I mett Miss P and Miss B H asked last to dance which me at ball tomorrow, but she does not go. So engaged her for assembly the Monday after. I had heard a good account her and her family and fortune.

Monday Jan 28   The Earl of Effingham, Sir John O'Carroll and severall gentlemen (I among the rest) gave a ball and cold collation to the ladies this night. I danced, and came away about 2 o'[clock] in morning. Miss T was there but did not dance. I spoke to her.

Tuesday Jan 29   Miss B H and Miss P came into Miss Consitts this morning when I was there to see my partner Miss B Consitt; we all walked out, and called at Mr H-b-n's.

Sunday Feb 3   Spoke to Miss B H at church this afternoon.

Monday Feb 4   I danced at the assembly with Miss Betty Hobson and thought her an agreable prudent girl. Miss T danced with Mr Lewis Disney[233] my acquaintance.

Tuesday Feb 5   Called in morning to see my partner walked out with the ladies; engaged her for Friday night. In evening I sat next her at play.

Thursday Feb 7   Called at Mr H-b-n's walked to Heslington with Miss C-n-tt etc and them. Mrs H asked me to drink tea with them tomorrow.

Friday Feb 8   I was at the concert in Great Room, having drank tea at Mr H-b-n's we went all together. I danced with Miss B H and thought her very amiable.

Saturday Feb 9   Called to see my partner, walked out with Miss C-n-tt and Miss N P and them.

Monday Feb 11   At the assembly I danced with Miss B H she was reserved and shy. In morning I went with Miss H-ns and Miss P to Legerdemain man.[234]

Tuesday Feb 12   Called to see my partner in morning staid above an hour.

Thursday Feb 14   This morning called at Mr H-b-n's; made my address to Miss B H-b-n. She was very coy. Spoke likewise to her sister and mother about it.

Friday Feb 15   This morning I had an interview with Mr H. He gave his consent and approved of my visits, but said she was very young being not 18 till July, and did not seem to approve of my proposal herself. But he would let me know more in 2 or 3 days. At concert I danced with Miss P who is at Mr Hs. I had not much conversation with Miss B H.

Saturday Feb 16   In morning called at Mr Hs to see my partner was left alone with her so talked to her about Miss B H. She said she was sorry her cousin could not approve of me. I was afterwards left with Miss B H she behaved as before, at last Mr C and his son in law Mr P came in and interupted us.

Sunday Feb 17   In afternoon saw Miss B H at church, but did not go to speak to her.

Monday Feb 18   At the assembly I danced with eldest Miss H had but little talk with the other.

Tuesday Feb 19   Called to see my partner in morning. We all walked out. At night Miss B H was at play with Miss P, Mrs Sterne etc and her father. I sat near but had not much conversation with her, she would not let me hand her out; but Capt M did.

Wednesday Feb 20   At night after supper I went to Mr H had great deal of conversation with him and his wife, they asked me to dinner tomorrow. I told them I would wait upon her. I was left alone with Miss B H. But she said so much and behaved so, that after almost an hours conversation I could not enter in any hopes of success.

Thursday Feb 21   I dined at Mr H-b-n's, and afterwards being alone with two old people I told them, I thought there was no prospect of success; but he said, he desired he might have a little more time to talk with her, and I found he would be almost willing to force her inclinations; this made me very desirous to put an end to an affair I was now very sorry had ever been begun. However at last he told me he would give me a determinate answer on Monday. I was greatly perplexed today.

Friday Feb 22   My birthday. I am now 31 years old thank God! Miss Hammond and Mr Goullett dined with us, and she and Mrs Milward and two Mr Disneys my old schoolfellows and acquaintance drank tea with us.

Saturday Feb 23   Having presented (last Wednesday night) Miss B H with 4 ticketts for Miss Phillips's benefit tonight I went to Mr H's this afternoon, drank tea and waited upon them all to the play. We were in one of the balconys I sat next Miss B H. When the play was over, she would not let me hand her out, I set them home, but she would not permitt me to touch her so I took my leave and wished them good night at door.

Sunday Feb 24   In afternoon saw Miss B H Mrs H etc at church in street when came out I spoke to them, asked Miss B H how she did etc and then left her and went into the Coffee House.

Monday Feb 25   In morning Mr H-b-n came to our lodgings, he my mother and self had an hour and half conversation. I found his daughter had a dislike to me, and that she was to have no present fortune, but he would settle what he had upon me. He was very desirous that I should pursue the affair. I told him I would consider of it. I dined at Mr C-tt's where were Mr H-b-n and Mr P. In evening before I went to the assembly, I wrote a letter to Mr H-b-n and sent it by my servant, acquainting him I was determined to lay aside all thoughts of pursuing this affair. There were none of them at the assembly.

Thursday Feb 28   This morning betwixt 9 and 10 left York mother and self in p[ost] ch[aise] and servants on horseback got to Leedes to dinner at New Inn.

Saturday Mar 2   This morning I went to see the cloth market which is a very curious and fine sight, to see so many thousand pounds worth of cloth exposed to sale, and their manner of buying it.[235]

Sunday Mar 3   In morning went to the newest church called Trinity,[236] with Mr and Miss Gaultier. In afternoon to the old church saw Mr Green there. Mr Gaultier showed me his dye house etc very curious.

Monday Mar 4   In afternoon I went and played on the organ in the old church. Supped at Mr Greens.

Tuesday Mar 5   Went to see cloth market again. In morning left Leedes and got to Wakefield before 1 o'clock; very bad day, and hearing the roads were impassable for a carriage to York any other way than by Leeds and the accomodations being very poor at White Hart, we resolved to return. I had not been at Wakefield since I left school 13 years wanting 3 months ago and yet could not stir out to see the old place or any of my friends. Dined and returned to Leedes. Went to an assembly made on account of a bride and bridegroom and danced.

Thursday Mar 7   Went to card meeting but did not stay long.

Saturday Mar 9   This morning about nine o'clock left Leedes (I wanted to have seen two Miss W-k-rs and heard them play and sing but had not that satisfaction). Got to York to dinner at Howards before 2 o'clock. We went to the play.

Sunday Mar 10   We drank tea at Mrs Milwards. She informed me how many foolish stories Miss C-n-tt had raised about me. NB I read several letters from aunt Peggy while I was at York and one from Mr Stonestreet, one from cousin Bere and one from Mr Raines.

Monday Mar 11   This morning betwixt 9 and 10 o'clock we left York dined at Barnby Moor and got well to Beverley thank God about 4 o'clock in afternoon. I found a letter from Mr Stonestreet.

Tuesday Mar 12   I wrote to Mr Stonestreet.

Tuesday Mar 19   This day I let my two closes in Newbegin near to Westwood to Mrs Burton. They were before in the tenure of Robert Saunders Esqr who quitted them at Candlemass last; from which time Mrs Burton enters upon them. This evening about 4 or 5 o'clock Lewis Disney Esqr came from York to see me, and spend a few days with me. He rode the grey horse (David) which I have bought of him 'tis 6 years old rising 7.

Wednesday Mar 20   Mr Disney and I walked about the town and to the Minster etc at night went to the assembly he played at cards.

Thursday Mar 21   This day I paid Mr Disney twenty pounds for his grey horse and two pounds fifteen shillings for his silver-plated bitt and stirupps; in all twenty pounds fifteen shillings [sic]. He gave me the saddle in. Dr Thackeray dined with us today.

Friday Mar 22   In the evening Mr Disney went away, it being then past 4 o'clock. He rode an hired horse sent him today by the carrier from York. He gave me an invitation to Lincoln. Received a letter from Mr Stonestreet with a bank post bill being my balance £84 4s in which is included Mrs Trubys dividend.

Sunday Mar 24   Wrote to my cousin Miss Bere.

Tuesday Mar 26   This morning Mr Dickons gave me the amount of the above bank post bill, being £84 4s and indorsed the bill and delivered it to him. I paid my mother ¼ years annuity due the 20th of February last £25.

Thursday Mar 28   I paid Mrs Truby her dividend on her £1460.

Wednesday Apr 3   This morning I went to the Town Hall and paid half years rent to the Chambermen Mr Nelson and Mr Armistead, for leasehold ground on which house without North Bar is built;[237] and also for gravel-yard. This day I sold my sorrell mare, which I have had now about eleven years and an half vizt from the year 1753 (the latter end of it) when it was bought of Alderman Atkinson[238] at [blank]. I sold it to [blank] Johnson a baker in this town for two guineas. I returned him a shilling, and gave him the bridle in. I paid the man who rode the mare in the fair 1s 6d. It was near 19 years old.

Thursday Apr 4   This day I let my close in Norwood (which Marshall quitts tomorrow) to Val[entine] Banks.

Friday Apr 5   Received a letter from Nat.

Saturday Apr 6   Paid Mrs Featherstons half year annuity due yesterday as per receipt. Mrs Wormeley and her son dined with us; they paid in £480, principals due to the executrixes of my late uncle F and also £10 19s interest thereon; we delivered her the bonds and notes; and my mother gave them a receipt in full of all demands. I paid Mrs F Johnsons hundred pounds due from the executrixes, and also 16s interest due thereon, got back the note and likewise took her receipts.

Tuesday Apr 9   Received a letter from Mr Stonestreet.

Thursday Apr 11   This morning I and servant on horseback, and mother with Mrs Milward and Mrs Cogdell in a post chaise set out from Beverley. Mother and I went to see my aunt Peggy at Hull who is under Dr Chambers care being not well. We dined at George. I got a bill at Peases to send up to buy stock for Mrs Truby as my aunt Featherston desired. Got from Hull about 6 o'clock in evening.

Monday Apr 15   I went to Hull this morning, returned to dinner. Mr Robinson dined with us.

Thursday Apr 18   Received a letter from aunt Peggy — she is better.

Friday Apr 19   Received a letter from aunt Peggy tonight.

Sunday Apr 21   Received a letter from Mr Stonestreet.

Tuesday Apr 23   This morning mother and I went to Hull in a chaise, dined and drank tea at Dr Chambers's, my aunt Peggy was there too. We returned in evening.

Friday Apr 26   Received of George Cook for my aunt Peggy £18 19s for hay eatage etc at Stork Hill.

Monday Apr 29   Went to Hull this morning on horseback, called to see my aunt Peggy; and at Mr Cayleys etc mett with Mr and Mrs Maddox at the inn, rode home all together. I got home about quarter past 3 o'clock to dinner.

Tuesday Apr 30   Received a letter from Lewis Disney Esqr.

Wednesday May 1   Made pomade divine by Miss Sinclair's receipt.[239]

Sunday May 5   Answered Mr Disney's letter.

Monday May 6   My aunt Peggy came from Hull with Dr Chambers who dined and drank tea with us.

Tuesday May 7   Made second sort of pomade divine.

Monday May 13   Our Militia came to town for exercises.

Tuesday May 14   Received a letter from Mr Disney. NB This afternoon I lent Mr Jack Robinson of Beverley, late of Welton 16 guineas, which he is to pay me again in January next.

Friday May 17   Received a letter from Henry Disney Esqr. Answered ditto and answered Lewis Disney Esqrs letter.

Tuesday May 28   Received a letter from Mr Stonestreet. Answered it. I wrote to Mr Wind at Harogate. Our races being today.

Friday May 31   Beverley races end today. Received a letter by Rev Mr Huthwaite from Mr Lewis Disney.

Saturday Jun 1   Revd Mr Huthwaite and Dr Thackeray dined with me. I answered Mr Disneys letter by Mr Huthwaite.

Monday Jun 3   This morning my mother in stage coach, and I and servant on horseback set out from Beverley, dined at Barnby Moor, and arrived at York about 5 o'clock in evening.

Tuesday Jun 4   At noon left York and after riding about 2 miles on horseback, it was so hot and dusty that I got into the post chaise; we dined at Tadcaster and got to Leedes before 5 o'clock in evening I drest, it being the Kings birthday and went to the ball; Sir George Saville and rest of the Militia officers of his battallion were there. I spoke to Sir George. I danced, minuetts and country dances.

Wednesday Jun 5   After dinner we left Leedes, and got to Marquis of Granby or the New Inn at Harrogate before 7 o'clock in evening. NB My aunt Featherston is at the Crown at Low Harogate.

Monday Jun 19   The ball was at our inn tonight. I opened it with Mrs Ward (late Miss Pemberton) and danced country dances with Mrs Arabine an Irish widdow lady of our house. We had another supper after dancing, and sat up late.

Wednesday Jun 10   We drank claret today after dinner, as we sometimes do by chance; I have not drunk so much since I was at Northampton.

Thursday Jun 20   My aunt Peggy came to the ball at Low Harogate in evening.

Monday Jun 24   The ball at our house. I opened the ball with Lady Clavering it was very splendid. I danced country dances with Miss Ragueneau. I have been at one ball at each of the houses and danced, vizt Queens Head, Green Dragon and Salutation.

Sunday Jun 30   In afternoon I walked to the Queens Head where had some conversation with Miss Kitty Rutter; whom I saw 3 years ago at Harogate. She is a vastly pretty sensible agreable young lady, she comes from Newcastle.

Tuesday Jul 2   In morning my mother, aunt Peggy and I about 9 o'clock set out from Harogate in a post chaise and got to York about 1 o'clock. My mother and aunt Peggy went to Dr Dealtry the latter to take his advice; we dined at Howards, and left York about 4 o'clock reached Harogate at 9 o'clock at night.

Wednesday Jul 3   I called tonight at Q[ueens] H[ead] and talked with Miss K[itty] R[utter].

Monday Jul 8   The ball at our house. Capt Sinclair opened it with Lady Clavering; twas more brilliant than I ever saw at Harogate. In the morning Miss K R---r came to visit a lady at our house. I asked her to dance tonight but she was engaged. She was drest with a large hoop, looked very pretty and genteel and danced vastly well. I had some conversation with her. I danced with Miss Willy Dottin.

Tuesday Jul 9   This morning Mrs Arabine told me there was to be a private ball at our house tonight and that Miss Brown and Miss K R were to be at it; and asked me if I would dance. I told her I believed I should. They accordingly set down all ladies and gentlemens names that were to dance, as I supposed to know the number that they might be equal. I went soon after to Q[ueens] H[head] and engaged Miss Kitty Rutter to dance with me. In the afternoon, I saw a new list made out, in which my name was left out, but Miss K R was set down to Capt Sinclair, a gentlemen who had the list in his hand, asked me if I did not intend to dance, I replied yes, I dance with Miss K R. Nay says he you see she dances with Capt S. I don't know, said I, but I imagine I shall dance with her for I asked her in the morning and she did not say she was engaged. Ah says he Mrs Arabine had promised Capt S to get her for his partner, but I will speak to her; — he did so — she was in some sort of confusion, but Capt S came to me and said, laughingly, you have been too sharp for me indeed Sir, you were very sly to engage the prettiest girl in the place. A little before this though I saw my name added to the former list and they had given me Miss S as a partner the plainest girl in our house. However, I had the pleasure of dancing with Miss Kitty Rutter, who was a most agreable partner indeed. I danced a minuet with her after country dances. We were the next couple to Mrs Arabine, and my partner and I talking about the above mentioned affair, I said to her aloud that Mrs A might hear me, that I had no notion of giving up my liberty in the choice of a partner, and would never be made to dance with any one. She is a most agreable young lady indeed.

Wednesday Jul 10   In morning my old friend Revd Mr Wind called to see me. He and I went to toyshop where I mett with my partner. I walked with her Miss K etc to Q[ueens] H[ead] we went into the Woodhouse; had several songs, I sung. Miss K R was vastly civil and good natured. I got her gloves for her, and played a little with her. In about an hour Mr Wind returned, we soon after all walked out and catched in shower we ran into the milliners. I bought some sweatmeats gave them to Miss K R and tother lady. Set them home and took my leave.

Thursday Jul 11   In morning went to Q[ueens] H[ead] talked with the agreable Miss K R again. She was very civil and free, quite gracious. Mr Wind engaged me to dine at Q[ueens] H[ead] tomorrow.

Friday Jul 12   I dined and drank tea at Q[ueens] H[ead]. I enjoyed Miss K Rs company almost the whole time; she did not go up to dress 'till almost supper time. She wanted me much to stay longer at Harogate and was so obliging as to say she would get Mr Stonestreet the best room in that house if he came. She would have had me staid the ball, but I was very sorry I could not. I came away before 7 o'clock.

Saturday Jul 13   In morning I went to the well spoke to Miss K R. She was in chaise with her sister Mrs O--, I talked to her a little, and then took my leave. At 11 o'clock my mother and aunt Peggy in post chaise and I and servant on horseback left Harogate and dined at Green Hammerton and got to York in evening; at night aunt Featherston arrived there also. I wrote to Rev Mr Wind tonight about Miss K R.

Sunday Jul 14   This morning my aunt Peggy got into her lodgings at Mrs Vevers in Stonegate; where she will stay some time under Dr Dealtry's care. At 12 o'clock at noon, my mother and aunt Featherston in a post chaise, and I and servant on horseback left York, dined at Barnby Moor, and got well home thank God, to Beverley, betwixt 7 and 8 o'clock in evening. NB This morning as I was walking in Stonegate with my aunt Peggy, we mett Miss B[etty] H[obson] alone. I pulled off my hat and she curtseyd. I have not seen her since the 24th February last. Vide. Mr Robarts came to me tonight and was unable to express his gratitude; for he said his son had wrote him that the Governor of Bombay had given him a most kind reception, and that he dined with him in great splendour, and that he had given him recommendations to Bengall. I wrote to Mr Stonestreet tonight.

Tuesday Jul 16   Received a letter from Mr Stonestreet.

Friday Jul 19   Received a letter from Revd Mr Wind. I answered it.

Sunday Jul 21   Received a letter from aunt Peggy. Answered it.

Monday Jul 29   This day my mother as one of the executrixes of my late uncle Featherston settled accounts with Mrs Truby and having paid her at £130 10s 9d balance of their last account and 1 years interest on the same to 8th May 1765 when said principal was paid in. I likewise settled accounts with Mrs Truby. We are now all clear with both Mrs Featherston and Mrs Truby. My mother likewise settled the account with Mr John Parsons and Mrs Truby and gave a receipt for the principal and interest £35 4s 2d for his use. All is now clear with all 3.

Tuesday Jul 30   Wrote to my aunt Peggy.

Sunday Aug 4   Received a letter from my aunt Peggy. Answered it.

Tuesday Aug 6   Received a letter from Revd Mr Wind.

Thursday Aug 8   My aunt Peggy came home from York tonight.

Sunday Aug 11   Wrote to Mr Stonestreet.

Tuesday Aug 13   Received a letter from Mr Stonestreet. Answered it.

Wednesday Aug 14   This afternoon Revd Mr Sinclair came to see us, we went all of us to drink tea at Mr Robarts, and Mr Sinclair supped with us. He goes to Scarbro' tomorrow and returns in about 3 weeks. He says Miss C---[240] is now at Nottingham that she says nothing but Mr and Mrs P--- [Peake?] talk often to him about me.

Saturday Aug 17   Mr Arden[241] called this afternoon to see me. He came from Birmingham about 2 months since. He told me he heard I had been there. I said yes never but once. He asked me if I had any commands, I said none at all. He goes there again next week.

Friday Aug 23   Received this morning two letters from Revd Mr Wind one of them should have come on Tuesday last and was much soiled. I spoke to Mr Bland our new postmaster, and he assured me it came only today to his hands. Vide the said letters with two enclosed therein, from Mr Squire to Revd Mr Wind and from a Mr Clarke to said Squires. Miss K R is reputed good natured, agreable in her temper and her conduct good. But her fortune 'tis said not very much, and family rather too numerous. Upon consulting therefore with my mother, and seeing it was proper to drop this affair, I wrote an answer this night accordingly to Revd Mr Wind.   Such is the issue of this affair.

Sunday Aug 25   I dined with the Mayor Mr Hoggard.

Friday Aug 30   Received a letter from Joseph Grove Esqr. Received a letter from Thomas Stonestreet Esqr inclosing a bill for £100 9s (I must pay Mrs Truby her dividend out of this, ½ year due Midsummer 1765, £33 4s).

Saturday Aug 31   This day my aunt Peggy went to her house.[242] God send her long health and happiness in it.

Sunday Sep 1   This day before dinner about half an hour past 12 o'clock Mr Stonestreet came to our house. I answered Mr Grove's letter. Mr and Mrs Robarts called this evening to see Mr Stonestreet and return him thanks.

Monday Sep 2   Paid my mother her quarter of years annuity due the 20th of last month £25 (settled accounts with Thomas Stonestreet Esqr).

Tuesday Sep 3 Dr Thackerway, aunt Featherston and Miss [sic] dined with us.

Thursday Sep 5   Revd Mr Sinclair breakfasted, dined, drank tea and supped with us. Mr R---s family etc drank tea with us, whose daughter I had often strongly recommended to him.[243] He fell in love with her and desired me to make his proposals to her father, which I promised to do, he goes home tomorrow.

Sunday Sep 8   This day I mett with a proper opportunity to talk with Mr R about Mr S's proposal — he seemed to think his income being mostly ecclesiastical, and going away at his death, in case of children would not answer. But said he would consult his family and consider about it. I wrote tonight to Revd Mr Sinclair.

Monday Sep 9   This morning I called to see my aunt Peggy as I had often done at her house; she was upstairs in her room, and looked but very ill; I had called in on Saturday morning last with Mr Stonestreet and she was then in her little parlour and seemed pure and brisk. But she told me, she eat 5 plumbs that day, and began to be ill about 5 o'clock in the evening. But had walked out a little to meet my mother coming from Mostcroft [Molescroft]; the day before she drank tea with us at my aunt Featherstons, Mr Stonestreet and Dr Thackerwray there too. She looked as well I thought as she had done lately, and was very chearful; as she was the day before that (Thursday) when Revd Mr Sinclair Mr Stonestreet and I called to see her. We all, my mother Mr Stonestreet and I dined and drank tea today at Mr Wakefields at Rowley (my aunt Peggy was to have gone with us if she had been tollerably well). We called at my aunt Peggy's in evening as returned and found her worse, Miss Appleton was with her. She looked, I thought very ghastly with her eyes and I was much alarmed.

Tuesday Sep 10   This morning went to my aunt Peggy's with my mother; found her worse, I sent my servant for Dr Chambers. Drank tea at aunt Peggy's in another room, upstairs. The doctor came in afternoon and prescribed.

Wednesday Sep 11   My aunt Peggy much worse this morning and very uneasy — Mr Stonestreet and I took a little ride. My dear aunt Peggy walked about room taking hold of my arm, and sometimes lay down upon the bed. Sent for Dr Thackwray tonight. She said Mr Stonestreet might come in evening. He did so, and sat a while.

Thursday Sep 12   My dear aunt Peggy much worse this morning. We dined at aunt Featherston's, and drank tea at my aunt Peggys in 'tother chamber. Dr Thackwray wrote at our desire to Dr Chambers to come again but he could not come. My dear aunt Peggy desired Parson Johnston might be sent for, and then told my mother and me that she would be burried near her mother, that she would have Nanny Job to have £100, out of which £90 is to pay off the mortgage on her two houses, which are both settled on her eldest son but my aunt Peggy desires that one may have one house and her other son, the other. She told us she would not have any of her furniture sold, but what we did not keep, she would have my mother give to Betty Brown; and she would have her aunt Blanshard have five pounds a year for her life; and upon my pressing her to tell me whatever else she had a mind to have done, she said she would have one of Neddy Blanchards daughters, who is her Goddaughter to have £10 and some little matter what thought proper to all relations; after which she said, This is my will — I have now made my will if I mend weel laugh at it, and if I die then 'tis my will. I promised her to do as she desired. She is quite sensible quick and clear, and bears the approaches of death with great fortitude. She begged me not to frett for her, but good God! how shall I help it. She said she would have me marry, Ay says I — I thought you would have lived to have seen that, she said it would to be sure have been a great satisfaction to her. I told her I should seldom come to that house of hers and garden if she died, she said yes, yes. Parson Johnston came and prayed with her she was got up and sat in elbow chair, my mother and I joined in prayers and tears. She was very attentive and joined as well as she could. Afterwards she laid down upon the bed again, then got up and laid down several times, complaining much of pain, in her bowells, her body being much more swelled than it was. She took but very little nourishment today. This is the most terrrible scene I have gone through since my dear father's last illness and death. She told me today I had always been a good child, and always would, O God grant I may through thy help.

Friday Sep 13   My dear aunt Peggy vastly ill, and full of pain today, on and off in bed severall times. I gave her all the comfort I could but wanted it very much myself. I was tore to peices with anguish. She was quite sensible, gave directions to her nurse and every body. Intirely resigned and desirous of being released; at night she grew worse and was in a cold sweat; she hardly took the least nourishment today. We did not leave her 'till near 12 o'clock at night. I kist her and wished her a good night, but had small hopes of seeing her alive in the morning. Mr Walker thought she could not hold out above 2 or 3 hours. I kist her she was cold and clammy. Received a letter from Mr Grove.

Saturday Sep 14   This morning we sent first to my aunt Peggy's, they brought us word she had sent for Mr Walker, and Dr Thackwray in the night or rather towards this morning and insisted upon being tapped. They used all possible arguments to dissuade her from so very hazardous an experiment but she had Mr Burton[244] sent for, he urged the great danger, but she was resolved she told him and if he would not do it she would send for another. Accordingly she was tapped. He took about a quart of glutinous matter, neither blood nor water, nor was it fetid.[245] I saw it when I came to her house today. They all said they never saw such before. When I went into her room this morning, she was in bed with curtains undrawn and door open, as soon as I came to the door she saw me, and stretched out her arm with joy saying — Is that you, come here — I went to her she told me she was better and a great deal easier. She was vastly pleased to see me. We dined at aunt Featherstons as usual and drank tea at my aunt Peggy's in another room. She was much easier all day and took jelly a little wine and water and other nourishment today often asking for it. But still we had no great hopes of her recovery. She saw Mr Stonestreet pass by her room door this evening and said to me I had a glance of Mr Stonestreet just now I saw him I told her it was him. She looked chearful and gave me a nod as she used to do when she was well (once today) to encourage me. Oh poor thing!

Sunday Sep 15   This morning my aunt Peggy much the same; sometimes warm, sometimes cold and clammy. About noon Mr Walker thought she was near her end. I asked her if I could do anything for her she said no I had done all I could and bid me go away. I went to my aunt Featherston's to dinner, and we thought not to have gone in to her again expecting she would be in the last extremities. But hearing after dinner that she continued much the same we went in again. We drank tea in the other chamber. I gave her a little tea myself. About 8 o'clock we left her, expecting to find her dead in morning. Received a letter from Revd Mr Sinclair.

Monday Sep 16   My dear aunt Peggy much same this morning, but rather weaker. She was very sensible and once when I asked her if I could do anything for her, she said yes, pray for my release, I told her I was extremely sorry to say that I was obliged to wish for it. I sent my servant for Dr Chambers, who came in afernoon, he went to see her, he said he would not prescribe any thing, for she was a dying. He said so too in her hearing. After which he went up to her bedside, and she asked him how long he thought she would continue and expressed her desire of being released; he told her, he hoped she would soon be released out of her misery. After he went away I comforted her and helped her all I could and asked her if should pray by her, she said I might if I would. I knelt down by her and said the prayer for a person at the point of death in Nelsons Fests and Fasts.[246] I found much difficulty in getting through it after this I repeated the Lords Prayer and a short blessing. She was in bed and up in elbow chair 'till the bed was made every half hour almost; when she was up in chair I held hartshorn,[247] and got herbs and flowers out of garden for her to smell too, she snuffed them up with seeming pleasure. I told her I hoped we should meet again in heaven, and I said she set us a glorious example and that she was almost to be envied; and often when I said to her God Almightly bless you my dear love, she would say, and you too. I gave her a little tea this afternoon again. She bid my mother take the key out of the closet saying there were papers and writings there. I asked her if there was anything she would have done more than she had told me, she said Ay there is one thing I had forgott I would have Nanny Richardson have £15, and when she dies she is to give £5 a piece to her grandson Whites. I asked her how she would dispose of the house at Norwood end,[248] told her I thought she used to talked as if she would reserve that for somebody else, and that I was not mercenary she very well knew, but she said, No, the reason she did not give me that, when she gave me the other lands etc were that she had a mind to have something left to dispose of. She told me she would not have me go much to Stork, for she believed that had been the cause of her death; for when [we] were at York last winter she went to see an hedge laid there, and stood and got wett, came home, and had a fit of the stranguary that night; but that she never durst tell us this before. We came away about 8 o'clock tonight, expecting as before to find her dead in the morning. NB This afternoon as my mother and [I] stood by her, she said 'What is this life! Nothing'; and she once said 'We have a good God, if we put our trust in him he will carry us through all, and whatever he orders is best'.

Tuesday Sep 17   Alass! Alass! My dear aunt Peggy died this evening quarter past 6 o'clock of a dropsy. Alass! Alass! Sent Betty this morning hearing she was alive we went, found her much weaker, but quite sensible but she spoke lower, they told us she had been 29 times (from 10 o'clock last night to 6 this morning) out of bed. We dined as before at my aunt Featherston's and drank tea at my aunt Peggy's. We gave her a little tea; soon after she wanted the quilt off, I took it off, I was at the end of room and she called with a weak voice, Jacky! Jacky! I went to her and she bid me lift her up a little, and told me to go on one side and my mother and on tother, I called Richard my servant (who assisted in helping her up very well and of whom she generally called before and seemed pleased with) to help her up higher and I stood by him to see he did it very tenderly. My mother asked her how she did, she kept constantly saying, Oh my back, Oh my back, and then told my mother she was upon the rack her belly pained her so, and said she was afraid she should burst. After she said to me in a low voice, 'Take away the clout'. I made them do so; and I believe these were the last words she spoke to me. I came out soon after about a quarter or perhaps half an hour past 5 o'clock, and about half an hour past 6 o'clock Richard came in to my mother, self and aunt Featherston and said Mrs Peggy is dead; she died about a quarter or 20 minutes past 6 o'clock evening. She had a little rattle in her throat and went off very easily. I did not see her after she was dead, nor my mother did not. Oh God this is an heavy stroke but thy will be done! Teach us O Lord to proffit by all the dispensations of thy providence and fit us for our latter end and finally bring us to thy everlasting glory through the merrits of Jesus Christ our Saviour Amen! We gave necessary orders and came home in a coach before 8 o'clock. My dear aunt Peggy has been in a bad way rather dropsical for 6 months past and I was often much afraid she would not recover, but I thought she would hold out perhaps a year or two, and sometimes had better hopes. Poor woman, she had been in her house not 3 weeks, and had got every thing made neat, several little peices of furniture she had not used, walk gravelled, and had made coverings for her chairs, and window curtains her last work, not above 10 or 11 days before she died. 'Tis very affecting to see these things. She has been a most tender and affectionate relation to me, and a chearful, constant and entertaining companion ever since I remember. I loved her next my dear father and mother, the best of any body in the world, and shall always revere her memory. I little thought when she left our house (going out without saying anything not caring I suppose to take a formal leave) that she would never come into it again. O God comfort us! Received a letter this morning from Revd Mr Wind. NB My dear aunt Peggy was a month or two turned of 50 years of age I believe. God was pleased to grant her her senses to the last, and great patience, fortitude, piety and resignation. May he, if he sees fit, grant us the same at our last hour, but above all may he give us life everlasting through Christ Amen! Amen!

Wednesday Sep 18   My aunt Featherston came to us and dined with us, we made preparations for funeral, as cannot keep the corpse longer than tomorrow.

Thursday Sep 19   This afternoon about quarter past 5 o'clock my dear aunt Peggy was burried in the church yard of St Mary's, near her mother, as she desired. My mother and I and cousin Neddy Blanchard and my aunt Featherston attended her corpse to the grave. Alass! Alass. She was burried in same manner as my father and uncle were; only instead of 8 poor men; 8 poor old maids in decent mourning of their own were the bearers. We went in a coach to her house a little past 3 o'clock in afternoon. I went in to see the coffin. NB Parson Johnston read the burial service. We returned to our own house. NB Mr Stonestreet was very much with us at my aunt Peggy's house during her last illness. My mother and I when she was so ill on the Thursday told her we were very sorry, she had come from our house; she said, no, she was better pleased to die at that house than at ours. I suppose she thought (such was her great tenderness for us) that it would be less shocking to us. O God comfort and support us miserable sinners! During her last illness I was often with her, and did all I could to help and comfort her. Teach us thy way O Lord make us useful members of society and finally bring us to eternal happiness through Jesus Christ thy son our Lord. Amen! Amen! Memoranda. One day when she was very ill, and I leaned down on the bed by her, she said to me, that she had not perhaps done all the good she ought to have done, I told her we should all be very miserable if God was not very merciful. This evening after tea, mother and I took cousin Neddy Blanchard on one side and told him what my dear aunt Peggy had bequeathed to her aunt Blanchard his mother, and to his Goddaughter and Mrs Job, and gave him five guineas in advance for his mother. He went home soon after. We desired him to call again soon.

Friday Sep 20   We sat in the back parlour.

Saturday Sep 21   It is but 3 weeks today since my dear aunt Peggy left our house and went to her own. She had long wanted to get there and she had her desire, but a very short enjoyment of it. Alass! Now my mother and I have nobody to rejoice when we come home from a journey, my poor aunt Peggy used to cry for joy, and we were vastly pleased to see her again and talk over matters to her. But this world passeth away, grant O God we may so use it as not to abuse it, and enable us by thy help and Holy Spirit to attain to an everlasting inheritance in heaven, through Jesus Christ our Lord. Amen! Amen!

Sunday Sep 22   This afternoon my mother and I appeared at St Mary's church in deep mourning, for my late dear aunt Peggy. Revd Mr Sinclair is come again to town came to see me, this afternoon.

Monday Sep 23   Mr Grove is come to town he called this morning he wrote a line to me first. Revd Mr Sinclair dined with us.

Tuesday Sep 24   Revd Mr Sinclair dined with us. He told me that matters were pretty well agreed betwixt Mr Ragueneau and him, and was in great joy.

Wednesday Sep 25   This morning Mr Ragueneau called again when [sic] Mr Sinclair to return me thanks for being the instrument under providence of promoting the alliance which he hoped would be between him and Mr Sinclair, at the prospect of which he expressed great pleasure. I am glad 'tis likely to be a match, as have reason to hope it will be an happy one.

Thursday Sep 26   I was obliged this morning to attend a meeting at the assembly room; they chose old Mr Penniman,[249] myself and Mr James Greyburn on the committee for the year. In afternoon my mother and I and Mr Stonestreet walked to my dear aunt Peggys house, were in room where she died brought away the securities. This first time I have been there since she was burried. Oh God. I pulled some nectarines. Alass! My aunt Featherston called this evening and brought two letters directed to Mrs Featherston at Beverley which she said she received today with a pot of electuary[250] from York; on opening the letters one was from young Mr Garencieres who had told Dr Dealtry how he found my poor aunt Peggy when he saw her little while ago, and he inclosed copy of what he prescribed in Latin and English; prescription was dated 18th instant and letter 19th. First being the day after she died and the other the day she was burried; as was the other letter which was from Mr Myers, about some lace for her curtains which he was to get her. Alass!

Sunday Sep 29   I gave Mr Easton surrender of Kirby's to deliver into court at Cottingham tomorrow.

Tuesday Oct 1   Mr Dickons gave me money for my bank post bill and I paid him his bill and several more bills, I likewise paid.

Wednesday Oct 9   This morning about 8 o'clock, Mr Stonestreet my mother and I in a post chaise went to Hull, we had some conversation at Cross Keys about his niece, and I saw Mr Stonestreet get into the boat to cross the Humber, in his way home. Twas very stormy.

Friday Oct 11   Received a letter from Nat.

Sunday Oct 13   Answered Nats letter.

Wednesday Oct 16   I paid Mrs Truby her dividend.

Thursday Oct 17   Received by Mr Gylby Mr Horsefields ½ year interest of £22 10s and also ½ year of my late aunt Peggy's due from him £11 5s.

Friday Oct 18   Received a letter from Mr Stonestreet.

Saturday Oct 19   Mrs Richardson and Mrs White dined with us and I paid Mrs Richardson the legacy my aunt Peggy left her of fifteen pounds, to be given at Mrs R death to her 3 granddaughters White.

Sunday Oct 20   Received a letter from Mr Stonestreet with a lottery ticket for Miss Appleton, which cost £12 7s 6d which I desired him to place to my account and she will repay me here. I delivered her said ticket today. I answered both Mr Stonestreets letters.

Monday Oct 21   In afternoon I took Mr Place counsellor at law his oppinion about the fine for Stork, and I showed him all the deeds etc — at same time I sent for Mr John Dickenson the steward[251] and he gave in his demand in which I acquiesced by Mr Places advice, and told him I woud pay him tomorrow.   I also asked Mr Place's opinion about what my late aunt Peggy desired me to do, in regard to paying of[f] the mortgage of the two houses at Hull of Jobs. He says he thinks I cannot safely do it 'till the eldest son come of age; but that then he may call his uncle to account for the arrears. In the mean time, I may pay Mrs Job ten pounds to put her in some way of business, and pay her interest for the remaining ninety at 5 per cent and when the eldest son comes of age, I may, please God pay off the mortgage in case he consents that his brother shall have one of the houses, as my aunt Peggy desired.

Tuesday Oct 22   I paid Mr John Dickenson an heir fine due from Elizabeth Courtney and late Margaret Featherston for a moiety of the copyhold estate late belonging to Ralph Featherston deceased at Hull Brig [Bridge] Stork and Sandholme, which was purchased of Mr Goodricke and wife due to proprietor of the late Sir Michael Warton's estate £36 2s 8d. Also paid to same for ditto twenty seven pounds two shillings for fine due from late Margaret Featherston on surrender of Ann Featherston to her of the other moiety of Stork etc purchased of Mr Dawson and wife. I told Mr Dickenson it should be said in his receipt to be for fine from Mrs M Featherston and me, and desired him to interline it he took pen in his hand but said he should be a witness and it did not signify. NB The first moiety <u>by mistake</u> was surrendered to uncle Featherston instead of to Anne his wife this mistake he was not aware of for in his will he leaves Stork to my aunt Margaret and directs his wife to surrender the copyhold to her. But she could only surrender the latter moiety, which she did to my aunt for her life and remainder to me at my aunt Margaret's desire. Vide April 25th 1764. So that my mother and aunt Margaret were heirs of the first moiety (notwithstanding my uncle's will) and consequently my mother is now in possession of it, and if she does not surrender it to me I paying £27 2s a year an half fine, I at her death if living must pay £36 2s 8d 2 years fine. I am to deliver Mr Dickensons receipts for the above £63 4s 8d to Mr Nelson[252] steward of the court who will deliver me a copy of the surrender court rolls. Memorandum. I paid Mr Dickenson also 1 quarter tyth rent due Michaelmas 1764 £3 7s 6d.

Wednesday Oct 23   I went to Mr Nelson's office, Mr Marmaduke Nelson and I looked over the rolls. I found a surrender of my uncle and aunt Featherston in 1753 to the use of her will. I gave him my two receipts for the fines paid Mr Dickinson yesterday, and am soon to receive copys of the surrenders. But am to talk with Mr Nelson senior the steward of the court, on Tuesday next, when we must endeavour to set things right.

Thursday Oct 24   Revd Mr Sinclair dined with us.

Tuesday Oct 29   This morning Sir Robert Hildyard breakfasted with us and according to his former promise to my late uncle he assigned to me, at my mothers desire, his security for Beverley and Hull Turnpike, on which remains £80, and my mother assigned to him the security for the Patrington Turnpike £100. Sir Robert paid me twenty pounds in cash; and then we adjusted the interest. I paid Mr Robinsons outrent at £6 4s 4d and my outrent for Anlaby £7 and also my outrent (late aunt Peggys) for Sandholme 2s 4d. Mr George the receiver did not take anything for the alienation of the last, as he said is was so lately taken. In afternoon I called at Mr Nelsons and looked over the rolls, he was of opinion that the surrender made by my uncle and aunt to the use of her will was invalid. I afterwards with my mother went to Revd Mr Johnston and my mother took administration to my late aunt Peggys effects; and then Revd Mr Samuel Johnston his son[253] and I looked over the books about the arrears of tyths due from my uncles tenant which he promised to pay Parson Johnston for. Tis a long confused account indeed.

Wednesday Oct 30   Revd Mr Samuel Johnston breakfasted with me. We examined again the affair of tyths. Afterwards, Mr Marmaduke Nelson and Mr Easton came and said my mother must pay for the quarter moiety that was my aunt Margaret's to which my mother was heir. After some conversation I acquiesced. Mr Nelson then said that his father could not make me out a copy of the surrender of that moiety by my aunt Featherston to my aunt Margaret for her life with remainder to me, as by the receipt it mentioned only fine as due from my aunt Margaret. I told him Mr Dickenson could set him right in that for that I mentioned that to him at the time and desired him to interline it, he consented seemingly and took it in his hand but then said why — it does not signify I shall be a witness for you; they said they would go to Mr Dickinson.

In evening I went to the assembly, first time since my dear aunt Peggy's death. Miss S---t [Smelt] was there. I spoke to her. Tis first time I have seen her since our affair vide April 1764. She came to Mr Goulton's last night to stay a while. Mr James Penniman[254] told me my late uncle Featherston about 4 years ago lent him two hundred pounds on his bond and he wanted to know to whom he must pay the interest. I told him I really did not know any thing about it, he said he would call upon me tomorrow.

Thursday Oct 31   Mr Penniman sent word he would call upon me on Saturday next. I called at Mr Nelson's and was much surprized to hear that Dickenson says the £27 2s 8d was only for my aunt Peggys fine, and that he told me he could not alter the receipt, which is an absolute falsity. I could not help being in a passion and desired Mr M Nelson would go with me to Mr Dickenson, which he did but he was gone out of town and was not expected home 'till tomorrow night. So I appointed to meet them on Saturday afternoon at Mr Nelsons. I paid my aunt Featherstons half years annuity due 10th instant. I see in York Courant today that Miss Thompson was married last week to Mr Walbank.[255] (Vide Wednesday February the 9th 1763).

Friday Nov 1   'Tis 9 years tonight since my dear father died. For he died the 1st November 1756; a little past 9 o'clock. Alass!

Saturday Nov 2   Mr Penniman was prevented calling on me today. In afternoon Mr Robart by my desire as a witness to what should pass, went with me to Mr Nelson's office where I mett him and Mr Dickenson by appointment. I desired Mr Nelson to produce the receipts for my payment of the two fines; he gave me them in my hand, and I then showed the receipt for the surrender fine to Mr Dickinson and asked him whether he did not take it in his hand in order to alter it at my desire, and that he afterwards said, why it does not signify, I shall be evidence for thee. He owned he did take it in his hand to alter it, but said that he told me he could not. I replied that I never heard him say any such thing, but asked him further what he then meant by saying he should be evidence for me, he replied that he meant, for the paying of the money. I asked him if he thought me such a fool as to desire verbal evidence when there was written evidence of that fact. He seemed to hesitate a little, but said it was only for my aunt Margarets fine. I desired him to tell me whether he was conscious, at the time I paid that fine, that it was all that was due and if he was why he treated me in such an unhandsome manner as not to acquaint me that that was not the whole of his demand, as from my objections to the receipt he saw that I apprehended it to be the whole. He replied that he did not know nor did he now know how it was he confessed. Very well, say I, Mr Nelson here would make you know whether you would or know, for he says that you (not he) are the person to settle the fine and that you went by your Book of Directions. But continued I, I will appeal to the rolls, and will not admitt your book as evidence. Yet I have something farther to say to you Mr Nelson, you told me, speaking of that surrender of my uncle and aunts to the use of her will, that it was not the stewards business to mind whether it was right or not, that you did as the surrender ordered you; now let me ask you one question, how are our estates secured to us. Are they not by court rolls, but if a surrender on your rolls be contrary to the custom of the court, it will be void, and the estate may come into hands which justice and equity would forbid to give it to; well in this case you say the surrender should have had council when he made the surrender, but I ask you does the most able council know all the different customs of all the coppyhold courts, will you if

Saturday Market Place, Beverley. The market cross was built in 1714.

they did allow them to set aside any of your customs; who then shall inform the surrenderer but the stewards of the custom of his courts; at least he should not insert upon the rolls a surrender which he knows is contrary thereto. I think indeed it ought to be at his peril if he does and that he ought to give very great security for the discharge of his office on his entering thereon. But however continued I, I insist upon precedents for the payment of such fines as you demand, he seemed to be in a great passion, but after some time he grew cool and said he would show me precedents. But he took a law book to look at those cases, and he showed me a paragraph which seemed to be against me, a little, but I looked a little more attentively and pointed out another fully in my favour; he was a little disconcerted and had recourse to the old excuse of the uncertainty of the law, and that one book said one thing and another book another. But however he promised to look out for precedents and I took my leave.

Tuesday Nov 5   This days newspapers brought the bad news of the Duke of Cumberlands[256] death on Thursday night last about 8 o'clock. I heard of it on Sunday. This afternoon I paid couzen Neddy Blanchard my aunt Peggys legacy of ten pounds to his daughter Bella, her Goddaughter, and I gave him likewise in her name a guinea each to his 3 other children being 3 guineas. I likewise gave to John Brown 6 guineas being a guinea each to his 6 children (Betty not included) in my aunt Peggy's name.

Wednesday Nov 6   It is nine years this evening since my dear father was burried. For he was burried betwixt 4 and 5 o'clock in the evening November the 6th 1756. Alass!

Thursday Nov 7   In morning I (with Mr Robarts) went to Mr Nelsons office. He seemed much cooler than before in his temper, and told me that he had searched the rolls but as only the sums paid are mentioned and not the rent of the land, they could give no satisfaction. This in great measure I admitted, he showed me a copy of some directions (from an old book which Dickinson has) about setting the fines and said it was customary to take 2 years and ½ rent for a life and a remainder; but that he thought 2 years a reasonable fine, and that he thought Mr Dickinson would agree to that, and advised me to comply, lest I might be obliged to pay 2 years and ½ rent. I don't see how they can well prove this. So I told him I would see and talk to Mr Dickinson about this. He said that this was the first fine of this nature that had happened since Mr Dickinson was steward and that he had a deal of business upon his hands etc but I insisted that when he made a demand upon me, it was reasonable I should know for what I paid my money. In afternoon Mr Ragueneau called to desire I would be a trustee for his daughter in the marriage articles, I told him I would with great pleasure.

Friday Nov 8   I attended a general meeting at the assembly room.

Saturday Nov 9   Mr Robarts dined with us. In afternoon Mrs Goulton and Miss S---t [Smelt] called. We talked about indifferent subjects. The latter looked very well, and with a smiling countenance. She goes away on Monday or Tuesday next. I wished her health and a good journey.   I feel not withstanding!   NB I saw today in this town the most surprizing exploits of Price, who rode on 3 horses, mounted and dismounted on full gallop, rode with his head upon the saddle and his feet in the air making the horse gallop etc etc. It was the most curious thing I have seen a long time.

Thursday Nov 14   Called with Mr Robarts upon Mr Dickinson; had some little talk with him.

Friday Nov 15   Received a letter from Nat. NB Last Sunday 10th November people went into mourning for late Duke of Cumberland. Men, black full trimmed, black buckles etc. But I don't alter my mourning.

Sunday Nov 17   Received a letter from Mr Stonestreet — he has bought £100 Old South Sea annuities for me. I answered his letter.

Monday Nov 18   Called upon Dickinson, with Mr Robarts; talked with him about fine he has got Mr Beatniffe's opinion, but had sent it to Mr Nelson senior, but will show it me when he gets it again. His opinion is that a fine for the remainder is to be paid if 'tis the custom of the court. This they must show me. There is to be a special court on Friday next, when I am to attend to have my mother found heir to the moiety that descends to her from my late aunt Peggy. I must afterwards endeavour to adjust the other matters.

Tuesday Nov 26   This morning about 9 o'clock I was at the wedding of Revd Mr Sinclair and Miss Ragueneau at St Mary's the ceremony performed by Revd Mr Ward. After breakfast about ½ hour past 11 o'clock in morning the bride and bridegroom and Miss Ragueneau set out from Beverley in a post chaise and four for

York in their way home. God grant them all health and happiness. I never saw a greater prospect of felicity nor friends on both sides as well as the parties themselves so thoroughly satisfied. Indeed this marriage gives universal satisfaction to everyone that know them. My mother and [I] breakfasted at Mr Ragueneaus but my mother was not at church. The last wedding I was at was Sir William Foulis and Miss Robinson; and the last I was at, at St Mary's was my late dear uncles. We came away from Mr Ragueneaus about 12 o'clock at noon. NB This morning after the wedding I signed the writings as one of the trustees.

Wednesday Nov 27   I paid my mother her quarters annuity due 20th instant £25. This day my mother and I attended the court at Hall-Garth and took the oath of fealty to the lords on being admitted tennants.

Sunday Dec 1   Mr Ragueneau received a letter from Miss Ragueneau that Mr and Mrs Sinclair and herself got well to Wilford last Thursday night; and found that everything exceeded what they expected; and were vastly pleased. (This day people changed mourning for late Duke of Cumberland men black full trimmed coloured buckles etc but I kept on in my mourning.)

Tuesday Dec 3   Received a letter from Mr Stonestreet.

Wednesday Dec 4   Paid my servant Richard one years wage due Martinmas last, nine pounds.

Friday Dec 6   Received a letter from Mr Robinson.

Saturday Dec 7   I surrendered my half moiety of the copyhold of my estate at Stork to the use of my will into the hand of the lords of the manor by William Jackson and W Blyth two copyholders. Mr Alderman Spendlove²⁵⁷ drew the surrender. NB I delivered the surrender to Mr Jackson he is to deliver it in at the next court. Memorandum the other half moiety is my mothers.

Sunday Dec 8   Answered Mr Robinsons letter.

Wednesday Dec 11   I paid Mr Dickinson, in prescence of Mr Robarts £18 1s 4d for my mothers hir fine for one fourth of copyhold estate at Stork etc; descended to her from aunt Margaret; and also my mother paid for the £9 2s 8d which with £27 2s 8d, paid before, makes up £36 for the surrender with remainder fine (about which had before some dispute); being two years rent. Mr Dickinson gave receipts which I carryd to Mr M Nelson who promised to make out the copies of the surrender from the rolls this week. NB I have paid for fines in all £90 and my mother is in possession of half of the copyhold, which if she was to surrender to me now £27 2s 8d more would be to pay; but this will not be done as 'tis all same betwixt us, and if I survive her shall heir it and pay £36 being 2 years rent.

Tuesday Dec 17   Mr Ragueneau called this morning and read us great part of two letters he has received from Mr and Mrs Sinclair, expressing in very strong terms their material happiness, and desiring their particular compliments to us.

Wednesday Dec 18   I got 3 copys of the court roll, relating to Stork etc for which I paid him £11 12s 6d. This afternoon I delivered to Mr Ramsey attorney at law £130 in cash and he delivered me a bond from Francis Best Esqr for the said sum (at 4 ½ per cent) dated 14th instant.

Sunday Dec 22   This day people went out of mourning for the late Duke of Cumberland; but I have had nothing to do with this mourning being in full mourning for my aunt Peggy.

Sunday Dec 29   Received a letter from Revd Mr Sinclair, thanking me, and acquainting me he was one of the happiest men in the world.

Monday Dec 30   This morning about 9 o'clock my mother and I went in a post chaise to Hull. I called at Mr Baxby's, Mr Thorley's about getting a new policy, and likewise paid insurance 6s for Stevenson's house. I also paid Nanny Job 1 quarter a years interest for £100 due 17th instant £1 5s and did several other little jobs. We got home a little past 5 o'clock in evening.

Tuesday Dec 31   This day I adjusted accounts with Mrs Truby and paid her her ballance £7.

Laus Deo! Amen!

MDCCLXVI [1766]

Wednesday Jan 1   Mr J Hoggard paid me six pounds being the interest due to me from Beverley and Hull Turnpike due 23d December 1765. Received annonymous letter and verses, from Jack Robinson.

Saturday Jan 4   This morning Revd Mr Samuel Johnston junior breakfasted with us and we proceeded to adjust the tythe, and in afternoon he brought me his account of arrears of tythe due from my late uncle Featherstons tenants from 1754 to 1763 (also offerings from him) which said account I allowed and paid him for the use of his father forty two pounds, sixteen shillings and two pence. NB My late uncle had promised to pay Parson Johnston the arrears when he would come to an account but he neglected to account with my uncle though he was often urged to it by him. I shall take of my tennants what judge reasonable of what I have paid for them, for which see my sketch of accounts.

Sunday Jan 5   This day I went into second mourning for my late dear aunt Peggy, and appeared at St Mary's church morning and afternoon in my light grey frock suit. I wrote to Mr Stonestreet and inclosed a letter from Mrs Webb to Mr G Park at Bombay desiring him to forward it.

Monday Jan 6   This day I went into first mourning again for the late Prince Frederick.[258] Being Twelfth Day I drank tea etc at Mrs Reynolds, where chose King and Queen. I was King and Miss Sally Goulton was Queen. I am to give an entertainment they say on Valentines Day.

Wednesday Jan 8   In morning I sent to all my tennants whom I had paid tiths for and talked to and made them following abatements vizt.

What I paid for each	What they are to repay
1. William Duggleby 15s	10s
2. Berriman £3	6d
3. Michael Reed £2 5s 10	[blank]
4. Nicholas Smith £3 10s	£3 3s paid
5. Widow Hewson £1 5s	6d paid
6. Thomas Barker £1 15s	5s
7. John Plaxton 16s 8d	10s 6d
8. William Hardy junior £1 6s 8d	16s 2d paid

(allowed for carriage hay over his close in my uncles time 10s 6d)

At the assembly tonight I began as usual, took out the bride Mrs Tullock, then asked Mrs Gethin and Mrs Wilberforce who did not chuse to dance, I then danced a minuet with Mrs Maisters, and asked her whom she called for her she said Mr Broadley who danced a minuet with Mrs Sterne etc soon after which on my asking Mr Tullock if he would dance a minuet, he flew out into a violent passion said he had been affronted at 3 assemblies, I told him it was more than I knew and asked him in what, which he would not tell me, but said that I was no steward, and had no business to direct, who was I, or what was I, and d--n Mr Broadley he knew not what right he had to dance before him etc etc. I told him that I had asked his lady to dance country dances when I first came into the room, that I had taken her out for the first minuet, and had ordered that no ticket should be carried to her partner that they might be the first couple, and farther that if had occurred to me, I would have told Mrs Maisters that there was a bridegroom there but he would hear nothing and continued in a violent fury. Revd Mr Best[259] standing by desired me to let him alone. Just after this Mr Gethin comes to me and asked me who were the stewards, I told him Mr Penniman and his lady when they were here, were the managers, but that Mr Penniman myself and Mr Grayburn were the committee for this year and further than this, Mr Penniman had desired me to officiate he still insisted I had no business to begin, and in an insolent manner asked me who or what I was. I made a pretty warm reply, yet repressed myself as much as possible seeing they were a little in liquor. However Capt Tullock coming up to me again, Col Appleton followed him and we sat down upon the bench at bottom of the room; here Capt Tullock talked in an higher strain, repeated what he had said who are you, and what are you, I told him of a good as family as he was; he muttered something of taking me by the nose or kicking me out ay by God said I do if you dare, I wish you would attempt it. Col Appleton seeing me going to break out into a passion took us out into the tea room, where we talked over matters again. Why says I what would the man be at would he have danced a minuet with his own wife. He exclaimed that he had been affronted at 3 assemblys but he said he could not think we intended it was our ignorance, I told him no — I could not allow that neither; nay if I would not allow that — and began to be furious — I told him I did not care. Capt Lester etc coming in we went in to Great Room again, as they said the ladies would wonder what was the matter. In the passage Mr Gethin repeated his insolent behaviour but I avoided as much as I could disputing with him. Mrs Tullock behaved very complaisantly, and Mr Gethin and Mr Tullock went to cards for the rest of the night, and began to dance country dances and was the bottom couple. Few people knew there had been any dispute all the night.

Friday Jan 10   My mother received a letter from Mrs Sinclair who warmly expresses her obligations and says she is the happiest of her sex.

Saturday Jan 11   Col Clarges, Mr Goulton etc all say that people think I acted in a very proper manner and condemn the behaviour of the gentlemen the other night.

Wednesday Jan 22   I received ½ years rent due Michaelmas last of George Cook my tenant at Stork. First I ever received for Stork and first paid since my uncles death. £31 10s paid him his note.

Tuesday Jan 28   Received a letter from Mr Stonestreet.

Saturday Feb 1   This afternoon, I had 14 ladies and gentlemen (all unmarried but Mrs Sterne) to drink tea etc. Treated them with plumb cake and wine, then played at Commerce. I had laid a wager with Miss Appleton of plumb cake about Mrs Sternes being with child which was the reason of this rout.

Sunday Feb 2   I answered Mr and Mrs Sinclairs letters, in one wrote by me to them both for my mother and myself.

Monday Feb 3   This morning my mother and I went to Hull, dined at Mr Cayleys. My mother had the opportunity while I went out about business, of having a long conversation with Mr and Miss C about Miss S [Smelt]. She asked them about the letter which Mr Medcalfe said had been wrote (vide Wednesday May the 16th 1764) they assured there were no such letters wrote — my mother then asked the reasons of that ladys refusal — Miss C said that she was very young and she believed would not have married a prince, but that she never knew her act in so childish a manner but that Mr Kitchingman was so very vehement in my favour that she was afraid she should have been obliged to marry me; if I had gone again — Miss C said likewise that Miss S always commended me very highly. Mr C said that girls would talk one among another and that if she had any little prejudices they might have been overcome, if I had gone again — my mother told him it could not be expected after that last letter she wrote to me — they owned she acted childishly therein — but gave no hints that if I now renewed the affair, I might find a change of sentiments, if they had my mother would have said something about my doing, but as they were silent on that head she said nothing. We saw Miss D[olly] S[melt] who is a very pretty girl and much grown. We invited her together with Mr and Mrs and young Mr C to come and dine with us very soon. We sent for chaise there and took our leave. We got home a little past 5 o'clock in evening. I drank a glass of cape wine at Halls wine merchants at Hull. Tis a light red and sweet. 36 shillings a gallon he says. Very dear.

Wednesday Feb 5   Only 4 ladies and 9 gentlemen at the assembly tonight so I returned at 8 o'clock. There was no dancing, only a party at cards rest went away. I never remember so bad an assembly before.

Saturday Feb 8   Mr George Thompson delivered me a bill or note.

Thursday Feb 13   This being Valentine Eve Miss Sally Goulton the Queen, Miss Goulton, Mrs Reynolds, and several young ladies, with Mr Grove and other gentlemen, there being 11 ladies and 4 gentlemen drank tea and supped with me as being chosen King on Twelfth Night at Mrs Reynolds. After tea we drew Valentines I drew my Queen Miss Sally Goulton. We then had songs and musick; and at supper I sat at the top of the table, having my Queen on one hand and her sister on the other; my mother sat with some ladies and a gentleman at a sideboard table. After supper we had a bowl of rack punch and vidonia Lisbon and port wine. Some songs and verses made on the occasion were read and a very pretty copy of verses made on the King and Queen, as 'twas said by Miss W---d, who was present. We broke up betwixt 11 and 12 o'clock. I was drest in my second mourning on the occasion.

Sunday Feb 16   I appeared at church in second mourning for my late dear aunt Peggy and Prince Frederick.

Thursday Feb 20   Queens birthday kept. I was at the assembly and went out of mourning for the night.

Friday Feb 21   Poor Mr Enter died last night — he had been ill about a forthnight — John Prattman came Tuesday night was sevnight and told me first of his being ill, and that he had paid him for his coffin, and given him money for burrying fees etc. I went to see him next morning and almost every day — sent him wine etc. He said he was very willing to die when God pleased, but still at last was taken desirous of getting out again to see his friends, last Saturday he sent me two old musick books with his compliments, and thanks for all favours. Poor man. He paid his landlady for his lodgings to tomorrow (when as it happens he is to be burried) and ordered John Prattman to send all his things to his nephew at Buxtehude in Germany. But to my great surprize John found 30 guineas in his trunk. However I ordered him to pack all up and go to Mr Bell of Hull as Mr Enter directed for orders how to proceed in sending his things and money to his nephew.

Saturday Feb 22   My birthday. I am now praised to God, thirty two years old. My aunt Featherston, Mrs Truby, Miss Parsons and Miss Appleton dined, drank tea and supped with us.

Sunday Feb 23   Revd Mr Pickwood read prayers in morning and preached in afternoon at St Marys. Fine delivery and good discourse.

Monday Feb 24   My mother called at Mr Goultons today and they acquainted her that poor young Mr Goulton died at Genoa some time ago they have known of his death some days, but kept it 'till lately from the young ladies. I am very sorry for him.

Tuesday Feb 25   My mother and I drank tea at Mr Goultons, there were no other company there.

Saturday Mar 1   Mr Ragueneau and I and John Prattman waited upon Mr Bell of Hull, at the Tiger, and John delivered him the ballance of the 30 guineas, remaining when apothecarys bill, 15s to himself, 6s to woman where Mr E lodged and 16s for a stone at his grave. I say John delivered Mr Bell £28 17s and received Mr Bells notes. So Mr Bell will remit it to Mr Enters nephew at Buxtehude; Mr Bells man who is an Hamburger was present. All musick papers, spinett etc are to be sent to Hull to Mr Bells. Thus we settled this affair.

Monday Mar 3   I drank tea at Mr Goulton's; they are in better spirits than they were last time I was there.

Sunday Mar 9   Miss Ingram dined drank tea and supped with us.

Monday Mar 10   Mr Cogdell and Mr Peirsons six children dined with us.[260]

Wednesday Mar 12   This day I destroyed my old will and made a new one; which was witnessed by Mr Robarts, Mr Clubley and Mr Christopher Elliott. Mr and Mrs Dicey the bride and bridegroom came to town today. Miss Nancy Ward who is married to young Mr Dicey son to the famous printer at Northampton.[261] Mr Goulton presented me with my mourning ring in rembrance of his son. He died 26th January last.

Tuesday Mar 18   Received a letter from Mr Stonestreet.

Wednesday Mar 19   At the assembly I danced with the bride Mrs Dicey.

Thursday Mar 27   This morning I rode to Stork — walked and rode about there was angry at George for plowing up a little bit of ground near his house for potatoes — told him I would not suffer such things to be done without leave from me. He promised he would not of the future. The bride and bridegroom Mr and Mrs Dicey, Mr Wards family etc drank tea with us this afternoon.

Sunday Mar 30   Easter Sunday. This day I went out of mourning for my late dear aunt Peggy, and for Prince Frederick.

Monday Mar 31   This afternoon I attended a meeting at the assembly room of the proprietors, but there being only Mr Penniman, Mr Nelson and myself, we adjourned 'till Friday morning.

Friday Apr 4   I was at a meeting at the assembly room.

Saturday Apr 5   This morning I called at Mr Goultons sat an hour there. Miss Sally was out; but in street I mett with her and walked along with her a good way, as far as Bar from Well lane; I pulled some songs out of my pockett in which I had inclosed a letter; I desired she would open them out when she was alone as there was a paper within, which I begged she would read in private; she put them in her pocket; we then talked about her mother and family etc. She is a most worthy amiable young lady.

Sunday Apr 6   I saw Miss Sally at church and she curtesyd to me.

Monday Apr 7   Mr G drank tea with us this afternoon. I said nothing to him.

Tuesday Apr 8   In afternoon I mett with the lady and Miss W walking in P Lane.[262] She was confused, there was no opportunity to speak.

Thursday Apr 10   I mett with Miss S G alone; she made some objections, told me that she had acquainted her father and mother, and desired time to consider of it. I waited upon Mr G in the afternoon. He gave me permission to wait on his daughter, and we had a good deal of conversation about it.

Friday Apr 11   Mrs G called this morning we talked about our affair. She said they would always have a fire in another room for me. I rode to Hull this morning dined at George, did some business I had there and returned in evening.

Saturday Apr 12   This morning I waited upon Miss S G but before I saw her Mr and Mrs G to my great surprise told me, they had been talking to her and she was quite averse to marryng. However she came in and they left us together for about half an hour, of which I made the best use, and she seemed to give me encouragement as I thought indeed, but when Mr and Mrs G came in on her going out they still persisted she would not have me. They, Mr and Mrs G I mean, were to drink tea at our house today, but not coming I went there when found one Mr Lee of Hull and Mr Strickland with Mr G. I staid them out and found they had been prevented coming by company and had thought each of them would send servant to let us know. We then discussed on the old subject. Mrs G said she sure it was no purpose for me to persevere, and that Sally meant to refuse me in the morning. In short after some further argumentation I told her I must then with great concern give this affair up. Had I thought Miss G had been indifferent about me, I would never have begun it; but anyone would have been deceived.

Sunday Apr 13   Mrs G called before dinner — confirmed what she had said yesterday. I told her I thought she meant her daughter gave me some encouragement she said that at night she asked her if we had talked about it; and when she told her she believed it was all over she came and kist her and said she had a great regard for me, but I was so much older and graver that she should have looked upon me as a father.[263] Mrs G said as Mr G had said before they hoped this would not interupt our friendship, of which I assured them it would not. I wrote to Mr Stonestreet.

Friday Apr 25   Drank tea at Mr G---s. Miss S G and Miss W were playing at chess when I went in — I suppose on purpose. By this means some confusion was prevented though she seemed very grave, and full of cold — and not well either in health or spiritts. It was my fortune whether by accident or design to be placed next her; had just a little common conversation. There were more company there.

Tuesday Apr 29   Received a letter from Mr Stonestreet.

Thursday May 1   I was at the meeting (being the first) of the trustees for the new turnpike road to Driffield etc Mr Keld was chose clerk and treasurer. I was engaged to vote for him, but there was no opposition. Revd Mr Thomas Bowman also engaged my vote for John Mason to be barkeeper at the bar nearest Beverley, which passed without opposition. The first bar is to be at Galley Lane end.[264]

Friday May 2   I receive a letter from Mr Henry Disney.

Saturday May 3   Paid my mother her quarters annuity due 20th February last.

Sunday May 4   Wrote to Mr Stonestreet.

Monday May 5   Received a letter from Mrs Spring.

Tuesday May 6   Wrote to Mr Henry Disney.

Thursday May 8   Sold my grey mare David for ten pounds at the fair. He cost me twenty.

Friday May 9   Received a letter from Nat.

Monday May 12   Today being old May Day my new man William Garnham (who lived with Mr Warton) came.

Tuesday May 13   This day my servant Richard Wallis (after I had paid him his half years wage being four pounds ten shillings, but I gave him four guineas and an half) went away. He has lived with me a year and an half and was a good servant.

Thursday May 14   I was at a private ball at Miss Byams.

Friday May 16   Received a letter from Mr Stonestreet inclosing two bank post bills.

Sunday May 18   I answered Nats letter.

Tuesday May 20   Beverley races began. I was at the assembly where were Miss B[etty] H[obson] and Miss S[ally] G[oulton]. I was near standing betwixt both, for Miss B H came and stood couple above me and Sally below but I got next the last a couple lower. I spoke to Sally just after I got into the room; the other came in at the other end. But I asked her how she did and how her father and mother, she smiled and said they were well. She is here for the races. There is a vast deal of company at the races.

Friday May 23   The races ended. Miss S G was not at the assembly toight. Miss B H was and has danced every night. I just spoke to her.

Saturday May 24   This morning I called at Mr G---ns. Mrs G not at home. Miss G and Miss S G Miss K and Miss M there — I told them I was going to Harrogate on Monday and told Sally that I heard she was going her journey next week she said she went on Monday. Some company Mrs B and Miss F my last nights partner came in; I got up and told Sally I wished her health and a good journey made my compliments to the rest of the ladies and came away.

Monday May 26   This morning my mother in stage coach (in which were Miss S G etc) and I on horseback set out from Beverley at 9 o'clock. All dined at Weighton; and we drank tea at Kexby; where my mother took an opportunity to talk with Miss S G but to no purpose. I saluted her wish her health happiness and a good journey and galloped on to York, being a very rainy day.

Tuesday May 27   In morning my mother and [I] mett Miss S G in Blake Street, first person we saw, walked little way with her and then took leave. We set out from York in a post chaise and got to Marquis Granbys Head at Harogate (having dined at Green Hammerton) little past 4 o'clock in afternoon, had the same rooms we had last year; found Mrs Arabine there, and Lord Ellcock one of the Lords of Sessions in Scotland, with whom I became acquainted, and he was a very agreable, sensible, good natured man, spoke several languages, and had been long in foreign parts; there were 4 or 5 people more.

Wednesday May 28   Mrs Arabine gave tea our old acquaintance Lady Margaret Dalzell, and one Mrs Scott and her two daughters etc drank tea with her, I happened to sitt next Miss Scotts, and being nearest the youngest talked most to her. They live in Staffordshire, and are very agreable ladies.

Saturday May 31   In evening Dr Smollett[265] (the famous historian) with his sister nephew with his lady and his sister came to our house. The doctor is very ill.

Sunday Jun 1   Dr Short[266] came to see Dr Smollett a curious interview.

Monday Jun 2   I went to Low Harogate this morning, where I have not been before since my dear aunt Peggy was there! Alass!

Wednesday Jun 4   Kings birthday. I was at a ball at Green Dragon given by General Oughton and gentlemen there. I danced with Mrs Arabine.

Saturday Jun 7   Mr Kock of our house gave a private ball, I danced with Mrs Telfer a niece of Lord Eglington's and lady to Dr Smolletts nephew. I am pretty well acquainted with the Dr and his nephew.

Monday Jun 9   First publick ball at our house this season; Mr Kock and I were masters of the ceremonies handed the ladies out of their coaches to their seats; I took ladies out and he the gentlemen for the minuets. I danced country dances with Miss Scott.

Tuesday Jun 10   I went to Studley with a large party Mrs Telfer and I were in post chaise. Dined and drank tea at Rippon; very agreably.

Wednesday Jun 11   I gave a private ball; danced with Miss Mackenzie. There were 7 couples. I read in York Courant this morning that Miss Harrison was married last Thursday to Gordon Skelley Esqr.

Thursday Jun 12   Mr Kock gave a private ball.

Tobias Smollett. John Courtney became acquainted with Smollett at Harrogate, and later took tea with him at Bath.

Friday Jun 13   I opened the ball at Salutation with Lady Campbell.

Monday Jun 16   I call in to see Dr Smollett now and then who is confined to his room; his nephew Mr Telfer desired me to write him how the doctor did. I danced with Miss Kitty Nelthorpe at Green Dragon ball. I was to have danced with Miss Nelthorpe, but she sent me a note last night desiring to be excused, as she durst not dance with the waters.[267]

Tuesday Jun 17   I breakfasted with Miss Nelthorpes and Mrs Woolmer and they drank tea, with my mother in afternoon.

Saturday Jun 21   Dr Smollett etc went away today.

Sunday Jun 22   I wrote to Alexander Telfer Esqr Dr Smolletts nephew. Mr Kinlock gave me an invitation to come and see him when I went into Scotland, I have received like invitation from others. I wrote to aunt Featherston.

Monday Jun 23   At the ball at our house tonight I and Capt Lind were masters of the ceremonies, I took out all the ladies for minuets, and he the gentlemen. I handed ladies out of their coaches etc. I opened the ball with Lady Campbell. Miss Scott sitting at top of room was the first young lady, after those that had precedence that danced a minuet. I danced country dances with her and we were first couple.

Wednesday Jun 25   Private dance. I danced with Lady Campbell.

Friday Jun 27   This morning I saw the famous Col Hector Monro;[268] he is good looking man; appears to be about 40. In evening I was at Salutation ball.

Saturday Jun 28   Private dance. I danced with Miss Scott. NB I have danced eleven times since I came to Harogate.

Saturday Jun 29   Went to chapel in morning, walked from thence with Miss Nelthorpe and Miss Scott took leave of the former and went with latter to Salutation, as did my mother sat and chatted a while with Mrs and Miss Scotts — they set us back to our inn; we took our leave. They live at Great Heywood near Wosely Bridge near Stafford, she gave us invitation to go and see her. We got a bitt of dinner in a room by ourselves and then took leave of all our acquaintance in the house, and left Harogate my mother and I in a post chaise about half past 2 o'clock, and got to York betwixt 6 and 7 in evening. We had very agreable company all the time we were at Harogate. Sensible and entertaining. Made several calls at York.

Monday Jun 30   This morning my mother went in the stage, and I left York half hour past 10 o'clock, being on horseback. It rained incessantly 'till I got near half way home. I got to Weighton just after company in the stage coaches had sat down to dinner. I dined with them; and soon after mounted my horse and got well, thank God, to Beverley betwixt 4 and 5 o'clock in evening. NB Miss Harrison was married at Yarm Thursday the 5th of June 1766 to Gordon Skelley Esqr son of the Revd Mr Skelley of Stockton and nephew to Lord Adam Gordon, to whose seat the new married couple set out immediately after the ceremony. I inquired about him, he has no fortune, is only a lieutenant, but has a good character and may get preferment. I wish with my whole heart she may be very happy.

Tuesday Jul 1   Wrote to Mr Stonestreet.

Tuesday Jul 8   Received an answer from Mr Stonestreet.

Saturday Jul 19   I leave with my aunt Featherston my rental and a receipt for John Stevensons year and half interest which he promises to pay next week to my aunt Featherston, by my desire; I also left a receipt for Miss Norrisons rent due to my mother, and also Revd Dr Clarkes bond for £50 with the account.

Monday Jul 21   This morning betwixt 10 and 11 o'clock, my mother and I in a post chaise, with William my servant on a post horse, set out from Beverley — dined at Hull — crossed Humber — drank tea with Lady Nelthorpe at Barton; lay at Brigg. Miss N not at home.

Tuesday Jul 22   Breakfasted at Spittle. Dined at Lincoln — in afternoon called to see Miss Caroline Houghton — she was not in town; drank tea at Glovers; after which went on to Sleaford, where lay.

Wednesday Jul 23   Breakfasted at Bourn[e], got to Peterborough at 11, saw Minster etc. Dined at Stilton, drank tea at Biggleswade, and lay at Stevenage.

Thursday Jul 24   Breakfasted at Hatfield and got to London, thank God, little past 1 o'clock to our lodgings at Mrs Denhams in Featherston Buildings Holborn.

Saturday Jul 26   Revd Mr and Mrs Sinclair and Mrs Russell at whose house at Chelsea they are came this morning to see us. Mrs Sinclair big with child. They are full of acknowledgements — and say they are very happy.

Sunday Jul 27   In morning was at Foundling Hospital chapel, we dined at Mr Eldertons. I was invited to dine at 4 places.

Tuesday Jul 29   Mr Stonestreet dined, drank tea, and supped with us.

Wednesday Jul 30   My mother Mr Stonestreet and I dined at Mr Russells at Chelsea with Mr and Mrs Sinclair who are there.

Thursday Jul 31   We all drank tea Mrs Wyche's.

Friday Aug 1   My mother and I dined at Northend, Hampstead, with Mr Davisons.

Sunday Aug 3   Was at St James's chapel but the King was not there. Drank tea at Mrs Browns.

Monday Aug 4   Dined with Mr Stonestreet at Islington and went with him and one of his sisters to Sadlers Wells in evening.

Tuesday Aug 5   Drank tea at Bagnigge Wells,[269] Mr Stonestreet with us.

Thursday Aug 6   [sic]   Called at Mrs Hogarths, she and cousin Miss Bere at Chiswick.

Friday Aug 7   [sic]   Dined drank tea and supped with Mr Kock in the city, where were Mr Davidsons etc.

Sunday Aug 9   [sic]   Were at St James chapel — saw the King and Prince Henry there. The Court in mourning for Queen Dowager of Spain, the King drest in purple.

Monday Aug 11   Was at Vauxhall.

Tuesday Aug 12   Mr Stonestreet dined with us, and we all drank tea at White Conduit House.[270]

Thursday Aug 14   This morning we set out from London, got a second breakfast with Mrs Hogarth and my cousin Bere at Chiswick. Dined at Hampton Court having first seen the palace and got to Windsor in evening.

Friday Aug 15   In morning saw Windsor Castle, and after dinner went on and saw the late Duke of Cumberlands lodge in the Great Park — drank tea at Bagshot and lay at Farnham.

Saturday Aug 16   Breakfasted at Alton — dined at Winchester — saw the Cathedral and College — and got to Southampton in evening to lodgings at one Mrs Knights in Butcher Row.

Monday Aug 18   I was at the play — The Wonder.

Tuesday Aug 19   I was at the ball and danced. Wrote to Revd Mr Ar-ch-r [Archer] about the old affair.

Saturday Aug 23   After dinner at 2 o'clock set out from Southampton passed through Romsey and got to Salisbury in the evening. Mett with Sir James Ibbotson and Capt Hamar at the 3 Lions there.

Sunday Aug 24   Went to the Cathedral to service and afterwards took a view of it. Received an answer from Revd Mr A which puts a stop to all future progress in a certain affair.

Monday Aug 25   Went to see Wilton, my Lord Pembrokes seat, with the most curious collection of ancient busts and statues.

Tuesday Aug 26   Set out from Salisbury after breakfast, saw Stonehenge. Dined at the Devizes and got to Bath in the evening.

Wednesday Aug 27   In morning went to the Pump Room — drank a glass of water.

Thursday Aug 28   Went to lodgings at Mr Paulins in Pierpoint Street.

Friday Aug 29   Went with Miss Byam, whom I mett with here to my surprize in morning, and one Mrs Wakeham to Spring Gardens where drank tea.

Sunday Aug 31   Went to the Abbey church. Mrs Wakeham and we are become very intimate, and we have got several acquaintance. Go to the Rooms often.

Wednesday Sep 3   Dr Smollett (who lives here) and his lady and Mrs Wakeham drank tea with us. He is much recovered.

Sunday Sep 7   Drank tea with Dr Smollett.

Monday Sep 8   Went to the other lodgings at Mr Trunells in Church Street, where we had just the number of rooms we wanted only. Mrs Wakeham lodges there.

Wednesday Sep 10   In morning Mrs Wakeham, mother and I in a post chaise went to Bristol, breakfasted at Hotwells[271] having first drank a glass of water in the Pumproom.

Then dined at Bristol and in evening went to the play with a large party from Bath who joined us, and we supped together after it.

Thursday Sep 11   We three breakfasted at Kings Weston 6 miles from Bristol — where have one [of the] finest prospects one can see almost. Dined at Bristol and then returned to Bath in evening.

Wednesday Sep 17   Tis a year today since my dear aunt Peggy died!

Thursday Sep 18   We drank tea and supped at Mr Byams.

Sunday Sep 21   Drank tea at Dr Smolletts.

Monday Sep 22   The King and Queens coronation. I was at the ball, danced a minuet, and country dances.

Wednesday Sep 24   This morning after breakfast, at 9 o'clock left Bath saw Porters Lodge at Badminton the Duke of Beauforts in our way. Dined at Cirencester and lay at Burford.

Thursday Sep 25   Breakfasted at Woodstock — saw Blenheim, and got to Oxford before 2 o'clock to dinner.

Saturday Sep 27   Having seen most curious colleges etc we this morning set out in the stage coach breakfasted at Tetsworth. Dined at Uxbridge and got to London in evening to Mrs Denhams.

Sunday Sep 28   In morning was at Lincoln's Inn Chapel in afternoon at St Andrews Holborn; where my father was christened.

Tuesday Sep 30   Mr Stonestreet dined, drank tea and supped with us. I showed him copy of my letter to Revd Mr A[rcher] with his answer.

Wednesday Oct 1   I was at Covent Garden theatre. Mr S dined and went with us. King Henry V and Coronation.

Thursday Oct 2   I was at Drury Lane theatre, with Mr S and my mother. Beggars Opera and Hermitt. I was at a meeting of proprietors of East India stock at Merchant Taylors Hall this morning but they soon adjourned.

Friday Oct 3   This day at noon, in St James's Park I mett the King in his sedan chair going from the Queens Palace to St James. We and Mr Stonestreet dined and drank tea at Mrs Wyches. A grand dinner, as usual.

Sunday Oct 5   In morning was at St Bennetts Fink,[272] and in afternoon heard anthem in Westminster Abbey — and was at service at St Margarets.

Tuesday Oct 7   Mr Stonestreet and Mrs Lambton dined with us.

Thursday Oct 9   I dined at Mrs Browns (my mother got a lax, which I also was beginning to have, and Mr Stonestreet too). Mr Dingley dined there.

Thursday Oct 16   I bought a pair of brown horses (9 years old) for my chaise. They cost thirty guineas.

Saturday Oct 18   Went with Mrs Wyche in her coach to the play at Drury Lane house, saw Garrick in Lusignan, in Zara, and Lord Chalkstone in Lethe. I saw him in Lusignan 11 or 12 years ago, first time I ever saw him.

Sunday Oct 19   Was at Temple church in morning, and [blank] in afternoon.

Monday Oct 20   This morning my mother and I went in our new post chariott for first time of using it, to see Mr Stonestreet in Islington.

Tuesday Oct 21   Mr Stonestreet dined with us — and I paid Mr Spencer coach-maker in Newman Street Oxford Road, seventy two pounds for my new post chariot. In evening my mother and I went to new comic opera Gli Stravaganti.

Wednesday Oct 22   We went in to City in our new chariot to Mr Stonestreets lodgings, and to the bank etc. He dined with us; drank tea and supped with us; we took our leave of him with many thanks for his kind favours.

Thursday Oct 23   This morning my mother and I in our post chariot, with our own horses, drove by our servant William, set out from London half hour past 9 o'clock. Dined at Hatfield. Lay at Baldock. Went 38 miles.

Friday Oct 24   Breakfasted at Biggleswade — dined at Bugden [Buckden], lay at Peterborough. Went 43 miles.

Saturday Oct 25   Breakfasted at Market Deeping, dine at Bourn[e], lay at Sleaford. Went 35 miles.

Sunday Oct 26   Breakfasted at the Green Man — dined at Lincoln, in afternoon went to Minster prayers. I spoke to Miss Caroline Houghton there. Called at Col Glovers, vastly civil. Drank tea at Mr Woolmers. Bells rung for me to my great surprize but would give ringers nothing. Went 18 miles.

Monday Oct 27   Before noon left Lincoln. Dined at Spittle lay at Brigg. Went 23 miles.

Tuesday Oct 28   Set out early. Got to Barton at 10 o'clock. Breakfasted at Lady Nelthorpes. Miss Nelthorpe played on harpischord and sung. Sir John invited me to come and see him. The young ladies were going to Lincoln, the coach was at the door. So we did not stay very long but took our leave and went on to the Waterside House[273] where we dined, and at 5 o'clock in evening embarked, and wind being fair and fresh, got to Hull in 3 quarters of an hour. Lay at the George. Went 11 miles by land and 6 by water.

Wednesday Oct 29   This morning after breakfast left Hull, and betwixt 11 and 12 o'clock in forenoon, got well, thank God, to Beverley. Went 9 miles.

Thursday Oct 30   Several people called to see us, and welcome us home.

Saturday Nov 1   Tis ten years tonight since my dear father died. For he died 1st November 1756 about quarter past 9 o'clock at night. Alass!

Sunday Nov 2   Wrote to Mr Stonestreet.

Tuesday Nov 4   My mother aunt Featherston and I went out airing in my new chariot or chaise.

Thursday Nov 6   'Tis 10 years now, this evening since my dear father was burried. For he was burried betwixt 4 and 5 o'clock in the evening the 6th November 1756. Alass!

Friday Nov 7   Wrote to Mrs Wakeham.

Sunday Nov 9   Wrote to Mr Stonestreet, to buy aunt F and me a lottery tickett each.

Monday Nov 10   I hired Will Turner, as my servant at 4 guineas a year, a full livery and frock, and a great coat if he stays 2 years, and second year is to have 5 pounds. I hire him from Old Martinmas, but he is to come before.

Tuesday Nov 11   Received a letter from Mr Stonestreet.

Friday Nov 14   Wrote to Mr Stonestreet.

Sunday Nov 16   This morning my mother and I, it being rainy, went to church in our new chaise for first time and returned in it.

Monday Nov 17   My new servant Will Turner came today. I call my other servant William.

Friday Nov 21   This day I received two letters one from Mr Stonestreet inclosing a bank post bill, and a lottery tickett for aunt Featherston and one for me. The other letter was from Hazards to acquaint me my tickett was drawn a blank the 17th which was the first day of drawing. My tickett was no 8M930, and my aunts no 29M460. The bank post bill is the ballance of Mrs Trubys dividend after deducting the cost of her daughters ticket. I answered Mr Stonestreet's letter.

Saturday Nov 22   I called at Mr Bowman's this morning to ask him about going to Hull on Monday.

Monday Nov 24   This morning at 11 o'clock Mr Bowman and I with our servants went to Hull, on horseback, to Cross Keys inn. Dined and drank tea there, and in evening Mr Maynard junior and Mr Groves mett us there; we all went to the assembly –

and I danced. I have not been at an assembly at Hull since December 1761 almost 5 years ago. Afterwards we all supped together. 'Tis a vile inn — I went there with Mr Bowman, but like the George much better.

Tuesday Nov 25   In morning at 11 o'clock I left Hull and got home betwixt 1 and 2 to dinner.

Sunday Nov 30   Wrote answer to Nat.

Monday Dec 1   I delivered Mrs Featherston her lottery tickett. I went this morning and reviewed my closes in Newbegin and Butt Lane.

Tuesday Dec 2   I was to review Stork, and Newbegin Closes.

Monday Dec 8   This morning went to Hull with Dr Thackwray. Went to the assembly danced with Miss C-yl-y [Cayley]. Heard a peice of news which much surprized me, that Miss N-lth-pe was just going to be married to one Mr C-rt-r a clergy-man near 50.[274] I was not vastly pleased, at my intelligence. We supped at the inn 3 or 4 of us.

Tuesday Dec 9   Dr Thackwray and I got to Beverley in morning. He dined with us.

Thursday Dec 11   Mr Hargrave, Dr Thackwray, and Mr Groves dined with us.

Friday Dec 12   Miss Peirson dined with us.

Tuesday Dec 16   Received a letter from Mr Stonestreet.

Sunday Dec 28   Wrote to Mr Stonestreet. Inclosed mine and aunt Featherstons lottery ticketts, that he may sell the blanks.

Wednesday Dec 31   I received Watkinsons rent — he says he has not heard lately of the man that claimed the estate, I mean his lease. 'Tis very well.

Laus Deo! Amen!

MDCCLXVII [1767]

Thursday Jan 1   There are no prayers at St Marys now. My aunt Featherston and Miss Parsons dined, drank tea and supped with us.

Monday Jan 12   Received a letter from Mrs Wakeham. NB The post did not come in 'till today. So much snow.

Tuesday Jan 13   Received a letter from Mr Stonestreet. My mother and I dined drank tea and supped at my aunt Featherstons.

Friday Jan 16   This morning the bellman came about on a little galloway, to give notice that there would be a way open betwixt here and Hull by eleven o'clock. I never saw I think, a greater fall of snow. It begun on New Years Eve.

Saturday Jan 17   Delivered Mrs Featherston the bank post bill I received from Mr Stonestreet 21st November last for £twenty two, seven shillings and 6 pence, being Mrs Trubys ballance.

Tuesday Jan 20   Neither Sundays nor this days post are yet come in, by reason of the great quantity of snow on the ground.   Mr and Mrs and young Mrs Bowman Miss Beilby and Capt Legard drank tea and supped with us. Revd Mr Bowman so ill of his cold he could not come. We played at whist.

Wednesday Jan 21   Mr Dunn the tennant of my house without the Bar, dined with us. This afternoon Mr Midgeley[275] the Mayor, Mr Bowman etc came to collect a subscription for the poor of this town. I subscribed and paid three guineas.

Thursday Jan 22   It has begun to thaw, and the snow goes gently away. I received a parcell of advertisements about a lost horse from the Revd Mr Wind; to disperse.

Saturday Jan 24   Mr Waines being at our house today — I told him I was very sorry the poor who had no settlements here were to receive none of the charity — and urged some arguments pretty warmly why they ought to be relieved at this severe season.

Sunday Jan 25   By a note Mr Waines sent me today I hope those that have no settlements will be relieved as well as those who have. I do not mean have as much, but have something given them.

Monday Feb 2   Revd Mr Johnston our good old minister, vicar of St Marys church died tonight in the eighty second year of his age, and having been above fifty years vicar of this parish. He married my father and mother, christened me, burried my father, aunt Peggy etc. He was a very valuable man and is a publick loss to the town! Though, as he has been almost bedridden for a year past, and lost in a great measure his memory, his life could not be desirable for his own or friends sakes. He lived above 10 years after my dear father. He was a chearful companion diligent minister and good man! He did duty when he was scarce able. The last time he preached I believe was Sunday 12th January 1766, which I think was the last time I saw him, poor man!

Thursday Feb 5   This evening Revd Mr Johnston was burried. I went to the church to see him burried: Mr Wilson read the service; young Mr Ward was there, and had a scarfe, there was none there but ordinary people, besides these and young Dickons, who I suppose was concerned in the funeral. Mr John Johnston and Miss Hayward were mourners. Poor Parson Johnston — I had a great respect for him.

Sunday Feb 8   Mr Robinson of Buckton dined and supped with us. I sent by him a letter and a guinea to my nurse at Burlington Key. Wrote to Revd Mr Wind. NB Miss Nelthorpe was married to Revd Mr Carter last month. I wish her all happiness.

Painting of North Bar Within, Beverley, by George Barrett c1780, showing the tower and west front of St Mary's Church. (Photograph by David Connell, by kind permission of John Chichester-Constable.)

Thursday Feb 12   In the York Courant of February 12th 1767 — I this day read as follows, vizt: 'On the 2d instant died at Beverley, universally lamented in the 82d year of his age after a long and painful illness, which he bore with a truly Christian fortitude and patience, the Revd Mr Samuel Johnston, Vicar of St Marys church in that town upwards of 50 years, during which time he never had a dispute with any parishoner. In him were united every social and domestick virtue; the tender husband the indulgent parent, faithful friend, and benevolent lover of mankind in general joined with an extensive charity and strict piety, compleated the character of the truly good Christian.' This is indeed I think a just character of our late worthy minister. Revd Mr A---r [Archer] of Stour Provost is dead.

Wednesday Feb 18   I bought a chesnut mare rising 5 years old about 14 hands and an half high of Mr James Watson of Hedon, who says he believes she was got by Jack Come Tickle Me. I gave 18 pounds for her.

Sunday Feb 22   My birthday. I am 33 years old, thank God. We keep it tomorrow.

Monday Feb 23   My aunt Featherston, Mrs Truby and Miss, and Capt Legard dined, drank tea and supped with us and Miss Appleton (who was to have been also at dinner) and Mr Groves drank tea and supped with us. Mrs Cogdell told me something this morning which rather surprised me, about which I propose to have more conversation with her.

Tuesday Feb 24   Mr Ragueneau called this morning brought me the receipt from the Society for Promoting Christian Knowledge[276] for the guinea I gave at admission, he also showed me the printed certificate of my character according to form, which he had signed to be sent to them.

Monday Mar 2   The corpse of one Mrs Brown who died last Tuesday evening and was burried on Thursday the 26th past was this day taken up by the coroner, who is Mr Midgely as Mayor, his order. One Mr and Mrs Brown came about 2 or 3 months ago and took Mr Hewitts house in our street, he was 30, she 45; he handsome, she rich, and had reserved her fortune in her own power. After much ill treatment in order to make her write a will to his mind, having obliged her to comply — he soon after made her take a bolus,[277] and broths and cordials in which 'tis believed he put strong poison; she languished several days, but a day or two before her death told Mrs Hewitt who was the only person who visited them, that she believed the devil and Mr Brown had been very busy with her etc seeming to intimate that she was poisoned. The day after the funeral Brown set out for London. Mrs Hewitt on the Sunday (yesterday) made a deposition before the Mayor; and the corpse accordingly was examined in the church of St Marys this day by the coroner, a jury, Dr Johnston, Dr Thackerway, Mr Burton etc. The maid and nurse were also examined. In short there appeared the strongest circumstances of the poison, and its being administered by Mr Brown. The jury adjourned to Wednesday next. Mr Arden is foreman. The Mayor wrote today to Mr Appleton who is in London to get Brown apprehended.

Wednesday Mar 4   The Jury mett examined Mr Bridges of Hull of whom Mr Brown had got mercury sublimate and glass of antimony. Others were also examined, as Smith an apothecary here of whom he had before got some hellebore, and had applyd to him also for the mercury etc but he had none. The jury adjourned to Monday next at the Town Hall.

Thursday Mar 5   This evening our new minister Revd Mr Drake arrived in town.[278]

Saturday Mar 7   I just saw Mr Drake who pulled of his hat as he was going to be inducted this [sic] and just after I had got by church I heard him ring the bell.

Sunday Mar 8   This morning our new minister Revd Mr Drake read prayers and preached, and read prayers in afternoon (Revd Mr Ward preaching). Mr Drakes text was, Draw nigh unto God and he will draw nigh unto you. He has rather a weak voice, but reads pretty well and made a good sermon. God send him good success in his ministry, and grant that we may reap true advantage from it!

Monday Mar 9   This morning I went to the Hall, and in the chamber I heard the maid and nurse, who attended Mrs Brown; examined, I saw the letter Mr Brown wrote to his maid, which came by the post on Friday last and was carried to the Mayor who opened it. I saw also Mr Appletons letter received by the Mayor yesterday, in which he tells him he had placed Justice Fieldings men at Doctors Commons[279] to wait for Brown, but that he durst not leave the warrant with them, but going to the Temple to talk with one Mr Perrott, whom he found was an acquaintance of Browns, as well as his; in mean time Brown went to the Commons, and found a caveat entered against the will; and I suppose has made his escape. The jury agreed in their verdict that Brown had poisoned his wife and I saw them sign it accordingly. I wish he may be taken and have his deserts. This day I having determined to cutt down most of the ash trees in Newbegin closes, I sold fifty two of them and two maples to Mr Middleton carpenter,[280] for thirty five pounds to be paid within 6 months. He to be at the expence of felling etc. Eleven ashes, 4 elms, and a few maples are to stand and not to be now felled, being not come to maturity.

Wednesday Mar 11   This morning they begun to fell the trees in my Newbegin closes. I went to see them.

Thursday Mar 19   This day I had eight score elms brought from Stork and begun to plant them in my Newbegin closes.

Tuesday Mar 24   Received a letter from Mr Stonestreet.

Thursday Mar 26   This day the labourers finished planting, staking and thorning my trees.

Saturday Mar 28   This morning when came downstairs my servant Will delivered me a letter, which he said a man brought and said he found it laid at the door. It was signed Jacques Laconick, and inclosed a copy of verses intitled Beverley Assembly or the Descent of Venus, being a panygyric[281] on the ladies, and especially on Miss S[ally] G[oulton] whom he feigns to be Venus. He desires I would either show them or use them as they deserve; the letter and verses are wrote in an attorneys hand — directed to me.

Sunday Mar 29   Wrote to Mr Stonestreet.

Friday Apr 3   Received a letter from Mrs Wakeham.

Monday Apr 6   This morning I went on horseback to Hessle to view my cottage there — John Taylor of Anlaby the carpenter was there to meet me. I believe it must be nearly rebuilt. I dined at the inn — Parson Tong dined with me as did the landlord. I went to look at the church saw poor Mr Perrotts grave. I returned in evening.

Friday Apr 10   Received a letter from Mr Stonestreet.

Monday Apr 15   This morning at St Mary's church before prayers I spoke to our new minister Revd Mr Drake, and wished him the enjoyment of his living etc.

Sunday Apr 19   Wrote to Mr Stonestreet, and to Mrs Wakeham. NB This day being Easter Sunday received the Holy Sacrament administered by our new minister Mr Drake (assisted by Mr Ward) for first time.

Wednesday Apr 22   My mother and I went in the chaise to Brantingham and dined with Mr and Mrs Bowman, whose brother and sister from Beverley are also there.

Sunday Apr 26   Wrote to Nat.

Thursday Apr 30   This morning my mother and I went in chaise to Hull, dined at George and returned in evening.

Friday May 1   Received a letter from Mr Stonestreet inclosing a bank post bill for the produce of aunt Featherstons blank and for Mrs Trubys dividend.

Sunday May 3   Revd Mr Drake our new minister and his lady drank tea with us, for first time.

Sunday May 17   Received a letter from Nat.

Monday May 18   Edward Webster brought me an order or warrant to him to summon jury, I being appointed headgrave this year of copyhold court of Beverley Watertowns, which meet on Monday next. I gave him half guinea for his fee and he is to have another at Michaelmas next, please God.

Tuesday May 19   I presented Revd Mr Drake a guinea for my offerings. Received a letter from Mr Stonestreet. Beverley races begin today.

Wednesay May 20   Rev Mr Drake and Mr Disney dined with us.

Friday May 22   Beverley races end today. I was 3 days upon the course, went in chaise with mother, and got out at stand.

Monday May 25   I paid my servant William Garnham his wage (deducting half guinea let him have last year at Harogate) nine pounds due old Mayday 1767. He is to have ten pounds this year, and livery and frock as before.

Wednesday May 27   The Militia officers gave a ball. I was there.

Thursday Jun 4   The Kings birthday. The gentlemen of the town gave a ball to the ladies and Militia officers. I was a subscriber towards it. My share came to 18 shillings. There were 29 subscribers. The sum total came to £26 9s or thereabouts.

Monday Jun 8   We supped at Mr Bowmans.

Friday Jun 12   Miss Dennis dined with us. I wrote to Mr Stonestreet.

Tuesday Jun 13   Received a letter from Mr Stonestreet.

Friday Jun 19   Received a letter from Mr Stonestreet, inclosing a bank post bill for one hundred pounds, being part of my ballance in his hands. This £100 I am going to put out at interest to Mr Goulton.

Saturday Jun 20   Mr Dickons paid me amount of bank post bill for £15 dated 22d October 1766 (which I got myself when I was at bank last year) at same time paid Mrs Dickons her note for William's livery. I delivered today the above bill for £100, and received his note to Mr Goulton, which was witnessed by Miss Goulton.

Monday Jun 22   This morning my mother and I in our chaise, and Will on horseback set out from Beverley, and got to York in evening.

Tuesday Jun 23   Mrs Arabine and Mr and Mrs Ragueneau are at New Inn at Harogate where we arrived this afternoon before tea. We found also one Mrs Burgh, a little boy her son who is ill, her daughter about 12 or 13 and her niece Miss Williams who is a most sweet young lady, all from Wales, and people of fortune.

Thursday Jun 25   I began to take notice of the beauty and amiable disposition of Miss Williams, and her sweet sensibility affected me much; Mr Ragueneau gave her very enconiums.[282]

Friday Jun 26   I was at Salutation ball, danced with Mrs Arabine, but engaged Miss Williams for Monday next when the ball is at our house; tonight at ball I had some conversation with her; she did not dance, but said to several she saved herself to dance with Mr C on Monday night.

Saturday Jun 27   This morning Mrs Arabine, Miss Williams and I in Mrs Arabines chaise, and a large party in ours and other carriages, went to Gauthorpe to see Mr Lascelles house.[283] I had much conversation with Miss Williams whose behaviour was most engaging. In evening we all went to the play.

Sunday Jun 28   The company here is very agreable. Sir Walter Blackett[284] sitts next me at dinner, and is very good natured and sensible man indeed; as is also one Mr Selwyn (for many years a noted barber at Paris) with whom I am very intimate.

Monday Jun 29   This evening ball at our house — I danced with Miss Williams; and was happy indeed. I had much conversation with her, and all my behaviour must show her that I was over head and ears in love with her. She is rather low, but her person every way agreable, her face expresses the greatest sensibility and the most perfect goodness of heart, her temper rather grave than gay, her age 22, her mind cultivated by the best education; her manner enchanting, her affection to her cousin Charles the little boy uncommon, her behaviour to me the most flattering to my wishes, and together with a modesty in all her words and actions, she joins the most engaging freedom; in short she was just such a woman as I would wish to be my partner for life, both in body and mind — her nose was the worst feature, being large and ill made, but yet 'twas to me more pleasing than any I had ever seen. She was the admiration of everyone in the house. What wonder that I was in love with so sweet a creature. I was Master of the Ceremonies tonight and opened the ball with Lady Rollo; and afterwards towards end danced a minuet with my dear Miss Williams.

Tuesday Jun 30   The play of Bold Stroke for a Wife was to be acted tonight, and when I went down stairs this morning I found a bill stuck up in Long Room, and some one out of joke had wrote at top by desire of two gentlemen at New Inn. I immediately guessed it was aimed at Mr Disney Roebuck, and me; but I took no notice but he immediately said they mean you and me; do they said I, there are not our names on the bill that I see; so I laughed and disappointed the author of this piece of fun.

Wednesday Jul 1   I spoke this evening to Mr and Mrs Raguenau, and told them of my affection for Miss Williams. They seemed pleased and said they had talked much to her about me and commended me very much, before and since I came, and they heartily wished me success as they had the highest opinion of her.

Thursday Jul 2   I was at play with Miss Williams, Mrs Arabine etc. In morning I had a long conversation with Mr Raguenau about Miss Williams, he gave me his advice. After we came from play she talked to me as walked up and down room with her and Mrs Arabine in the kindest manner, told me she had an invitation to Beverley and should certainly come, she was serious she said and said many other things which would have given any man encouragement. Mr and Mrs Raguenau took leave tonight, being going away tomorrow, which is a great loss to me.

Friday Jul 3   I was at Queens Head Ball with Mrs Arabine and Miss Williams, danced with Mrs A and a minuett with Miss W. But my partner only dancing one country dance I sat beside her and Miss W rest of night. Very happy, and came home in chaise with them.

Saturday Jul 4   I offered ticketts to ladies at our table for play, but Miss W said she should not go, however Mrs Burgh saying she must take my tickett, she said she would, but I told her I would not have her go against her inclination, but she took my tickett and said she would. After dinner when I went in to Long Room she said to me, Why so grave Mr Courtney; Why, said I, because I was afraid you would not take the ticketts because 'twas I that offered them; she then said Mrs Arabine could witness for her that she had said before she should not go, and farther she would assure me that she had never had so great a regard for any person upon so short an acquaintance as she had for me. Oh how happy this made me. So we all went to the play.

Sunday Jul 5   After breakfast I took an opportunity to speak to Miss Williams. I told her I had a question of importance to ask her, etc which was I desired to know if her affections were preingaged, she replyd they may you know without ones friends approbation, I hope Madam said I that is not the case, and then told her the state of my heart adding that I hoped the more she saw of me she would not like me the less, she said she dared say she should not but that she had a mother, who was the fit person to apply to and that she had an aunt also who was at Harogate, to whom I might speak if chose. Her manner at same time was very flattering; and I imagined I was in a fair way to succeed in my wishes; we had not any more conversation on this subject today.

Wednesday Jul 8   I believe 'twas today that Miss Williams and Mrs Arabine Mrs Burgh etc and Miss Routh mother and I went to Mr Metcalfes to tea; in return, Mrs Arabine driver was drunk, horses run away, we saw them stop at last, overtook them, Miss Williams jumped out, ran to me I took her in my arms she said, Oh Mr C how frightened I am, I was afraid she was going to faint; however she presently sprung from me and would fair have got into the chaise again, but chaiseboy could not be got off horseback without danger, and he drove against us and swore and curst at a terrible rate, with the utmost difficulty I persuaded her to get into my chaise; I mounted on my servants horse and rode home in my laced coat bag wig and silk stockings, rejoiced that my sweet girl had got well back again.

Saturday Jul 11   I was at play with Miss Williams and family — Drummer and Harlequin Revells. I sat by her and talked to her she was kind in words and looks. NB I spoke to Mrs Burgh on Tuesday or Wednesday morning last, she was short in her answers but said she would mention it to her mother when got home, I told her my fortune upon her asking me whether I could make settlements for £10,000. She said she supposed I would make all clear I said yes to be sure; she desired that I would show not particularities while they were there. In mean time my mother had a conversation with Miss in great room; she had spoke to her 3 or 4 days before and had then received great encouragement, for on mother's saying she hoped she had no dislike to her son, she said, no, that she would assure her she had not, but that even my mother herself would not like to have such an affair concluded too hastily. On her talking to her this second time, she said I hope he will let me go to see my mother, my mother said to be sure, she likewise said more things, giving great hopes nay almost assurances that nothing was wanting but her mothers consent. All her looks gave me great encouragement too, and sometimes her words.

Sunday Jul 12   This morning when came downstairs heard that Mrs Burghs were all gone to York for Dealtry's advice for Master. I did not see them all day as returned late.

Monday Jul 13   At breakfast talked as usual to Miss Williams who was free as before, but Charles was very ill which made her very uneasy. I had no opportunity of private conversation all day; but in evening at ball I leaned on her chair and told her in a low voice, that I was much concerned and distressed at hearing they were going to Knaresborough on Masters account, and that I was afraid I should not be able to acquitt myself as Master of the Ceremonies tonight but I should make sad blunders. She replied, I wanted to tell you that we were going to Knaresbro', but why are you distressed about it, it is not so far off, besides says she if you are so concerned you will not be able to go through the business of tonight she spoke this in a kind manner at last said go away we are noticed. I opened the ball with Lady Rollo, but often gave as usual my dear girl a kind look, which she sometimes returned I danced a minuet with her, but she would not dance country dances, so I sat beside here a good while and talked to her told her how much I loved her etc etc. She said if her mother did not give her consent perhaps I might never see her any more. You should prepare yourself for it. I replied she killed me by saying so, but I hoped she would etc etc. All seemed to go on well.

Tuesday Jul 14   This morning we sat a long time with Mrs Burgh and Miss Williams, but could only talk of common matters, except that my mother asked Mrs Burgh if we might go to Knaresborough and she said don't mention it yet. Just before they went, Miss Williams stood looking over stairs down upon me a good while, I looked up two or three times, and she smiled and looked very kindly at me. About noon they went way to Knaresborough I handed her in to the chaise. My mother asked her whether I should attend her on horseback, but she would not permitt me.

Wednesday Jul 15   This morning Mrs Arabine mother and I went in our chaise to see them at Knaresbro'; Miss Williams and all very civil and glad to see us. She looked very kindly on my giving her some tender glances. I was at Knaresbro 2 or [sic] times more this week, all went right, though no opportunity of talking but by the eyes.

Monday Jul 20   In morning I sent to know how Master did after an operation he had undergone, they sent word he and they all were as well as could be expected. I was at Dragon ball and danced as usual with Mrs Arabine.

Tuesday Jul 21   Mrs Arabine mother and I drank tea Mr Bagshaw's at Knaresborough; after tea we went mother and I only to Mrs Burghs. Miss Williams and little Miss came down to us; she was very free and looked very kindly; desired I would give her compliments to Mr Raguenau when I wrote next, for whom she always exprest the highest regard, which I thought a good sign. We staid an hour I believe with her; and came away vastly pleased, and she said to me I wish you a very good night Mr Courtney.

Thursday Jul 23   In morning mother and I and Miss Dottins (for Miss W would not permitt me to go there alone) went to Mrs Burghs, and were much surprized to find Mr Field there, as he went home but last Monday; (however I dont think he made his addresses to her). Her behaviour was rather altered, and I had not one kind look from her today, but I thought 'twas because of company being there.

Saturday Jul 25   This morning I went on horseback to Knaresbro', but outstaid Mrs Arabine and Miss Dottins. Miss Williams being left with only Master and Miss at last with a grave tone said to them go out, I have something to say I would not have you hear. My heart sunk — they went out. She then told me that as I probably staid at Harogate on her account, she thought proper to tell me that she had considered of my offer, and she desired I would not think of her any more, I expostulated in vain, I told her I had flattered myself with hopes, she said there were none from the first and that if I followed her 20 years I might hinder her from marrying any body else but she should not marry me; she said she had no dislike to me, that I had done nothing to offend her, but that she did not chuse to marry; the old lady came in I durst not tell Miss W what encouragement I had received from her before old lady. I expostulated for half an hour without effect, Miss at last got up and went out. I talked to old lady till Mr Richardson the surgeon came in to see Master; when I took leave; mounted my horse and galloped home dinner, with a whirlwind of contending passions in my mind. I saw and spoke to Miss Smelt this morning at Wells.

Sunday Jul 26   We told Mrs Arabine whole affair about Miss Willliams who had made her acquainted with it. She says she likes a young clergyman whom her friends did not approve of, but that she fancies they may now have given some hints it might be approved of which causes this change, for she believes she thought of me once. She will talk to her. Miss Williams was all last night with Mrs F whose husband died today. Oh how kind; my heart was torn with various passions today.

Monday Jul 27   I was engaged to dance with Mrs Arabine which I did at our ball, but got excused being Master of Ceremonies. Miss Smelts and Mrs Metcalfe were at ball, staid till 3 o'clock. Capt Mansfield and I sat up with them, I talked to Miss Smelt who was very free. She is a very pretty girl. Next to Miss Williams she is the girl I like best.

Wednesday Jul 28 [sic] I went with mother and Miss Dottin to Mrs Burghs. No kind looks.

Saturday Aug 1   I rode in morning to Mr Metcalfe to ask them and Miss Smelts to tea on Tuesday. Miss Smelt very free, played a little on harpischord; a pretty girl. But oh Miss Williams.

Sunday Aug 2   Miss Williams all lost.

Tuesday Aug 4   Miss Smelts, Mrs Metcalfe etc drank tea with us; they had called at Knaresborough to see Mrs Burgh and had seen Miss Williams in tears, Master being very ill. I talked to Miss Smelt and was civil to her. Pretty girl.

Saturday Aug 8   I called at Knaresborough, only saw little Miss.

Sunday Aug 9   Mother with Mrs Davidson etc saw Miss Williams at Knaresbro', she seemed very kind, laid her hand on my mothers and she thought all was right again.

Monday Aug 10   About 11 this morning I went to Mrs Burghs found Mr Selwyn there, staid him out; spoke to Miss Williams on old subject, in a low voice she said could not hear me so was obliged to speak before all family she gave me no hopes, and said she desired I would say no more as it was a subject very disagreable to her aunt at last I got up saying I believed my company was disagreable, but told her I would call as came by when went away on Wednesday; she said hastily and getting up, if I do not see you, I heartily wish you your health and happpiness — I told her should call, but I from my soul wished her all health and happiness and wished it had been in my power to have contributed to her happiness. However I did not take my leave as intended to call again. Our ball tonight I asked as usual Mrs Arabine she would not dance; I'd agreed with Miss Arden whom I had danced with some years ago at Scarborough.

Tuesday Aug 11   Jonas the conjurer performed this evening at our house. Very curious indeed.

Beverley Race Stand, built in 1767. (From G Oliver, *History of Beverley*, 1829.)

Wednesday Aug 12   Mrs Arabine mother and I talked about Miss Williams and Mrs Arabine thought we had better not call as went by, which I intended, she said they would think I was piqued; but I desired she would talk to her, and that she would write to me, which she said she would do. We told her we thought it a very odd affair. She said she knew the old lady had often taken Miss Williams away out of the room and been very harsh with her on my account and that she believed she was not my friend. We took our leave of Mrs Arabine Mrs Davidson and rest of her friends and left Harogate about 11 o'clock in morning passed by Mrs Burghs at Knaresborough, saw none of them at windows and got to York to dinner before 3 o'clock.

Thursday Aug 13   This morning left York, dined at Weighton and got well, thank God to Beverley, about 5 o'clock in evening. Mr and Mrs Sinclair are at Beverley and little child. NB I could not be particular about Harogate as one affair chiefly engrossed my attention, my heart being deeply interested therein.

Saturday Aug 15   I told Mr Raguenau the whole story of my late affair he thinks it very odd behaviour. I paid 3 guineas to Mr Ellis and received a silver tickett for the Beverley stand no 230.[285]

Sunday Aug 16   Received a letter from couzen Nat Courtney.

Monday Aug 17   We drank tea at Mr Raguenaus. I saw Mr Sinclairs little girl. Fine child.

Friday Aug 21   Received a letter from Mr Stonestreet, with two bank post bills being my ballance one hundred and thirty eight pounds, fourteen shillings and threepence.

Mr Robarts called this morning has received a letter from his son who has been in a terrible storm, lost all he took out with him. But desires I would not mention the latter part of his account.

Sunday Aug 23   Received a letter from Mrs Wakeham. Wrote to Nat.

Tuesday Aug 25   This morning my mother and I in chaise went to Cave, dined and drank tea at cousin Neddy Blanchards, and his mother my great aunt, old Mrs Blanchard dined with us. His wife lies in. I have not been at South Cave since my grandmother died, and we have not dined there since my dear father died. We returned home in evening.

Wednesday Aug 26   I went to vestry to pay Revd Mr Drake tith for my mothers close near house. We had some little conversation about my closes that are tith free.

Thursday Aug 27   This morning mother and I went in chaise to Hessle to see after the rebuilding of my cottage there and returned home to dinner.

Sunday Aug 30   I wrote to Mrs Arabine.

Tuesday Sep 1   Wrote to Mrs Wakeham.

Saturday Sep 19   Received a letter from Christopher Goulton Esqr by his son. Revd Mr Neat (who took his degree at same time with me) and his lady and Mr King and his lady; (latter Mr Neats sister) came to town tonight. Mother and self waited upon them at the Tyger.

Sunday Sep 20   Revd Mr Sinclair and his lady, and Miss Ragueneau Revd Mr Neat and lady, and Mr King and his lady dined with us. Mr Neat went out of town before tea.

Tuesday Sep 22   Received a letter from couzen Nat. Wrote to Mr Stonestreet.

Wednesday Sep 23   I asked my servant what Bonner said about Master Burgh. He said that he was worse, he saw him day before he left Harogate (that is near a week ago) in a chair and that they said he was wearing away. I am very sorry to hear it indeed. Mrs Arabine went away day before Bonner came away, which surprized me much.

Friday Sep 25   Received letter from Mr Stonestreet.

Sunday Sep 27   Received a letter from Mr Stonestreet.

Wednesday Sep 30   This morning my mother and I went in chaise to Buckton to pay visit to Mr Robinson and Mrs Brown and Mrs Wyche who are there. I have not been there these 4 years; not since my uncle and aunt Peggys deaths.

Friday Oct 2   We went to Burlington Key [Bridlington Quay] — heard there news of Duke of Yorks death 17th last month at Monaco. We returned to Buckton to dinner.

Saturday Oct 3   My mother and I returned to Beverley. Left Buckton about 10 o'clock called at Bransburton [Brandesburton], but no meat to be had in the town, so were obliged to go without our dinners, and got home, thank God, about 5 o'clock in evening.

Sunday Oct 4   Received a letter from cousin John Courtney — answered it to Nat. Wrote to Mr Stonestreet. This day I went into the mourning for the Duke of York.

Tuesday Oct 6   Received a letter from Mrs Arabine — she says Miss Williams is determined — but her situation and all family is deplorable, Master is weaker every day, and there is very little hopes of his recovery — Miss W declared she has an high opinion of my character, and Mrs Arabine thinks my suspicion of somebody saying something to my disadvantage is groundless and wishes to give up this fruitless pursuit. She says she herself leaves Harrogate the next day (which was yesterday) and would have persuaded the distrest family to go to York — but they would not hear of it. This letter gives me great concern.

Wednesday Oct 7   I received cash for my bank post bill no 28525, for £38 14s 3d of Mr Overend, and indorsed and gave him the bill accordingly.

Saturday Oct 10   Mr Middleton paid me thirty five pounds for 52 ash and 2 maple trees, which I sold to him 9th March last. This day I lett Stork to George Coke for a further term of 3 years from Ladyday next at the same rent of £63 pounds per annum.

Monday Oct 12   There were fireworks exhibited in Markett Place tonight by some Italians by subscription. I subscribed half a crown. I had never seen any fireworks before. They were very pretty indeed.

Sunday Nov 1   Tis eleven years tonight since my dear father died. For he died November 1st 1756. Alass!

Wednesday Nov 4   I had a party of ladies and gentlemen at cards, at Pope,[286] this afternoon.

Friday Nov 6   'Tis eleven years this evening since my dear father was burried. For he was burried 6th November 1756, betwixt 4 and 5 o'clock in evening. Alass!

Sunday Nov 8   Wrote to Mr John Stevenson in York Castle and to Mrs Hannah Thirsk at York.

Tuesday Nov 10   Received a letter from Mrs Hannah Thirsk.

Thursday Nov 12   Received an answer from Mr John Stevenson.

Sunday Nov 15   This morning Mr Atkinson, surgeon, of York, called to talk to me about Mrs Thirsk's affairs. He desired I would wait about 4 months in which time they should either sell the house, or pay me in the money I have upon it, so I say desired I would defer Dr Sykes's assigning the mortgage; I told him would consider of it, and write him word. I asked him how his patient Master Burgh did he said that the matter came from the inside of him, but that he was young and had that chance on his side — he says the family are all with him at Knaresborough, and as I understand him had taken a house there, but my mother thought he said at York, for the winter. Mr Atkinson was not with me above 5 minutes, and being in such an hurry, I could not talk so much to him on this head as I wished. So Miss W[illiams] will be in Yorkshire all the winter.

Monday Nov 16   I went to the vestry at St Marys church to speak to Revd Mr Drake about demand of tyth made for my Newbegin and Buttlane Closes. I told him they had never paid tyth, I believed, and that they were also in the parish of St Johns — he said there was no such parish, they were in St Martins — I replied that could not be, for all my writings mentioned these closes were in the parish of St Johns and writing ought to be authentick certainly.[287] He said he would not by any means have any disputes with his parishoners, and that he had wrote to the Archbishop to make enquirys in proper offices and that Mr Midgeley was to state the case, and Mr Yorke or some eminent council opinion was to be taken. (NB I must see this case before it be sent to Mr Yorke.) It lies upon Mr Drake to prove his right in his affair, and not on me to prove an exemption. I told him that I should be one of the last in the world to abridge him of his rights, but that I thought it proper at the same time to assert my own, and waited upon him then, lest he might think I aquiesced in the demand, especially as Val Banks one of my tennants had paid him for one close which he ought not to have done without my knowledge. He said it was very right, and that I might depend he would let me know of all the steps he took in the affair, and I told him I was very well satisfied.

Tuesday Nov 17   This morning my mother and I in chaise went to Hull, I called upon the Mayor George Thompson Esqr and he paid me 2 years rent by a bill for £24 11s 6d, cash £1 10s 6d — £26 2s. Called at Mr Halls paid for wine — returned in evening got home betwixt 5 and 6.

Thursday Nov 19   I went into second mourning for late Duke of York (should have done so last Sunday).

Saturday Nov 21   Received from Christopher Goulton Esqr a bond for £200 with interest at 4 per cent per annum.

Thursday Nov 26   Answered Mr Stonestreets letter.

Sunday Dec 6   Received a letter from Mr Stonestreet with 2 bank post bills inclosed, 1 for my dividend and 1 for Mrs Trubys dividend. Answered Mr Stonestreets letter. Mr Tufnell our present member, and Mr Anderson[288] came to town as candidates today.

Monday Dec 7   Received a note from Mr Anderson tonight to desire my company to breakfast with him tomorrow and to canvass this town. I wrote an answer that I desired to be excused waiting upon, did not design to canvass with any party and was not yet absolutely determined in regard to the little interest I might have in the affair of the election.

Tuesday Dec 8   This morning Mr Tufnell and his brother Mr Jolliff called — he said did not come to canvass, should not declare till after a chamber meeting on Thursday, when if the majority were inclined to any neighbouring gentleman he would decline. I told him I could not then say any more than that I wished him well, and might perhaps be of some little service to him. In afternoon, Mr Anderson and Mr J Penniman etc called — I told him I thought the family had a right to have one Member, as had been such benefactors to the town, but that in case two were to offer on that interest — I would oppose both. He said he should have no connections with any one — I told him I knew nothing to the contrary but that I should give him my interest. Memorandum. Paid my servant Will Turner 1 years wage due Martinmas last being 4 guineas. Agreed with him for five pounds for the current year, and in case of his good behaviour I may give him six pounds.

Thursday Dec 10   Wrote the following note to Mr Davison of Blue Boar, and sent it by my servant Will Turner, vizt: 'Beverley 10th December 1767. Mr Davison, I am informed you have taken a lease of the inn known by the sign of the Blue Boar and Horns for a term of years, but this lease being granted without my knowledge, is not valid without my consent — and I hereby acquaint you that I make it void to all intents and purposes whatever. Yours J C'.

Monday Dec 14   Mr Davison called said was sorry he had not known that Stephenson could not let him a lease, twould be be a great loss. He was very civil and said he would speak to him about settling matters in some way or other.

Tuesday Dec 15   Mr Bethell called in morning but I was out to invite me to breakfast and canvass town with him, and sent a note in evening but I declined it.

Wednesday Dec 16   I mett Mr Bethell and 40 gentlemen I believe canvassing as I came from riding, I told him I gave him whatever interest I had — he asked me to dinner. I excused myself civilly.

Sunday Dec 20   My mother received a packett from Miss Routh, with some patterns and a purse for her and song for me.

Monday Dec 21   Delivered Mrs Truby the bank post bill no R6299 for £34 4s being her dividend due Michaelmas last.

Tuesday Dec 29   My aunt Featherston Mrs Cogdell, and Capt Legard dined, drank tea and supped with us.

Thursday Dec 31   Honourable Mrs Molesworth drank tea with us today when I played on organ a good while and sung, she thinks the organ very fine.

Laus Deo! Amen!

MDCCLXVIII [1768]

Friday Jan 1   Began the year at Beverley. I was at prayers at St Marys this morning —
Mr Bell of Hull called while I was at church. He called again in afternoon, talked
about the undivided estate at Weel and Tickton of which he has now a third.

Sunday Jan 3   Wrote to Mr Stonestreet.

Tuesday Jan 5   Mr and Mrs Bowman, Revd Mr and Mrs Drake, Miss Raguenau
Honourable Mrs Molesworth and Mr Jacomb and Mr Thomas Goulton drank tea and
supped with us. Miss Goulton was invited but had a cold.

Sunday Jan 10   Received a letter from cozen Nat.

Saturday Jan 16   Sent my letter to Miss Routh at Durham by Capt Graham, who is
going home to Newcastle. My mother and I dined at Mr Goultons.

Tuesday Jan 26   Received a letter from Miss Routh and one from Mr Stonestreet.
We supped at Mr Bowmans.

Friday Jan 29   Received a letter from John Croft Esqr.

Monday Feb 1   We supped at Revd Mr Drakes. I played at cards — a young party at
Pope.

Tuesday Feb 2   Wrote to Mr J Croft.

Friay Feb 5   Received another letter from Mr J Croft.

Wednesday Feb 17   We drank tea at Mr Ragueneaus who had a little concert; there
was a great deal of company and among them Miss Sm–lt; I sat by her a while and
talked to her, she told me she should learn to play on harpsichord again with Hawdon
while she was at Hull. She looks very well.

Thursday Feb 18   I drank tea at Mr Wards. A young party at cards. Miss Sm–lt was
there; but I did not play at same table with her.

Friday Feb 19   Received a letter from Mr John Croft.

Monday Feb 22   Miss Smelt and Miss Goulton called this morning to see us. My
birthday. I am thank God 34 years old. Aunt Featherston, Miss Parsons, Miss Appleton,
Capt Legard and Mrs Cogdell dined drank tea and supped with us. Memorandum. I
was in treaty with Sir George Metham at this time about an estate called Yoalkfleet.[289]

Wednesday Mar 2   I had a private discourse with Mr Cayley at his house at Hull
about Miss Smelt.

Saturday Mar 5   Received a letter from Mr Cayley today.

Monday Mar 7   This morning I waited upon and had an happy private interview with my dear Miss Smelt and dined and drank tea at Mr Cayleys at Hull.

Tuesday Mar 8   Wrote to Leonard Smelt Esqr.[290]

Sunday Mar 13   In afternoon received a letter from Leonard Smelt Esqr who has got to Hull.

Monday Mar 14   Mr and Mrs Smelt breakfasted with us.

Tuesday Mar 15   My mother and self went to Hull, I had private interview with Mr Cayley and afterwards with Miss Smelt. Dearest best of women! Mother and I dined at the inn and afterwards we went to Mr Cayleys together and I introduced her to Miss Smelt, and left them together, they agree very well and we all drank tea there together.

Friday Mar 18   This morning I breakfasted with Mr Anderson and Mr Bethell the two candidates at the Barr,[291] after which attended them to the Hall staid the polling and election there, and returned they being in the chairs to the Barr and dined with them along with rest of gentlemen. I came away about 7 o'clock in evening.
  Poll was vizt[292]
  For Hugh Bethell Esqr   850
  For Charles Anderson Esqr   844
  For G F Tuffnell Esqr   3
  For [blank] Pelham Esqr   1

Monday Mar 21   I was at Mr Anderson's ball; which was opened by Mr Penniman and Mrs Molesworth at top and myself and Miss Anderson at the bottom. About 35 couples at country dances.

Tuesday Mar 22   I wrote to my cousin Miss Bere informed her I hoped to be married to Miss Smelt ere long, etc. I wrote before to Mr Stonestreet on same subject. I have also told aunt Featherston and Mr Ragueneau.

Wednesday Mar 23   This morning at Hull going into Mr Cayley's I mett with Sir George Saville at the door we talked together and went into Mr Cayleys study together; when he went away, I walked into the parlour to Miss Smelt.

Thursday Mar 24   I was at Mr Bethell's ball. 35 or 40 couples. (NB I often go to Hull to visit Miss Smelt.)

Wednesday Mar 30   I was at Hull, and returned in evening — supped at Mr Ramsey's; played at whist.

Monday Apr 4   My mother and I dined and drank tea at Mr Cayley's at Hull.

Tuesday Apr 12   I told Mr Robinson of Buckton, that I hoped ere long to be married to Miss Smelt.

Saturday Apr 16   This morning Miss Smelt, Mr and Miss Cayley etc called and drank chocolate with us in their way to Burton, Revd Mr Cayleys.[293]

Sunday Apr 17   I wrote to my dear Miss Smelt at Burton.

Saturday Apr 23   Miss Smelt and Miss Dolly Mr and Miss Cayley and 3 grandchildren dined and drank tea with us in their way to Hull.

Saturday Apr 30   Received a letter from Miss Smelt, which much surprized me, and hurt me extremely; galloped to Hull in an half an hour; had an interview with my dear Miss Smelt and made up all matters to our mutual satisfaction, and removed all her scruples.

Sunday May 1   My dear mother was taken very ill this morning. I sent for Dr Chambers; and wrote a line to Miss Smelt.

Monday May 2   I received an answer from Miss Smelt yesterday Dr Chambers came today.

Thursday May 5   My mother being something better I went to Hull and dined at Mr Cayley's.

Saturday May 7   My dear Miss Smelt came this afternoon to see my dear mother.

Wednesday May 18   I dined (as often before) at Mr Cayley's; he gave me a draft of marriage articles.

Saturday May 21   I sent my servant over to Mr Beatniffe with draft of my marriage articles for his opinion which he returned and I gave Miss Smelt the draft to deliver Mr Cayley with a letter. Miss Smelt dined and drank tea with us. My mother, thank God, better than she was.

Sunday May 22   I went into mourning for Princess Louisa.[294] Undrest. Dark grey frock.

Tusday May 24   Beverley races begin. I went into our new stand with my silver tickett, and was at assembly as usual.

Friday May 27   Beverley races ended.

Monday May 30   My dear Miss Smelt and Miss Cayley drank tea with us. NB I am often at Hull.

Tuesday May 31   I was at the Militia ball; and danced with Miss Wakefield. Very apropos! being both engaged. Mr and Mrs and Miss drank tea with us.

Thursday Jun 2   Dined at Mr Cayley's. After dinner we signed the marriage articles.

Wednesday Jun 8   Gentlemen of the town (I among rest) gave a ball to ladies and militia officers. I was there but did not dance country dances.

Wednesday Jun 15   I dined and drank tea at Mr Cayley's. After dinner I went to Revd Mr Clarke's and got a licence. We fixed on tomorrow sevnight the 23d June to be the wedding day. (NB The Kings birthday is to be kept that day.) We are to be married at Low church (St Marys) at Hull. My mother not well enough to be present at the ceremony, which I should have been vastly glad she could.

Saturday Jun 18   I received a very pretty letter from my dear Miss Smelt.

Sunday Jun 19   I went into second mourning for Princess Louisa; but shall go out of mourning on wedding day and shall not put it on again for her.

Monday Jun 20   This morning I went to Hull, dined and drank tea at Mr Cayley's; I got a ring of Jones. We settled all matters about Thursday. Before dinner I had as usual an happy interview with my dear Miss Smelt.

Wednesday Jun 22   My aunt Featherston drank tea with us. We talked over all matters of tomorrow. My aunt Featherton will be at our house all day with my mother; and I am to go to Hull in my chaise in the morning.

Thursday Jun 23   This morning about 9 o'clock I set out from home in my post chaise, being drest in a new plain white suit and got to Mr Cayley's before 10 o'clock; found the bride ready drest in a white night gown, with a white hat etc and in about half an hour we all went to St Mary's commonly called the Low church. Miss Smelt and Mr Cayley in Mr Cayley's post chaise — myself Miss Cayley, Miss Dolly Smelt, little Master Cayley and 2 little Misses (Mr Cayley's grandchildren) in an hackney coach. Nobody but Mr Cayley's servant and mine were in the church. Revd Mr Thompson the minister of the church, married us. I brought back my bride in Mr Cayley's chaise; and her sister Mr and Miss Cayley etc were in the coach. We dined at Mr Cayley's. The bells rung at both churches — I gave half guinea to High and a guinea to Low church ringers. About 5 o'clock in afternoon my bride and I in our own post chariot and her sister Dolly and Miss Cayley in Mr Cayley's chaise, all servants having plain white favours[295] and Miss Dolly and Miss Cayley silver and white, set out from Hull, and got to our house at Beverley about half an hour past 6 o'clock; paid our duty to my dear mother, drank tea and supped with her and aunt Featherston and Miss Parsons. NB We used our best agate knives, which were never before used, but reserved for my wedding day. (The bells at St Mary's and Minster were ringing as Kings birthday was kept this day; but they came to me, I gave a guinea to St Mary's and half a guinea to the Minster ringers.) After supper servants came in my bride and I danced a minuet together, I danced with rest, and then we danced two country dances my bride playing on harpischord. Soon after the bride retired to bed, in the best chamber and I followed. Hear me O most gracious God and send thy blessing upon us, grant that we may, if it be thy will, increase and multiply — lead a virtuous and useful life, be ever pleasing and agreable one to the other, behave dutifully and tenderly to my dear mother, whom I beseech thee to restore to perfect health and long to preserve; and may we likewise happily enjoy health and spirits with as many of

St Mary, Lowgate, Hull, 1790, the church at which John Courtney was married.

the good things of this life as thou seest convenient for us; and finally this life ended may we attain everlasting felicity in the world to come, through the merritts and mediation of our blessed Lord and Saviour Jesus, to whom with thee O Father and the Holy Ghost be all Honour and Glory for ever and ever. Amen!

Notes

1   John Spring was married to Courtney's cousin, Susannah (see appendix 1).
2   Ralph Featherstone (see appendix 1).
3   St Mary's church, Beverley, where John's father was buried in 1756.
4   Cornelius Cayley (1692–1779), lawyer, Recorder of Hull. His wife Elizabeth was related to Mary Smelt, John Courtney's future wife.
5   Thomas Stonestreet of Islington was a family friend who had connections with the East India Company. He acted as Courtney's broker. John Robinson (d. 1769) of Buckton was also a friend of Courtney, both their fathers having lived in the East Indies. He married Hannah Grimston, daughter of John Grimston of Bridlington and moved into Grimston's house (The Avenue) in Westgate. Hannah died in 1741 (a few months before her father) and soon after John Robinson built a house on his family's estate at Buckton, north of Bridlington. The date of Buckton Hall has hitherto been uncertain, but a reference in the Grimston family papers indicates that building work started nine months before John Grimston died, giving a starting date of spring 1742. John Courtney stayed there as a child.

6   Christopher Goulton (1706-83) lived in North Bar Without, Beverley. 'Parson Johnston' was
      Samuel Johnston (1685-1767), vicar of St Mary's church, Beverley, for many years. He died in
      1767 at the age of 82. His father Samuel was a doctor, as was his older brother John, whose son
      and grandson also entered the medical profession. One of his own children, Samuel, followed
      him into the church; another became an apothecary and later personal physician to William
      Constable. 'Mr Lister' was probably a member of the Hull merchant family of that name. In the
      original text an 's' has been added to each of the surnames; this may have been deliberate, signifying
      that other members of their families were present, but this seems unlikely.
7   See 29 March 1762.
8   Stephen Whisson (d. 1783), Fellow of Trinity College, Cambridge from 1741. He is buried in the
      College chapel.
9   The Perrotts of Hessle and Hull, a prominent local merchant family. Courtney records the death
      of Andrew Perrott (who died in much reduced circumstances) in January 1762. His house at Hull
      and raff yard, staith, vaults and granaries were advertised to let in the *York Courant* the following
      June.
10   George Ferraby was a member of a well-known family of Hull booksellers and printers. He had
      a shop in the Market Place in Beverley every Saturday (market day). On April 6 1805 John
      Courtney wrote 'This day was the last day of Mr Ferraby the bookseller coming to this town
      where his grandfather, father and himself have come every Saturday from Hull to an open shop
      in the Market Place'.
11   Jonathan Furnas.
12   Sledmere on the Yorkshire Wolds, seat of the Sykes family with whom Ralph Featherstone,
      Courtney's uncle, had close connections.
13   Richard Beatniffe (d. 1792), lawyer. He succeeded Cornelius Cayley as Recorder of Hull in
      1771, and in 1779 was appointed Recorder of Beverley.
14   Revd Mark Sykes (1711-1783), rector of Roos, son of Richard Sykes of Hull, merchant. He
      succeeded his brother Richard to the Sledmere estate in 1761, and was created baronet in 1783.
15   Probably Jane Collins, widow, the daughter and heir of William Ashmole, a Hull alderman and
      merchant.
16   'Mr Constable' was probably Marmaduke Constable of Wassand (d. 1762) or his son Marmaduke.
      A spinet is a keyed musical instrument, similar to a harpsichord, which was popular in the
      eighteenth century. The more usual form of 'sevnight' is 'sennight', meaning a period of seven
      days.
17   Anne (1709-59), daughter of George II.
18   The York assembly rooms, designed by Lord Burlington, were opened in 1732. An engraving of
      the rooms by W Lindley is dated 1759, the year of John Courtney's first visit.
19   Catherine (Kitty) Fourmantel, a popular singer with whom Laurence Sterne, author of Tristram
      Shandy, had a fliration during her stay in York.
20   John Taylor of Bridlington, attorney.
21   For John Courtney's mother, Elizabeth Courtney, see appendix 1. Revd John Clarke was appointed
      Master of Beverley Grammar School in 1736. He resigned in 1751 and was replaced by William
      Ward who remained in post until 1768, when he was forced to retire due to ill health. Ward died
      three years later, at the age of 63. See also note 85.
22   James Hebblethwaite's estate at Norton, near Malton.
23   Peter Wyche was the grandson of Sir Peter Wyche, and son of Barnard Wyche, a merchant in
      Surat in the East Indies, where Peter was born. John Courtney's father served as Governor of
      Surat. Wyche was also related by marriage to John Robinson of Buckton, another East Indies
      merchant. See also the entry for 6 November 1763.
24   John's grandmother was Elizabeth Nelson (formerly Featherstone) and 'aunt Peggy' was her
      unmarried daughter, Margaret Featherstone, Elizabeth Courtney's sister (see appendix 1).
25   For John Eaton Dodsworth see the entry for 6 May 1759.
26   In this context a 'housekeeper' was a householder.

27 A report in the *York Courant* 1 October 1765 described how Thomas Scott of York, peruke maker, successfully rode his horse to London in under 34 hours, for a wager of £100. He supplied John Courtney with two fashionable wigs — a bag wig, which had the back-hair enclosed in a bag, and a bob-wig where the locks turned up into bobs of short curls.

28 The Tiger (nos 41-47 North Bar Within) was the town's principal inn at this date. It closed in 1847, when it was subdivided.

29 At this date the assembly rooms were in North Bar Within. Mr Enter, a German, gave professional concerts. For an account of his death see 21 February 1766.

30 The Ragueneau family (often spelt incorrectly) were apparently of French Huguenot descent, but came to Beverley from Leghorn (Livorno) in Italy. 'Miss Raguenau', the eldest daughter, was called Martha. Miss Goulton was probably Mary, elder daughter of Christopher Goulton of Beverley. Miss Smelt was presumably Mary Smelt, a visitor to the town (see appendix 1). Miss (Mary) Waines and her younger sister Hannah were the daughters of William Waines, draper. Miss Legard and Jenny Legard were probably related to the Legards of Ganton, who at this date lived at Etton, near Beverley.

31 A drink invented by Colonel Francis Negus, consisting of wine and hot water flavoured with lemon and spice.

32 Joseph Pease (1688-1778) was a wealthy Hull merchant. He opened the first bank in Hull in 1754.

33 William Territt, Fellow of St John's College, Oxford, became rector of Bainton, a few miles north of Beverley, in 1741. He remained there until his death in 1783.

34 Richard Sykes (1706-61) of Sledmere and his half-brother, Joseph Sykes (1723-1805), a merchant who lived at West Ella near Hull.

35 Spital-in-the-Street, a staging-post near Caenby Corner on the road from the Humber to Lincoln.

36 William Ridlington (d. 1770), Regius Professor of Law at Cambridge, 1757-70.

37 John Randall (1715-1799) was organist at King's College, Cambridge from 1745-99, and Professor of Music from 1755.

38 The chapel of the Foundling Hospital in London to which John Courtney refers became fashionable after Handel gave performances of the Messiah there.

39 A Cambridge term for common room.

40 Felice de Giardini (1716-96), born in Turin, was an eminent violinist. Thomas Vincent was an oboist and composer ('hautboy' being the French term for the oboe). The German musician and composer Karl Friedrich Abel (1723-1787) wrote much music for the bass viol or 'viola da Gamba'.

41 George, 4th Viscount Torrington, who was admitted nobleman at Trinity College, Cambridge, in 1759 at the age of 17. He died in 1812.

42 Admiral John Byng (1704-57), fourth son of Viscount Torrington, was defeated at Port Mahon in 1756, court-martialled for neglect of duty and sentenced to death.

43 Lynford Caryl (d. 1781), Master of Jesus College, Cambridge 1758-81 and prebend of Southwell, Lincoln and Canterbury.

44 See 21 May 1762.

45 Sizars received an allowance from the College to enable them to study. At Cambridge students who paid for their own 'commons' were known as pensioners.

46 Almost certainly Edward Place (1726-1785), who came from Bedale in Yorkshire and was Dean of the collegiate church of Middleham.

47 Henry 2nd Viscount Palmerston.

48 Richard Neate (d. 1817), son of Richard Neate of Horbury, Yorkshire.

49 At this date 'Caput' was the term used for the ruling body or council of the University of Cambridge.

50 Second or third year students at Cambridge were originally known as 'sophisters' and later 'sophi(o)mores', a term still in use in American universities.

51 It was common practice for the gentry to leave close friends a small sum of money each with which to purchase a mourning ring, to wear as a memorial.

52 An organization for conveying letters or packages for one old penny. The 'official' penny post was not established until 1840. Before then the amount charged varied according to the distance the letter was carried, and was payable on delivery.

53 Edward Young (1683-1765), poet. In 1742 he published *The Complaint; or Night Thoughts on Life, Death and Immortality* which achieved immediate popularity.

54 Marylebone Gardens, opened in 1650, and enlarged in 1738. Assembly rooms were built the following year.

55 The pleasure gardens laid out on the grounds of Ranelagh House, Chelsea were opened in 1742. The grounds are now part of Chelsea Hospital gardens.

56 The Theatre Royal, Drury Lane, was opened in 1663. William O'Brien (d. 1815) was an actor and dramatist. Mrs Hannah Pritchard (1711-68) was one of the leading actresses of her time.

57 In 1683 a 'musick house' was built by Thomas Sadler as a side attraction to a medicinal well. The theatre was rebuilt in 1765.

58 The Royal Exchange, where J Hazard & Co, stockbrokers, had their offices, was in Cornhill. In the eighteenth century the vaults of the Royal Exchange were let to bankers, and to the East India Company for the stowage of black pepper. East India House, the premises of the East India Company, with which John Courtney's father had served, stood nearby in Leadenhall Street, close to which was the Jerusalem Coffee House, which was patronised by merchants, brokers and others concerned with the East India Trade.

59 A spirituous liquor. It was sometimes used in punch, hence 'rack punch' which is mentioned later in the diary.

60 Vauxhall Gardens, opened c1660, a popular venue providing illuminated walks, musical entertainment and firework displays.

61 Julian Bere (see appendix 1) lived with the celebrated artist William Hogarth and his wife Jane. The Hogarths lived in Leicester Square but also had a small villa in the country at Chiswick. Hogarth's four satirical pictures titled *An Election* were painted in 1754.

62 John Courtney's father was baptised at St Andrew's, Holborn on 17 December 1679 (see appendix 1).

63 Ambrose Uvedale (d. 1818), son of Revd Samuel Uvedale of Barking near Needham Market, Suffolk. He was a contemporary of John Courtney at Wakefield School and Trinity College, Cambridge.

64 More properly known as the Chapel of Our Lady of the Crag. There is a carving of a figure once thought to represent Robert of Knaresborough, the hermit 'saint' who lived in a cave, which Courtney also visited. The sites were obviously popular with visitors; Mary Hardy, a Norfolk diarist, records a similar visit to the chapel and 'dreary cavern in a rock' in 1775. (Norfolk Record Society vol 37, p17.)

65 The Plompton estate near Harrogate had recently been purchased by Daniel Lascelles, son of Henry Lascelles of Harewood.

66 At this date there were two assembly or 'long' rooms at Scarborough — Browns and Cooks.

67 Medicinal spring waters were discovered at Scarborough in the early seventeenth century and by the end of the century the first spa house was under construction.

68 John Thomas, bishop of Lincoln from 1744 until 1761, when he was appointed bishop of Salisbury. He was succeeded at Lincoln by John Green, a native of Beverley.

69 Kimbolton Castle, south-west of Huntingdon, was rebuilt by Vanbrugh 1707-14 for the 4th Earl of Manchester.

70 Alexander Hunter (1729-1809), a well-known physician and author, who was based in Beverley at this date. He practiced in York from 1763, when John Courtney mentions them dining together there. Many years later John consulted him at York.

71 Samuel Johnston (d. 1775), son of Dr Samuel Johnston (d. 1767). He was related to John Johnston (d. 1799) who was also in the medical profession, but gave up his business as an apothecary in Beverley in 1769 to become personal physician to William Constable of Burton Constable Hall, whom he accompanied on the 'Grand Tour'. The latter must be the 'Mr J Johnston' mentioned later in the diary.

72 Servants were usually hired at Martinmas (11 November). However, in 1752 the Gregorian calendar was adopted in place of the Julian calendar, and the official start of the new year moved from 25 March to 1 January. Eleven days in September 1752 were 'lost', 2 September being followed by 14 September. This meant that in subsequent years festivals celebrated on the correct date were actually taking place eleven days earlier than in previous years. Sometimes people chose to hold events at the traditional time rather than on the correct date, which led to terms such as 'old Midsummer' and 'new Midsummer'. A full year's wages for a servant hired at Martinmas 1751 would not be due until 22 November 1752, and payment in subsequent years might therefore continue to be made on that day of the month.

73 In America 'Thanksgiving' was celebrated on the last Thursday in November. It is not clear why Courtney thought it significant.

74 Militia forces were billeted in Beverley at several periods, and the presence of gentlemen officers enhanced the limited social circle of the town. Henry Pleydell Dawnay, 3rd Viscount Downe, was mortally wounded at the battle of Campen and died on 9 December 1760.

75 Nathaniel Courtney (see appendix 1).

76 The first lottery in England took place in 1566, to raise money for harbour repairs and other public works. State lotteries were abolished in 1826.

77 Randolph Hewitt of Beverley, grocer.

78 The assembly room was in Dagger Lane, Hull. The 'High Church' was Holy Trinity.

79 No subsequent record of this publication has been found. It was probably a failed venture.

80 The Tufnells were related to the Meekes. Anna Meeke, daughter of William Meeke married John Jolliffe Tufnell of Essex, brother of George Tufnell, in 1748. Mr Grimston was John Grimston (1725-80) of Kilnwick on the Wolds.

81 William Bethell, brother of Hugh Bethell of Rise, in Holderness.

82 Sir Digby Legard of Ganton (1729-73). The family also had an estate at Etton, near Beverley.

83 Mrs Truby was Ann Featherstone's mother (see appendix 1). Mary Appleton (d. 1787), the unmarried daughter of Robert Appleton senior, and sister of Robert and Teavil, lived near the Courtneys in Walkergate. Matthias Hawdon became the first Minster organist (see note 143).

84 Miss Newsome, who occurs later in the diary. See note 109.

85 Revd John Clarke (d. 1761), former master of Beverley Grammar School, 1736-51, and Wakefield School, 1751-8. John Courtney was one of the pupils who followed him to Wakefield to complete his education. Clarke's death in 1761, and the subsequent sale of his library, are recorded in the diary.

86 Dr Andrew Perrott of York (d. 1762), a relative of Andrew Perrott of Hull.

87 Robert Appleton of Beverley, attorney.

88 Probably a reference to the Tiger Inn (see note 28) of which John Todd (d. 1765) was landlord.

89 See appendix 1.

90 John Dealtry (d. 1773), a York doctor.

91 For the Grimes (Greames) and Newsomes see note 109. Revd Laurence Sterne (1713-68), the novelist and grandson of an archbishop of York, held the livings of Sutton-on-the-Forest and Stillington, and in 1760 also obtained the living of Coxwold, where he settled at 'Shandy Hall'. He also had a house in Minster Yard, York. Later in the diary John Courtney refers to Sterne's wife as 'Mrs Tristram Shandy'.

92 The prescription suggests he had a skin disease.

93 Dorothy (Dolly) Perrott of Hull, the sister of Andrew Perrott of Hull, and cousin of Dr Andrew Perrott of York.

94 Mary, daughter of Revd Mark Sykes (later Revd Sir Mark Sykes, baronet, of Sledmere) and wife of John de Ponthieu. She died at the age of 21 and was buried at Roos in Holderness, where her father was then rector.

95 Sir William Foulis of Ingleby Manor, and his wife Hannah, daughter of John Robinson of Buckton, and their son William, baptised 30 April 1759.

96   The black marble floor slab, with deeply incised coat of arms, commemorating the deaths of John Courtney senior (d. 1756) and his wife Elizabeth (d. 1770) is in the choir of St Mary's church, Beverley.

97   George Whitefield (1714-1770), leader of Calvinistic Methodists. The courtyard where he preached was at Hotham House in Eastgate, Beverley, a magnificent Palladian mansion built 1716-21 but never occupied by the family. It was sold in 1766 and subsequently demolished.

98   Proclamations were made at the fine early 18th-century market cross, in Saturday Market. Randolph Hewitt lived in 'Dings' the area of the market place near the cross.

99   The text is unclear but the word is almost certainly 'frock', short for frock coat. A fasting or fasten penny was a small sum of money paid on hiring a servant, to secure the agreement.

100 A conventional badge of mourning, in this context a strip of white linen or muslin (worn on the cuff of a man's sleeve).

101 Vails were gratuities paid to servants, more specifically payments made by house guests. Courtney's entry for 23 November 1763 refers to the abolition of this practice in Yorkshire.

102 Beverley returned two Members of Parliament. John Jolliffe Tufnell of Langleys, Essex was MP for Beverley 1754-61, but did not stand in 1761. His brother George Forster Tufnell of Turnham Green, Middlesex and Chichester, Sussex was elected in the 1761 election and served as MP for Beverley until 1768 and again from 1774-80. Michael Newton of Barr's Court, Gloucestershire and Culverthorpe, Lincolnshire, was also elected. He was great nephew of Sir Michael Warton of Beverley and inherited a share of the Warton estates. 'Young Mr Penniman' was probably James Pennyman — see note 254.

103 The wife of Revd John Clarke — see note 85.

104 Hugh Bethell (1727-72) of Rise and Watton Abbey. He served as MP for Beverley 1768-72.

105 William Gee was the son of James Gee of Bishop Burton — see 3 December 1761. 'Mr Boynton' may have been Griffith Boynton who inherited the Burton Agnes estate the following year, or another member of that family.

106 Catherine Dickons, widow of Peter Dickons of Beverley, mercer.

107 Miss Parsons was related to the Featherstones (see appendix 1). 'Mr Feanside' was probably Jonathan Fearnsides 'mathematican' who rented a newly-built house in Highgate (no 15) from the Corporation of Beverley in 1753. Thor bass is an abbreviation for thorough bass, i.e figured bass.

108 Ralph Featherstone, John Courtney's uncle, was pall bearer at the funeral of Richard Sykes of Sledmere, and was left 20 guineas in his will.

109 Mary Greame, widow of John Greame (1664-1746), the builder of Sewerby House (later Hall) near Bridlington, her daughter Elizabeth Newsome and grand daughter Mary Newsome. John Courtney subsequently mentions several other members of the family (usually by their initials) — Mr Newsome of London, Mary Newsome's grandfather, Mary and Anne Greame, her spinster aunts, and Thomas and Christiana Greame of Towthorpe, her uncle and aunt. The name Greame is often spelt 'Grime' in contemporary documents suggesting this is how it was pronounced.

110 The farce 'Miss in her Teens', first performed in 1747, was one of David Garrick's early successes as a playwright. Many plays are mentioned in the diary, most of which can be identified.

111 A rough draft.

112 Thomas and Christiana Greame of Towthorpe, Wharram Percy parish, near Malton.

113 Thomas Haxby of York (1729-1796), instrument maker. He opened his shop in Blake Street in 1756. His known works include building an organ for St Marys church, Scarborough in 1762.

114 Successful candidates at parliamentary elections were placed in a chair or seat and carried aloft in triumph.

115 John Bowman of Beverley, draper.

116 The Blue Bell in North Bar Within, later renamed the Beverley Arms.

117 Warton Pennyman Warton (1700-1770) lived in Newbegin House, Beverley, which Courtney purchased after his death.

118 Horse racing took place on the area of common pasture known as Hurn, near the Westwood.

119 Thomas Wakefield was rector of the parish of Rowley from 1734 until his death in 1787.
120 Revd Thomas Bowman, son of John Bowman senior of Beverley, and brother of John. He was appointed vicar of Brantingham in 1757.
121 For the Courtneys' house in Walkergate see appendix 2.
122 Sir Septimus Robinson (1710-65), brother of Richard Robinson, Lord Rokeby.
123 Francis Dodsworth was born at Thornton Watlass, and was a pupil at Beverley Grammar School before entering Cambridge in 1748. 'Revd Mr Wells' was most probably Robert Wells (c.1734-1807), son of Revd Thomas Wells, whom he eventually succeeded as rector of Willingham, Lincolnshire.
124 Probably Lady Margaret Dalzell (d. 1781), unmarried daughter of Sir Robert Dalzell, 6th Earl of Carnwath.
125 Studley Royal, seat of the Aislabie family.
126 George, 6th Earl of Northesk (d. 1792), a naval officer of some distinction.
127 For Hinxman see note 137. The work by Tobias Smollett was probably his *History of England*.
128 Sir Robert Hildyard (1716-81). The family seat was at Winestead in Holderness, although Sir Robert also rented a house in Lairgate, Beverley.
129 Edward Augustus (1739-67), eldest brother of George III.
130 Probably Barbara, wife of Richard 4th Earl of Scarbrough (sic). She was the sister of Sir George Savile of Rufford, who is also mentioned in the diary.
131 John Wind, curate of Thirkleby, and rector of Kirby Knowle.
132 Sir Brian Stapylton of Myton-upon-Swale (d. 1772).
133 William George (1697-1756).
134 Probably James Grayburn of Beverley, oatshiller. Grayburn Lane, on the west side of Lairgate, is named after the family.
135 Probably Thomas Constable, second son of Sir Marmaduke Constable of Wassand. See also note 263.
136 A coarse cloth made of cotton and flax.
137 A notice appeared in the *York Courant* in December 1761 notifying the public that John Hinxman, bookseller and stationer of Stonegate, York, had let his shop to John Todd and Henry Sootheran.
138 Courtney refers on 11 June 1766 to the marriage of a Miss Harrison, who was presumably related to the Perrotts.
139 The coaching inn at Barmby Moor, on the Beverley to York turnpike road. The township was often called Barnby Moor at this date.
140 St Michael-le-Belfrey, in Minster Yard.
141 Captain Cooke and Miss Newsome.
142 Bacon Morritt lived at Grays Court, adjoining the Treasurer's House in York. His daughter Elizabeth was well-known locally for her needlework pictures, some of which are at Rokeby Hall, North Riding.
143 Haxby's design was rejected in favour of that of John Snetzler who built the organ installed in Beverley Minster in 1769.
144 Roger Ellerker of Risby Park near Beverley, who kept a pack of hounds.
145 An enigmatic representation of a name, word etc by pictures suggesting its syllables.
146 John Barry, attorney.
147 The 'uphill assembly' was the one held at the County Assembly Rooms, in Bailgate, built in 1745.
148 John Courtney saw the actor-manager David Garrick perform on several occasions. Two of the leading actresses of the day were Susannah Cibber (1714-66) and Catherine (Kitty) Clive (1711-85).
149 Dr Edmund Pyle, King's chaplain 1738-76.
150 Caldwell's Assembly Rooms.
151 The Royal Society of Arts held the first organised art exhibition in the country in 1760. The Society was based at Beaufort Buildings, Strand.

152   John Taylor (1703-72), an itinerant oculist, commonly known as the 'Chevalier'.

153   A person with chambers in the Inner Temple or Middle Temple, two of the Inns of Court.

154   William Boyce (1710-79), organist and composer, master of the orchestra of George III.

155   An ornamental covering for the chest, often covered with jewels, and worn under the lacing of the bodice.

156   Influenza broke out in London in early April 1762, and had pervaded the whole of the city by the end of the month.

157   William Sigston of Beverley nurseryman and seedsman.

158   No relationship between John Courtney, the grandson of a London stonemason, and the Courtneys of Devon has been established.

159   Francis, 10th Earl of Huntingdon (1729-89), son of Selina, Countess of Huntingdon, who founded the nonconformist sect known as 'Lady Huntingdon's Connexion'.

160   A card game in which barter is the chief feature.

161   An eating house where meals were provided at a fixed price.

162   A shout of exultation or applause, cf hurrah.

163   Sir George Montgomery Metham (1716-93) of North Cave near Beverley. He was MP for Hull 1757-66.

164   Robert, Ann and Catherine (Kitty).

165   Sir George Savile (1726-84) of Rufford Abbey, Nottinghamshire. He was MP for Yorkshire 1754-83.

166   Bridget Johnston, daughter of Revd Samuel Johnston.

167   Bernard Delacourt of Beverley, watch and clockmaker.

168   Sally Webster was appointed.

169   Probably Henry Wilson (d. 1797), usher of Beverley Grammar School until 1751, and of Wakefield school 1751-6. A number of exhibitions (scholarships) to Cambridge were available through the Corporation to pupils of Beverley Grammar School. See also 31 December 1762.

170   Daughter of John Thompson of Kirby Hall, Little Ouseburn, West Riding — see 31 October 1765.

171   Robert Clive (1725-74), 'Clive of India'.

172   Crimson.

173   Sir Edward Clive (1704-71), justice of common pleas.

174   The treaty of Paris marking the end of the Seven Years War was signed on 10 February 1763.

175   The assembly rooms in Norwood, opened in 1763, were designed by John Carr. In 1935 the building was pulled down to make way for the Regal cinema, which was demolished in 1998.

176   Sir Griffith Boynton of Burton Agnes (1743-78) who succeeded his father in 1761.

177   The Thorntons were a Hull merchant family.

178   Miss Archer, daughter of Revd Benjamin Archer, Rector of Stour Provost, Dorest.

179   Almost certainly Mrs Smelt, Mary's mother. Her father died in 1755.

180   Mary Smelt would have been travelling to Hull to stay with her relatives, Mr and Mrs Cayley.

181   Edward Winn, second son of Sir Rowland Winn of Nostell Priory.

182   Perhaps earth-oil or petroleum, obtained from the area close to the river Irrawaddy in Burma. Stonestreet had strong links with the East Indies.

183   John Hoggard of Beverley, tanner.

184   The Wilberforce family settled in Beverley in the sixteenth century, and a Mrs Wilberforce was still living in Saturday Market, Beverley in 1766. 'Mr Wilberforce' was perhaps Robert Wilberforce of Hull (d. 1768), a member of the same family, and father of William, the famous philanthropist.

185   See note 101.

186   William Chambers junior, physician. He trained at Leyden University and practised in Hull from 1725 until his death in 1785.

187   Neddy Blanshard, John's cousin (see appendix 1).

188   Flannels soaked in a medicinal substance and applied to the body.

189 An incised black marble slab marks Ralph Featherstone's grave, which is in the south choir aisle of St Mary's church.

190 Butt Lane in Beverley, at the south end of the town. The surrounding land has recently been built on.

191 The closes lay on the south side of the street now called Westwood Road.

192 William Nelson of Beverley, attorney, died in 1763.

193 Formerly part of Cottingham, but now within the Hull boundary.

194 The will had to be proved in the ecclesiastical court at York.

195 Ultimately two trusts were formed, the first of which controlled the road from Beverley via Market Weighton to Kexby Bridge, to the east of York.

196 An expression of thanks.

197 William Dodd (1729-77), chaplain of the Magdalen House 1758, appointed royal chaplain in 1763 but later struck off. He was hanged at Tyburn on 27 June 1777 for forging a bond in the name of Lord Chesterfield.

198 The Ridotto was a social assembly of music and dance.

199 'Change' was the Royal Exchange in Cornhill. Exchange Alley lay opposite. Theresa Cornelys, a Viennese opera singer and courtesan, rented Carlisle House and established her fashionable assembly rooms there in 1760. She was declared bankrupt in 1772.

200 The theatre at Covent Garden was opened in 1732, and destroyed by fire in 1808.

201 The British Museum was opened to the public in 1759. At this date admission was by written application only.

202 Revd Richard Kitchingman, son of Valentine Kitchingman of Thirkleby. Rector of Sessay 1749-77. His wife was aunt to Mary Smelt, John's future wife.

203 Leases, a house near Bedale, where Mary Smelt was brought up. Following the death of her father in 1755 it had presumably passed to his brother Leonard, Mary's uncle.

204 Dorothy (Dolly) Smelt, Mary Smelt's younger sister.

205 Stork, to the north-east of Beverley, formed part of the manor of Beverley Water Towns. The manorial court was held in a building on Hall Garth, where the archbishop of York formerly had a manor house, just south of Beverley Minster.

206 Mary Smelt's uncle.

207 In the East Riding of Yorkshire a deeds registry was established in 1708, and is now part of the East Riding Archive Service. Similar registries exist for the North and West Ridings, and for Middlesex. The volumes into which the deeds were copied are an invaluable resource for historians. The transaction noted here can be found in volume AE, page 392, no 746.

208 Thomas Hassell (d. 1773) of Thorpe Hall, Rudston.

209 Revd Thomas Metcalfe (1706-74), rector of Kirkby Overblow, Yorkshire. He was married to Anne, daughter of William Smelt of Kirby Fleetham, Mary's aunt.

210 His dancing room was in Toll Gavel, Beverley.

211 The road between Beverley and Hull was turnpiked in 1744. The Act was renewed in 1764, the new branch being the road between Newland and Cottingham.

212 Daniel Draper was at school with John Courtney. It was probably through John Courtney's father that Draper entered the East India Company. He married Eliza Sclater in Bombay, a woman who achieved a certain degree of notoriety through her relationship with Laurence Sterne, whom she met on a visit to London in 1766-7. Eliza eventually returned to her husband in Bombay but later left him and settled in England.

213 Mortimer's Hole was named after Roger Mortimer, 1st Earl of March (c.1287-1330) who was captured at Nottingham. The house referred to is Newdigate House, where the Frenchman Marshal Tallard spent several years after surrendering to Marlborough at Blenheim in 1704.

214 George Robinson, son of Sir John Robinson of Kingsthorpe, Northants, went up to Trinity College, Cambridge in 1749, and was made Fellow in 1765.

215 The Peacock Inn in the Market Square at Northampton, an eleven-bay building dating from the late seventeenth century, survived until the 1960s.

216   Lady Betty Germaine (1680-1769) of Drayton House, Northamptonshire.

217   Dressmaker.

218   The Creeds had an estate at Tichmarsh, near Oundle. The aloe, an exotic flowering plant, was first introduced into England from the Cape at the end of seventeenth century.

219   Revd George Sinclair (d. 1775), rector of Wilford, near Nottingham. He went to Beverley Grammar School and Trinity College, Cambridge, but was several years older than John Courtney.

220   Henry Lascelles' wealth came in part from the ribbon trade. The house he purchased as part of the Harewood estate was known as Gawthorpe. His son began to build a new house (Harewood House) in 1759 and Gawthorpe was later demolished. The tomb in the church is that of Sir William Gascoigne (d. 1419), on which he is shown in judge's robes.

221   The identity of the family from Newcastle is not revealed.

222   An area on the east side of the river Hull.

223   The Blue Boar and Horns on the west side of Toll Gavel (no 18), Beverley. It was rebuilt and renamed the Holderness Hotel c.1830, and later converted to shops.

224   Probably William Iveson of Hedon (d. 1786), attorney.

225   For details of property in Beverley owned by the Courtney/Featherstone families see appendix 2.

226   Sinclair was rector of Wilford, south of Nottingham.

227   John Baskerville (1706-75). Before establishing himself as a type-founder and printer Baskerville specialised in the manufacture of japanned goods, including tea trays.

228   The present Theatre Royal in St Leonards Place is on the same site. The first theatre there was built in 1744, over the vaulted undercroft of the medieval hospital of St Leonard. When the new theatre opened in January 1765 the *York Courant* described it as 'by far the most spacious in Great Britain Drury-lane and Covent Garden excepted, and, for convenience and elegance ... equal, if not superior, to either of them'.

229   Mary, eldest daughter of Alderman William Waines and his wife Hannah married Richard Sterne of Elvington.

230   Betty Hobson.

231   Miss Consitt.

232   Molly Thompson.

233   Lewis Disney (1738-1822) son and heir of John Disney of Swinderby and Lincoln. The family originally came from Norton Disney in Lincolnshire.

234   A conjurer or juggler.

235   The Coloured or Mixed Cloth Hall in Leeds, designed by John Moxson and opened in 1758, was described as exceeding 'any building of its kind in Europe'. (D Linstrum, *West Yorkshire Architects and Architecture*, p 282.)

236   Holy Trinity, Leeds, built 1721-7.

237   Details of this house, which was leased from the Corporation, are given in appendix 2.

238   Peter Atkinson of Beverley.

239   A receipt was a recipe, in this case for a scented oinment applied to the skin, especially to the skin of the head, or hair.

240   Miss Carver — see December 1764.

241   John Arden, natural philosopher, who lectured on astronomy and other subjects, came to Beverley in 1756. His daughter Jenny, born at Beverley in 1758, (when her father is described as 'chemist') was a friend and correspondent of Mary Wollstonecraft (1759-97), author of *A Vindication of the Rights of Woman*, who also lived in the town as a young woman. John Arden's son, John, a doctor, served as Mayor of Beverley nine times.

242   See appendix 2.

243   Martha Ragueneau.

244   Robert Burton of Beverley, apothecary.

245   The unpleasant procedure of 'tapping' involved piercing the body wall and drawing off accumulated fluid.

246   Robert Nelson *A companion for the festivals and fasts of the Church of England,* first published in 1720.

247   Hartshorn was the name commonly given to a solution of ammonia, used as smelling salts.

248   The late seventeenth-century house, until recently known as the Valiant Solder (currently known as 'The Cornerhouse'), at the junction of Norwood and Old Walkergate in Beverley (see appendix 2).

249   Probably Ralph Pennyman, who died in August 1768. He was buried at St Mary's church, Beverley.

250   A powdered medicine mixed with honey or a similar substance.

251   John Dickinson (1701-78), surveyor, and steward or agent for the Warton estate. The Wartons held the manor of Beverley Water Towns, of which Stork was a part. Following the death of Sir Michael Warton in 1725 the estate passed to the families into which his three sisters had married, the Pelhams, Newtons, and Pennymans. It was not formally divided until 1775.

252   Several members of the Nelson family were attorneys, and in this capacity acted as stewards of the manor court.

253   Revd Samuel Johnston (d. 1791), son of Revd Samuel Johnston.

254   James Pennyman (later Sir James Pennyman of Ormesby, 6th bart) (1736-1808), son of Ralph Pennyman of Beverley. From 1765 James lived at Lairgate Hall. He was MP for Beverley 1774-96.

255   John Courtney proposed to Molly Thompson, daughter of John Thompson of Kirby Hall, Little Ouseburn, West Riding, in February 1763. The report in the *York Courant,* 29 October 1765, describes her as 'an accomplished and beautiful young lady with a large fortune'. She married Childers Walbanke of Kirkbridge, North Riding.

256   William Augustus, Duke of Cumberland (1721-65), second son of George II.

257   Suckling Spendlove of Beverley (d. 1777), attorney.

258   Prince Frederick (1750-65), brother of George III. He died on 29 December 1765.

259   Francis Best, rector of South Dalton near Beverley.

260   Francis Peirson of York married Sarah Cogdell, daughter of John Cogdell of Beverley, grocer, deceased in 1754.

261   The Northampton printer referred to was almost certainly William Dicey, son of Cluer Dicey.

262   Probably Pighill or Pickhill Lane, Beverley, now called Manor Road.

263   John Courtney was 32. Sarah (Sally) Goulton was only 17. In 1769 she married Revd Thomas Constable, rector of Sigglesthorne, second son of Marmaduke Constable at Beverley, who was three years older than John Courtney. The following year her brother Thomas married Dorothy, daughter of Leonard Smelt, and cousin of John's wife, Mary.

264   Gallows Lane, at the boundary between Beverley and Molescroft, on the road leading north from the town.

265   Tobias Smollett (1721-71), author of *The Expedition of Humphry Clinker.* This work deals with the adventures of a provincial gentleman at Bath, Harrogate and Scarborough just at the time when John Courtney was at these places.

266   Thomas Short (d. 1772), who practised at Sheffield. His published work includes *Treatise on Cold Mineral Waters.*

267   Catherine Nelthorpe and her elder sister Charlotte, daughters of Sir Henry and Lady Nelthorpe of Barton on Humber, Lincolnshire.

268   Col Hector (later Sir Hector) Munro (1726-1805) served in India, and suppressed the mutiny at Patna in 1764.

269   A popular eighteenth-century spa, located in King's Cross Road.

270   A tea and coffee room at Islington.

271   Bristol Hotwells, the spa at Clifton.

272   St Benet Fink, Threadneedle Street, rebuilt by Wren 1670-81 and demolished in 1842-4 to make way for the new Royal Exchange.

273   The inn at Barton haven. Part of the building survives.

274   Charlotte Nelthorpe married Revd Robert Carter Thelwall of Redbourne, Lincolnshire.

275   Jonathan Midgley of Beverley, attorney, who built one of Beverley's finest Georgian houses, Norwood House.

276   The Society for Promoting Christian Knowledge (S.P.C.K.) was founded in 1698.

277   A large pill.

278   Revd Francis Drake, son of the antiquary of the same name, held the living of St Mary 1767-1791.

279   A colloquial name for the College of Advocates and Doctors of Law situated near St Paul's Cathedral.

280   William Middleton (1730-1815), a Beverley builder and architect.

281   A panegyric, or writing in praise of these Beverley 'ladies'.

282   Expressions of praise.

283   Harewood House — see note 220.

284   Sir Walter Blackett (1707-77) of Calverly near Leeds and Wallington Hall, Northumberland, MP for Newcastle 1734-77.

285   Money to build the new race stand was raised by subscription; 330 silver admission tickets to the stand were issued.

286   Pope Joan, a card game played by three or more persons, using a pack from which the eight of diamonds has been removed.

287   Following the suppression of the College of St John in 1548, Beverley Minster became a parish church, serving both the town parish of St Martin, and a new parish of St John the Evangelist, comprising the outling townships of Molescroft, Storkhill, Thearne, Tickton, Weel, Woodmansey, Beverley Parks, Eske and part of Aike.

288   Charles Anderson Pelham (formerly Charles Anderson) of Brocklesby, Lincolnshire. He was the great nephew of Charles Pelham, son of Sir Michael Warton's sister Elizabeth, and inherited a share of the Warton estates. He became Lord Yarborough in 1794, and died in 1823.

289   Yokefleet, south-east of Howden.

290   Mary Smelt's uncle.

291   In the seventeenth century two families, the Hothams and the Wartons, had political control of the town. The 'Bar interest' was so called from the Wartons' house which adjoined the medieval brick gateway known as North Bar. Charles Anderson Pelham, one of the heirs to the Warton estates, took over the Bar interest from Michael Newton in the 1768 election.

292   The poll was a technicality, Hugh Bethell and Charles Anderson Pelham being returned unopposed.

293   Revd William Cayley (d. 1784), son of Cornelius Cayley, Recorder of Hull. William was vicar of Burton Agnes from 1760.

294   Princess Louisa (1749-68) was a sister of George III.

295   Ribbons or cockades worn at weddings and other ceremonies.

Appendix 1

Family members mentioned in the diary, and their relationship to John Courtney

Julian Bere (d. 1790), 'cousin'. Sometimes called Julien. Daughter and heiress of Charles Bere of Hammersmith Esq. She may have been related to the first wife of John Courtney I. Her will makes no reference to members of the Courtney family. She lived at the house of the artist William Hogarth and his wife Jane in Leicester Square. In her will, drawn up in 1763, she left 20 guineas to 'my dearly beloved and good friend Mr William Hogarth as a small token of the love, friendship and high esteem I bear him' and a pair of diamond ear-rings and some silver cutlery to Jane Hogarth. She outlived them both; William died in 1764, leaving her a ring worth five guineas, and Jane in 1789. Julian Bere died in October 1790.

Edward (Neddy) Blanshard (d. 1788), mother's cousin. Son of Edward Blanshard of South Cave, butcher and his wife Margaret. Margaret was the sister of John Courtney's grandmother, Elizabeth, wife of Thomas Featherstone.

Elizabeth Courtney (formerly Bourdenand, née Featherstone) (1702-1770), mother. Daughter of Thomas and Elizabeth Featherstone, sister of Ralph and Margaret. Her first husband, John Bourdenand, whom she married in 1721, died in 1724. Eight years later she married John Courtney, father of the diarist. She died on 22 June 1770.

John Courtney I (1679-1756), father. Son of George Courtney, stonemason of Saffron Hill, Holborn, London and his wife Susanna, daughter of William Toyne, stonemason. He was baptised at St Andrew's, Holborn in December 1679. John spent his working life with the East India Company. In September 1717 a marriage took place at St Andrew's, Holborn between John Courtney and Isabella Williams, at which time John is known to have been in England, on leave. He returned to Bombay in December, perhaps with his new wife who may have died in India. His career culminated in his appointment as Governor of Surat. He retired from the East India Company in 1731 and the following year married Elizabeth Bourdenand (née Featherstone) of Beverley, a young widow. Their only son, John, was born in 1734. John I died on 1 November 1756.

Nat[haniel] Courtney, cousin. Perhaps the son of James, brother of John Courtney I, and almost certainly the Nathaniel Courtney who had a son, James, baptised at St Andrew's, Holborn in 1722. In the diary there is a reference to the forthcoming marriage of Nat's son John, presumably a brother of James. Nat was obviously not a wealthy man — John Courtney sent him a guinea during a spell of bad weather. No other relatives from this side of the family are mentioned in the first two volumes of the diary, apart from Julian Bere (q.v.) whose relationship to the Courtneys is unclear, and the Spring family (q.v.). John I certainly had other nieces and nephews, including Richard Courtney who went out to India in 1720, and Elizabeth Courtney, who was granted permission to visit her uncle in Bombay four years later. Although first cousins of John II, they would have been considerably older than him, and no contact seems to have been maintained, assuming they were still alive when the diary was written. In the later volumes of the diary and associated correspondence a troublesome 'cousin', Edward Courtney, makes an appearance.

Ann Featherstone (c.1719-1789), aunt. Daughter of Ann and Thomas Truby, wife of Ralph Featherstone. She died on 3 March 1789.

Margaret (Peggy) Featherstone (1715-65), aunt. Daughter of Thomas and Elizabeth Featherstone, and unmarried sister of Elizabeth (Courtney) and Ralph. She died on 17 September 1765.

Ralph Featherstone (1700-1764), uncle. Son of Thomas and Elizabeth, brother of Elizabeth (Courtney) and Margaret. Ralph served an apprenticeship with Richard Philipson, a Beverley tanner, and received his freedom in 1722. He married Ann Truby on 5 May 1748. He was apparently a figure of some influence in the local community, serving as surveyor and treasurer of the Beverley and Hull turnpike trust and as a trustee for members of the Sykes family of Sledmere, with whom he was closely associated. He was a pall bearer at the funeral of Richard Sykes in 1761. He died on 2 January 1764.

Elizabeth Nelson (formerly Featherstone, née Banks) (1682-1760), grandmother. Co-heiress of Stephen Banks of Broomfleet, yeoman (d. 1686). Married Thomas Featherstone, a shoemaker from Hornsea, in 1698. At this date she was living in Beverley, and was perhaps related to Robert Banks, a prosperous shoemaker in the town. By 1707 Thomas and Elizabeth had settled in Beverley, where Thomas is described as innholder. They had at least nine children of whom three, Ralph, Elizabeth (John's mother) and Margaret were still living when John began his diary. John's grandfather, Thomas Featherstone, died in 1719 and in 1732 his grandmother married Thomas Nelson of Beverley, butcher. He died in 1745 and she died on 11 May 1760.

Ann Featherstone Parsons (c.1748-1831). A young relative of the Featherstones, who later became companion to Ralph's widow, Ann ('aunt Featherstone'). She is referred to often in the later volumes of the diary. In 1794 Ann Parsons married Revd Rowland Croxton, vicar of Wetwang, and moved to Croom, near Sledmere. She died in February 1831.

Mary Jesse Smelt (1744-1805), future wife. Daughter of William Smelt of Leases near Bedale. Married John Courtney on 23 June 1768, the last event recorded in the second volume of the diary. Mary gave birth to at least ten children, two of whom died in infancy, one in childhood and another aged 20. The eldest of their six surviving children, John, was born on 26 June 1769 and the youngest, Dorothy, on 8 October 1781. Mary died on 24 December 1805, a few weeks before her husband.

John Spring of Brigg, cousin's husband. Married to Susannah, daughter of Blackett Midford and his wife Susannah (née Courtney). The latter was John's aunt (his father's sister).

Mary Truby (c.1692-1770), aunt's mother. Widow of Thomas Truby, mother of Ann Featherstone.

Appendix 2

Beverley property with Courtney connections

Walkergate House

John Courtney was brought up in a house on the site of the present Walkergate House, a property which apparently belonged to the Bourdenand family. In December 1721, not long after his mother Elizabeth's marriage to her first husband, John Bourdenand, a deed was drawn up between Bourdenand and Ralph Featherstone, Elizabeth's brother. This related to various property in Walkergate, including the house in question, and may have been a mortgage. Three years later, following the death of John Bourdenand, another deed was drawn up between Elizabeth, his widow, and members of the Bourdenand family. This dealt with all the Walkergate property apart from the principal house and associated land, in which Elizabeth must have had a life interest. She probably continued to live there, perhaps with her widowed mother, Elizabeth Featherstone.

Following Elizabeth Bourdenand's marriage to John Courtney in 1732 (the same year that her mother married Thomas Nelson) the couple lived briefly in North Bar Without in one of the Featherstone properties (see below). Soon after the birth of their only son, John, they moved to the house in which Elizabeth had previously lived in Walkergate, and where her mother was perhaps still living. From 1735 John Courtney was assessed for poor rates on the house in Walkergate in place of Mr Thomas Nelson (his wife's stepfather).

John junior went up to Cambridge in 1752 and from around this time until after his father's death in 1756 the house in Walkergate was rented to Marmaduke Constable Esquire of Wassand. John's parents probably spent the last few years of their married life living with the Featherstone relatives. On his return to Beverley John and his widowed mother moved back to Walkergate, where they remained until her death in 1770. The house then passed back to John Bourdenand's relatives, the Hunters. The present house dates from the 1770s, and was probably rebuilt soon after Elizabeth Courtney's death.

North Bar Without

John's relatives, the Featherstones, lived in North Bar Without. His uncle, Ralph Featherstone, had begun to purchase property in 1721, as soon as he came of age, presumably with money he had inherited from his father, Thomas, who died in 1719. In July 1721 Ralph purchased a house with a yard, garden or orchard and close in North Bar Without (a site now occupied by nos 50-54 North Bar Without). Five years later he took a 99-year lease from the Corporation of Beverley of one of the properties they held in trust for the upkeep of the Minister. This lay on the south side of his freehold property. Under the terms of the lease he was granted permission to take down the house and rebuild it, which he probably did soon after taking the lease. John Courtney's parents lived there briefly; John describes the leasehold house (no 48 North Bar Without) as the one in which he was born. When his parents returned to Walkergate the following year the house was let. It was still let to a tenant in 1752, when Ralph Featherstone made his will, but around 1757 he and his wife Ann moved there. Ann's mother, Mrs Truby, may have lived with them. Ralph died seven years later, but his widow remained in the house until her death in 1789. Her companion, Ann Parsons, continued to live there until her marriage in 1794.

When Ralph died in 1764 his unmarried sister Margaret ('aunt Peggy') was living in the old house next door. Under the terms of his will, this freehold house was left to Elizabeth Courtney (the only member of the family with a child to inherit), and the leasehold property was left to Ralph's wife, Ann, for the remainder of her life. Soon after Ralph's death Margaret moved in with the Courtneys in Walkergate, whilst the freehold house was substantially altered or rebuilt. On 31 August 1765 she returned there, but died only three weeks later. The house was later divided into two, and in the second half of nineteenth century a third house built, partly over the entry which separated the freehold and leasehold plots.

Between 1731 and 1760 Ralph Featherstone also leased property on the opposite side of North Bar Without, which belonged to St Mary's church. A late nineteenth-century house, no 45, stands on the site.

The fine house on the east side of the street known as Ash Close (no 62) also has Courtney connections. John Courtney lived there for a year, almost certainly in 1770-1, following the death of his mother and prior to his purchase of Newbegin House.

The Valiant Soldier, Norwood
The 'house at Norwood End' which John inherited from his aunt. It had been left to her by John's grandmother, Elizabeth, whose first husband was Thomas Featherstone, innholder. In 1812 the inn, which stands at the junction of Norwood and Walkergate, was sold to the Corporation by John's son, John Courtney III, for road widening. Part of the building was demolished at this date. The name 'Valiant Soldier' survived until the late twentieth century. In 2000 it was called The Cornerhouse.

Newbegin House, Newbegin
Built c.1689 for Charles Warton, son of Michael Warton of Bar House. In 1714 the house passed to his nephew, Warton Pennyman, who took the additional surname Warton. He was living in Newbegin House when John wrote the first two volumes of his diary. Warton Pennyman Warton died in 1770 and the house was inherited by his six daughters, who sold it to John Courtney in 1771.

Appendix 3

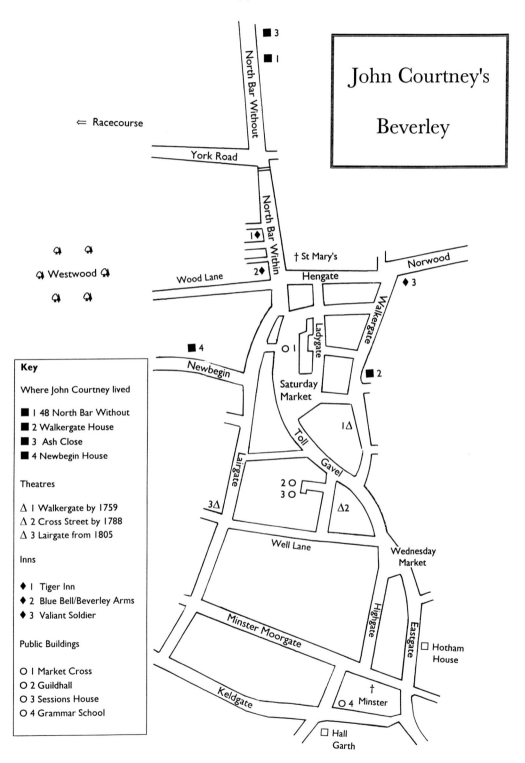

John Courtney's

Beverley

⇐ Racecourse

York Road

■ 3

■ I

North Bar Without

North Bar Within

I♦

2♦

† St Mary's

Norwood

Hengate

♦ 3

Walkergate

Wood Lane

Westwood

Ladygate

■ 4

Newbegin

O I

■ 2

Saturday
Market

I△

Toll Gavel

Lairgate

3△

2 O
3 O

△2

Well Lane

Wednesday
Market

Highgate

Eastgate

□ Hotham
House

Minster Moorgate

Keldgate

†
O 4 Minster

□ Hall
Garth

Key

Where John Courtney lived

■ 1 48 North Bar Without
■ 2 Walkergate House
■ 3 Ash Close
■ 4 Newbegin House

Theatres

△ 1 Walkergate by 1759
△ 2 Cross Street by 1788
△ 3 Lairgate from 1805

Inns

♦ 1 Tiger Inn
♦ 2 Blue Bell/Beverley Arms
♦ 3 Valiant Soldier

Public Buildings

O 1 Market Cross
O 2 Guildhall
O 3 Sessions House
O 4 Grammar School

INDEX

References to immediate family members (mother, uncle and aunts) occur many times; therefore only their deaths (where applicable) have been indexed. For information about these and other relatives see Appendix 1. Incidental references to places are not included in the index. The entries for Beverley are selective.

St Clair, Gen 46
St Robert's Cave 18, 152
St Robert's Chapel 17, 152
St Valentine's Eve (celebrations) 117
Sandicroft, Revd Mr 17
Salisbury 125
Sarratina, Sig 16
Saunders family (of Beverley) 22, 28, 33, 48, 56, 64, 71, 77, 90, 97
Savile, Sir George 62, 77-9, 87, 99, 146, 156
Scarborough 18-19, 28, 45-6, 61, 87
Scarbrough, Lady 45, 155
Scott family (of Staffordshire) 121-3
Scott, Mr 46
Scott, Christopher 83
Scott, Thomas 9-10, 19-20, 151
Selwyn, Mr 135, 139
servants (hired by JC) 20, 30, 47-8, 50, 54, 73, 90, 120, 128, 134, 144, 153-4
Sessay 80
Short, Dr Thomas 121, 159
Siddall, Mr 17-18
Sigston, William 59, 156
Simpson, Mr 19
Sinclair, Capt 100
Sinclair, Miss 87, 92-3, 98
Sinclair, Revd George 87, 89-93, 102-4, 107, 109, 112-14, 117, 124, 140-1, 158
Sinclair, Martha (née Ragueneau) 113, 116, 124, 140
Skelley, Gordon 121, 123
Smelt family x, 10, 53-4, 58-60, 70-2, 79-82, 110, 112, 116, 139, 145-9, 151, 156-7, 159, 160, 162
Smith, Capt 47, 60, 63
Smith, Ensign 46
Smith, Mr 33, 40, 46
Smith, Mr (apothecary) 132
Smith, Mr (servant to Lord Manners) 58
Smith, George 1
Smith, Nicholas 115
Smollett, Tobias x, 121-2, 125-6, 159
Soaper, Master 12
snow (heavy fall of) 129-30
Society for Promoting Christian Knowledge 132, 160
Sootheran, Henry 50, 155
South Cave 141
Southampton 125
spa (at Scarborough) 18, 45, 152
Spain (declaration of war against) 50
Spencer, Mr 127
Spendlove, Suckling 113, 159

Sperin, Abraham 17
Spring family (of Brigg) 1-2, 19, 120, 149, 162
Squire, Mr 102
Staines, Mr 12
Stanley, Mr 57
Stapylton, Sir Brian 45, 155
Staveley, Mr 83
Staveley, Michael 25
Sterne, Elizabeth 34
Sterne, Revd Laurence x, 26, 150, 153, 157
Sterne, Mary (née Waines) 94-5, 115-16
Sterne, Richard 94
Stevenson, Miss 17
Stevenson, Mr 89, 114
Stevenson, John 123, 142
Stilton 56
Stonestreet, Thomas 1, 5-6, 8-13, 16-22, 24-30, 36-7, 40-1, 45, 47-8, 50-1, 56-63, 65-7, 69-72, 75-6, 78-81, 83, 89-91, 97-9, 101-4, 106-8, 112-13, 116, 118-20, 123-4, 126-30, 133-5, 140-3, 145-6, 149, 156
Stork (property at) 81-2, 98, 105, 108-9, 113, 116, 129, 133, 142, 157
Strickland, Mr 119
Studley Royal 44, 121, 155
Summergangs (property at) 89
sun (eclipse of) 80
Sussex, Lord & Lady 85
Sykes family (of Hull and Sledmere) 5-6, 8, 10-11, 17, 19, 22-5, 27, 33, 40, 49-50, 53-4, 82, 143, 150-1, 153-4, 162

Tadcaster 25, 34
Tallard, Marshal 85, 157
Tancred, Mr 6
Taylor, Miss 18
Taylor, Mr 92
Taylor, John (attorney) 6-8, 150
Taylor, John ('Chevalier') 57, 156
Taylor, John (builder) 89, 133
Telfer, Mrs 121
Telfer, Alexander 122
Tenducci, Sig 58
Tennyson, Mr 28-9, 90
Tennyson, Mrs 27, 90
Territt, Revd William 10, 41, 50, 60, 151
Thackeray, Dr 97, 99, 102-4, 129, 132
theatre see entertainments; London; York
Thirsk, Hannah 8, 142
Thomas, Miss 58
Thompson, Miss 23
Thompson, George 81, 89-90, 117, 143